HOOKING OFF THE JAB

NIGEL COLLINS ON BOXING

"Nigel Collins has remained one of the essential voices analyzing and contextualizing boxing for half a century. In his writing, there emerges both an enduring passion for the sport and a brutal honesty about its toll."

—Eric Raskin, Showtime Boxing Podcast

"In 1987, I was in my thirteenth year of working for ABC Sports. I had begun my stint there covering college football, and eventually touched every sport imaginable through my exposures on *Wide World of Sports* and Olympics broadcasts. Then I was suddenly assigned to boxing, a sport in which I had experience only as a viewer. In a panic, I began foraging for every byline that might educate me and keep me from failing my new responsibility as a storyteller in the most revered storytelling sport. And the first name that became a basic staple was Nigel Collins, at that time the executive editor of the magazine that was seen as the Bible of Boxing.' His writing and reporting helped to keep me afloat. It was a form of poetry that 28 years later we entered the International Boxing Hall of Fame together. He didn't need exposure to me to achieve that recognition, but I know I wouldn't have gotten to Canastota without his work."

—Jim Lampley

"Nigel Collins is, simply put, one of the best to ever write about the sport of boxing. He's vastly experienced, enormously insightful and he's been in the small halls, the outdoor stadiums and everywhere in between. He's met champions, journeymen, promoters, has-beens, never-weres and, of course, his fellow Hall of Famers. He has carefully and colorfully chronicled boxing for more than 50 years, and his excellent must-read work will stand the test of time for generations to come.

–Tris Dixon, author of *Damage: The Untold Story Of Brain Trauma In Boxing*

Additional books by Nigel Collins

BOXING BABYLON

Behind The Shadowy World of The Prize Ring

TRAVELS WITH MARY JANE

Confessions of a 70-Year-Old Stoner

HOOKING OFF THE JAB

NIGEL COLLINS ON BOXING

NIGEL COLLINS

WINDING ROAD STORIES

NEW YORK   LOS ANGELES

Jacket design by Michael Kronenberg
Jacket Copyright 2022 by Winding Road Stories
Interior book design by A Raven Design

ISBN#: 979-8-9866043-5-0 (pbk)
ISBN#: 979-8-9866043-6-7 (ebook)

Published by Winding Road Stories
www.windingroadstories.com

Table of Contents

BEHIND THE SCENES

THE HAPPY WARRIOR

LEGENDS OF THE RING

IRON MIKE

For Gavin

Foreword

"Hi. This is Nigel Collins from *The Ring*."

I was in my cubicle, working for a god-awful health insurance company. A few weeks earlier, I had faxed a revised version of a feature I'd submitted on spec to *The Ring* about fighters who had been ruined by a single fight. The first version had been rejected, rightly so, by Steve Farhood because it lacked a hook that made it timely. Not long after, the excellent featherweight Kevin Kelley barely survived journeyman Ricardo Rivera after having his ass handed to him by Alejandro Gonzalez, and I had my hook. I added the bit about Kelley and faxed the whole thing to the number on Farhood's stationery. It was April 1995.

"We liked your feature on ruined fighters and would like to buy it. Does that sound all right?"

I didn't hear anything he said after that. The ocean roared in my ears. Something or somebody was trying to convince me that Nigel Collins was on my phone about something I had written. And he liked it. He wanted to buy it for *The Ring*.

I was nine years old. A Saturday morning. My father and I were at a barbershop in Morgan, a couple of towns over. He sat in the barber's chair, smoking, getting a crew cut. I grabbed a *Boxing Illustrated* from the magazine rack next to me. Several pages in, there was a photo of George Foreman carrying a cow. Other photos and stories about fighters: Jack Dempsey, Barney Ross, Zora Folley. I read them but kept going back to the photo of Foreman and the cow. Carefully, silently, I started ripping the paper around the edge of the photo. I didn't know why. The barber heard something, looked up. I stopped. He went back to his clippers. I finished tearing out the photo, folded it, put it in my pocket.

A few years later, I'm pedaling my green three-speed to the shopping center about a mile from my house. There's a stationery store there with a stocked magazine section, and every few weeks they get new issues of *The Ring, World Boxing, International Boxing, Boxing Illustrated.* The guy is just unlocking the door when I pull up on my bike. I let it clatter to the sidewalk and rush past him. Three new ones this week. I snatch them off the rack and run to the register. The guy rings them up and puts them in a paper bag. I pay him in coins, tuck the bag under my arm and pedal home as fast as I can.

"Er, uh, yeah, thanks, that sounds, that sounds fine, um, Nigel."

The conversation lasted all of 20 seconds, but it changed everything that could be changed, launching me into a career and a life that is just as it was supposed to be but only if everything fell right into place, if the right person was there to help cultivate it, if it were abetted by wisdom and intelligence and generosity.

Years later, I would learn that the business of sports journalism, like most business, is governed mainly by a kind of lifeboat ethic that mandates that the incompetent powerful do whatever they can to retain their position, including, and especially, undermining the success of those beneath them. If that means editing every bit of copy into a banal, lifeless, inoffensive mishmash with the singular goal to remain employed one more day, so be it. This is not how it was at *The Ring*—at least, not so long as Nigel Collins was running things. I promptly learned that all that mattered was the quality of the work.

A month or so after Nigel called that first time, I sent in another piece, then another, before the first one had even come out. Nigel bought those, too, and soon I was pitching lists of story ideas. Some he green-lit, some he didn't, but he was ever receptive, ever accommodating, responding to my queries with a phone call or handwritten note. Soon, he was assigning me stories. The thrill at getting the call and assignment was always followed by panic and dread and a certainty that I couldn't do it, that I'd be found out, finally, as a fraud, and this fantasy I'd been living that I belonged to the same world as the Nigel Collinses and Steve Farhoods and Peter Kings and Bobby Cassidys had been just that, fantasy.

I'd file my stories in the dead of night, just under deadline, after six hours of chain smoking and frenzied typing. A thousand times I'd think, "Fuck it, I can't do this, I'll just call him tomorrow and tell him to give it to someone else." But he believed in me. He wouldn't have given it to me otherwise. I'd smoke some more, pound the keys and send it in. Next day, he'd call me at work to thank me and say I'd done a great job. I'd float around the office.

Eventually I was writing all the fight reports for *The Ring* and its sister magazines, plus features, sections, the *TV Page,* a column on the website. I took whatever I could get. Nigel put my name on the magazines' masthead: "Senior Writer." I felt like I'd won a Pulitzer. "It's not going to get you any extra money, but it's something," he said, and there was no reason he had to do that beyond generosity of spirit.

It never got boring because Nigel encouraged his writers to take risks: to be funny, off-color, dramatic, morbid when it was called for, truthful even when it was inconvenient. When two of his writers, Ivan Goldman and the fictitious "Jim Bagg" got into a feud in their columns, he didn't squelch it. He knew it was fun for the readers and played along. And even as the owners cut staff, reduced his budget, and made his job as difficult as it could be, he never succumbed to the easy choice of lower standards. His writers had to perform.

Because everything ends eventually, *The Ring* was sold and the new owners, Golden Boy Promotions, made things even worse before cleaning house altogether in 2011, firing Nigel and other members of the old guard. This made Nigel's overdue induction into the International Boxing Hall of Fame four years later particularly sweet.

In 2015, Michael Kronenberg founded *Ringside Seat*, a quarterly boxing magazine dedicated to the highest standards achievable in boxing writing and journalism. By some accident of the universe, I became its editor-in-chief, Nigel its most senior writer.

We soon discovered that the years and heartaches of leading an ever-shrinking crew charged with pumping out multiple magazines ad nauseam—"It feels like we're running a M.A.S.H. unit," Nigel once told me—had to some degree handicapped Nigel's writing. He'd always been a wonderful read, his stories standing out among the best in the genre, all wise and elegant and knowing.

But freed from the mayhem that is editing, his writing reached new heights, finding the unobvious, delivering profundity, poignancy and a gentle wisdom in every piece. He does not write "about boxing," he has often said, but about life as experienced through the prism of boxing, and I can't think of a better way to describe it than that. Neither will you as you read the stories on the pages that follow this one.

I am no longer the kid who couldn't read enough boxing magazines. I am a man who has spent a good part of my life living in their world, largely because one who held the keys to the door to that world unlocked it for me. And if I have written anything at all over the past almost-20 years that is worthwhile, it is because he gave me the chance to develop a voice. If (less plausibly), I am worth anything as an editor, it is because I am mimicking him to the best degree that I can. Inevitably, no man can live his dream without another's help, and he who finds that help is a lucky man. I have been a lucky man indeed.

—William Dettloff

Introduction

The lobby of the old Philadelphia Arena smelled like hotdogs and mustard. It was always crowded until the first pair of boxers entered the ring and scuffed their boxing boots in the rosin box.

I was with my father the night Bennie Briscoe fought George Benton there, December 5, 1966. It was an all-Philly showdown between the past and the present, and we had good seats halfway up the risers. Former light heavyweight champion Harold Johnson sat behind us, eating popcorn.

I remember the noise and the adrenaline rush when Briscoe rallied down the stretch. He had Benton in a bad way when the doctor ordered referee Joe Sweeney to stop the fight at the end of the ninth round. My mind buzzed as we headed for the car, lingering in the afterglow of a memorable night at the fights.

You see, the seed was planted early. I didn't start covering boxing because I wanted a career in journalism. I did it because I wanted a career in boxing.

Grandfather told me tales of bareknuckle fighters that actually turned out to be true. Dad liked to tell a yarn about boxing an exhibition with future light heavyweight champion Freddie Mills, aboard a transport ship bound for India during World War II. What's even crazier, Dad claimed he won on a foul. The only things I can vouch for is that both men were in the Royal Air Force and my father was stationed in India.

My turn with the gloves came in the U.S. Army, where I foolishly volunteered to box in a tournament at Fort Sam Houston. A few sparring sessions and two bouts convinced me I had no future between the ropes. I wasn't surprised or unhappy. After all, I didn't come from a family of boxers. What my father and grandfather really did best was tell stories, which apparently also goes for me.

I got my first job in boxing because of a dead man. Boxing lifer Archie Pirolli worked for Philadelphia's Hall of Fame promoter Herman Taylor. Trainer Willie Reddish called him a "pencil man," a guy who'd ghost sign Sonny Liston's autograph on photos of the champ.

Prior to his death, Pirolli was *The Ring*'s Philadelphia correspondent since the quill and parchment days and filed bareboned fight reports that didn't reflect the uptick in Philadelphia boxing. I convinced promoter J Russell Peltz I was the perfect replacement, and he helped me nab the juiciest beat east of L.A.

What a thrill it was to document the renaissance of Philadelphia boxing. To witness "Miracle Matt" Franklin's (later Matthew Saad Muhammad) mindboggling knockouts of Marvin Johnson, Bill Douglas, Richie Kates and Yaqui López. To see Bennie Briscoe's wars with Eugene "Cyclone" Hart, Karl Vinson and Lenny Harden. To be ringside for the rise of future bantamweight champion Jeff Chandler, and the cunning speed of brilliant southpaw Tyrone Everett.

During those years, I wasn't just ringside for *The Ring* and the British weekly *Boxing News*. I was closer to the nitty-gritty of the sport than ever before, hanging out at various gyms on a regular basis, getting to know the boxers and their trainers. A boxing gym is a world unto itself, and it wasn't long before it felt like I belonged, accepted, the writer dude who knew a little bit about boxing.

Once the Spectrum boxing program ended in 1980, the action shifted to Atlantic City, where casinos invested millions of dollars in boxing. Due to my proximity to A.C. (60 miles), my workload tripled and raised my profile, as did *Ring* cover stories on WBC light heavy champ Saad Muhammad and WBA bantamweight titleholder Chandler, a couple of guys I'd known since their days as four-round prelim fighters. The boxing feeding frenzy in Atlantic City made it one of the biggest go-to sites in the country, and I was at the center of it all.

One summer evening in 1984, I was sitting at the kitchen table, rolling a sheet of paper into my typewriter when the phone rang. It was someone from *The Ring* informing me that if I was interested in a fulltime position, I should call editor and publisher Bert Randolph Sugar in the morning. Three weeks later, I was at my desk in a dusty office suite on the top floor of an old three-story building in Manhattan's garment district.

I was happily sucked into Bert's orbit, a creative yet wildly extravagant realm where money was no object and having a good time was second only to getting the next issue to the printer on time. Bert was putting out a far superior magazine than his predecessor and was getting a lot of positive media attention. Unfortunately, money was flowing out in far greater quantities than it was coming in.

The let-the-good-times-roll ethos ended abruptly when Bert was fired for plunging the magazine into maelstrom of red ink. Regardless of the financial mess he left behind, I am eternally grateful to Bert for giving me my first fulltime job in boxing. After he left *The Ring*, whenever he wrote a new book, he would send me a copy inscribed, "To Nigel Collins who is still trying to buy back his introduction to ... Bert Sugar." We remained friends until his death in March 2012.

After another culling of the staff and moving to a smaller office, I became Editor-in-Chief with the January 1985 issue, and I soon realized I wasn't working in the boxing business anymore. I was in the publishing trade.

Though we operated on shoestring budget, publisher Denis Blanck always found a way to send me to witness history in Las

Vegas: Thomas Hearns-Roberto Duran, Marvin Hagler-Thomas Hearns, Ray Leonard-Marvin Hagler and Mike Tyson-Trevor Berbick, indelible memories from an extraordinary time.

Tyson's popularity helped keep *The Ring* afloat. Putting his face on the cover, as we did 12 times between the May 1986 and the May 1989 issues, always boosted sales. Nevertheless, we could not recover from the debt we inherited. Only four issues of *The Ring* were published in 1989. When the paychecks stopped, we all went home.

With more free time on my hands, I wrote my first book—*Boxing Babylon: Beyond The Shadowy World Of The Prize Ring*. A riotous party launched the book at Dirty Frank's, Philly's beloved dive bar at 13th and Pine. Citadel press bought drinks for friends, writers, book buyers, boozers and boxing people, including WBA bantamweight champion Jeff Chandler and his pixie-like manager, "KO" Becky O'Neill. Promoter Peltz showed vintage fight films and my father stopped by for a few bourbons.

The launch party was like Mardi Gras, a bacchanal before a period of austerity. I woke the next morning looking down the barrel of unemployment.

After a few freelance jobs, including some TV work for HBO, I was offered a rematch I couldn't refuse. In 1993, *The Ring* was sold to Kappa Publishing, located in Ambler, Pennsylvania, a half-hour drive from my home. I happily accepted an offer to rejoin the staff as managing editor, and after my friend and colleague Steve Farhood moved on in 1997, I was promoted to my second term as Editor-In-Chief, a position I held until the November 2011 issue.

During my second stint heading up the "Bible of Boxing," I took direct aim at the leeches that have led to the abomination known as the "four belt era." I reintroduced *The Ring* belt and created a new championship policy.

The belt itself was and still is coveted by boxers, so much so that I once traveled to the Philippines to put it around Manny Pacquaio's waist (an event recounted in this book). Most recipients understand *The Ring* belt is emblematic of the true champion, but that doesn't stop their managers and promoters taking enormous sums of money out of a fighter's purse to pay sanctioning fees to the alphabet outfits.

My second time at *The Ring* was among the most memorable of my career. We brought the magazine into the 21st century, switching from pulpy black and white newsprint to all glossy paper with color photos in the December 2000 issue. I was also able to recruit some of the most talented young freelance writers in the sport such as Eric Raskin, William Dettloff, Don Stradley, Ted Lerner, Don Stewart and Michael Rivest, along with more established journalists such as Bobby Cassidy Jr., Ivan Goldman, Jeff Ryan, Gavin Evans, Pete Ehrmann, Brian Doogan and David Mayo.

We brought fans close to the action, providing my eyewitness accounts to legendary battles: Shane Mosley-Oscar De La Hoya I & II, Oscar De La Hoya-Ike Quartey, Marco Antonio Barrera-Naseem Hamed; Floyd Mayweather-Oscar De La Hoya, Arturo Gatti-Micky Ward I, II & III, Mike Tyson-Michael Spinks, Lennox Lewis-Mike Tyson, and Bernard Hopkins' masterpiece against Felix Trinidad. All told, I saw Manny Pacquiao fight live seven times, including his knockout victories of Oscar De La Hoya, Ricky Hatton and Miguel Cotto. Yes, indeed, those really were the days.

In 2007, Oscar De La Hoya's Golden Boy Promotions would acquire *The Ring*, creating a state of affairs that could easily become a conflict of interest. De La Hoya told the media, "These magazines will be held in an editorial trust where they will be operating totally independent of any influence from me or others from the Golden Boy Companies as it relates to editorial direction or content."

After a few years of a honeymoon period, little by little, the pledge of editorial freedom was violated, and when I fought to protect it, I quickly became persona non grata. As much as I loved my job, it was a relief when the axe finally fell after the November 2011 issue.

Though I felt my boxing writing career might be entering the final round, six months later, I was hired by Matt Sandulli, executive producer of ESPN's *Friday Night Fights* to handle social media during the show. Not too long afterward, I began writing columns for

ESPN.com on a regular basis. Moreover, Matt was gradually giving me facetime during the show, first writing and narrating short documentaries, and then on the set discussing that night's card and recent boxing events.

After several years of doing some of my best boxing writing, my time at ESPN came to an end in 2020 with no hard feelings. During those years, my work reached the largest audience it ever had.

These days, thanks to designer Michael Kronenberg (the man who designed the cover of this book) and editor William Dettloff (the gentleman who wrote the forward), I'm delighted to be writing for *Ringside Seat*. Only now, I get to include International Boxing Hall of Famer in my bio, an honor I was bestowed in 2015.

Any success I've had is only partly mine. I owe a huge debt to the fighters, without who there would be no boxing. I know how fortunate I've been to go places where most people can't. To experience fighters not only at their highest moments but at their most vulnerable as well. They've inspired me and broken my heart, sometimes at the same time. Those two extremes and everything in between has been my muse.

The book you hold in your hand is a compendium of that journey into the soul of boxing from 1980 to 2022. I hope you enjoy reading it nearly as much as I enjoyed living it.

—Nigel Collins

"I was standing on a street corner one night in Philadelphia and saw two winos start to fight, and I swear they were both hooking off the jab."

—Randall "Tex" Cobb

MUHAMMAD ALI

WAS ALI REALLY THE GREATEST?

HIS COMMON TOUCH WAS THE GLUE THAT HELD IT ALL TOGETHER

ORIGINALLY PUBLISHED BY ESPN.COM, JUNE 4, 2016

MUHAMMAD ALI TOLD us he was "The Greatest" before he was Muhammad Ali, back when he was still Cassius Clay and few people took him seriously. That all changed, of course, but even after he had the world at his feet, nobody ever believed in Ali more than he believed in himself. That, perhaps, was his greatest strength. He didn't think he was The Greatest. He knew he was.

But was Ali the greatest boxer of all time? And what does greatness mean, anyway? What are the qualifications and benchmarks for such exalted status? And who decides these things?

If you look strictly from a pound-for-pound point of view, Ali was not necessarily the greatest. Pound-for-pound rankings are a game played in the arena of the mind, where boxers from all weight classes compete on equal footing.

Could Ali have beaten a heavyweight version of Sugar Ray Robinson or Roberto Duran? Could a middleweight version of Ali have beaten Carlos Monzón or Marvin Hagler?

Unless you take it too seriously, this sort of speculation is harmless fun, but it also reveals one important truth: You can't evaluate a boxer on fighting ability alone, not when you're dealing with the very best of the very best. The field is too tightly bunched at the top.

When you read the fighters' plaques at the International Boxing Hall of Fame, you see some vital stats and a list of the inductees' accomplishments. But true greatness is much more complicated than that. Intangibles play a major role in pushing a fighter beyond the ring and into the consciousness of the masses.

One of those intangibles is charisma, an overused word that should not be confused with popularity or financial success, though all three often coincide. True charisma is like a spell that draws people to the source, often for reasons they can't quite elucidate.

Ali was unique, something the world of sports had never experienced before and something from which it would never recover. He launched the era of unrestrained braggadocio and unabashed self-promotion that has since influenced athletes in every athletic endeavor. But nobody has ever done it better.

His poetry, prediction and artwork were all part of the package, but they weren't the brainstorm of a publicist; they flowed naturally from Ali with childlike candor. The authenticity was palatable.

Although much of what Ali said seemed to be tongue-in-cheek, the power of his words was almost as formidable as his fists. The nicknames he gave his opponents (George Chuvalo: the "Washerwoman;" Earnie Shavers: the "Acorn;" and George Foreman: the "Mummy") elevated them in a strange way, regardless of any affront they suffered in the process.

Those who fought him looked back on sharing the ring with Ali as an honor, even, as was usually the case, they lost. To fight Ali was to be a piece of history.

Ali was charming, witty, brash and funny, but with an edge. Alternatively, mischievous and malicious, he alienated almost as many as he attracted at first but converted most to his cause by the time he was done.

For some, it was Ali's bravery in the ring that won them over, especially as he aged but continued to persevere and overcome. For others, it was his fearless stand against the Vietnam War for which he sacrificed what could arguably have been his peak years as a boxer. Whether you agreed with him or not, you had to respect the courage of his convictions.

He was a hero of the civil rights and antiwar movement, an advocate of religious tolerance, ahead of much of the United States in his foresight and outrage. The counterculture was in his corner from the start, and as the mood of the country began to change, he was a rallying point, somebody who led by example.

The only other two boxers who came close to having the sociopolitical impact of Ali were Jack Johnson and Joe Louis. Both are seminal figures in the history of boxing and the United States, and the only other boxers whose historical impact compares to Ali's.

Johnson, the first black heavyweight champion, was a rebel reviled by most of white America. Louis became a symbol of America's strength by knocking out German Max Schmeling on the eve of World War II.

Ali was a little of each, a rebel with a cause who spoke truth to power. Rooting for him gave folks of all stripes a common cause, which eventually spread beyond the ring and into more profound realms of life.

Of course, all of this wouldn't have mattered anywhere near as much if Ali were not a magnificent fighter. Boxing was the vehicle that kept him relevant until his iconic legacy became secure, part of our collective psyche.

And what a fighter he was, the champion of the world at a time of unparalleled riches in the heavyweight division—Joe Frazier, George Foreman, Ken Norton, Ron Lyle, Jerry Quarry, Earnie Shavers, Ernie Terrell and Oscar Bonavena.

He fought them all and beat them all, at first with unmatched speed and an unorthodox style, which mystified and frustrated all who stood against him. Later, with guile, courage and a willingness to fight on, he was confident he would prevail when others would have faltered.

Ali's common touch was the glue that held it all together. He loved mingling with the people, hopping out of a car to playfully spar with random people on street corners or kids in playgrounds. He'd do the Ali Shuffle, crack a few jokes and make everybody feel part of him. He was the champion of celebrities and fat cats sitting ringside as well as the downtrodden who couldn't afford the price of a ticket.

Ali was The Greatest because he said he was, lived his life accordingly and convinced the world it was true. In the end, it's the people who decide such things—and the people have spoken.

MEMORIES OF MUHAMMAD ALI

HE MADE ME PROUD TO BE A BOXING FAN

Originally published by ESPN.com, June 10, 2016

As my plane flew south toward Louisville, Kentucky and Muhammad Ali's funeral, memories of "The Greatest" came and went like windows into the past—a series of flashbacks that reminded me how much he was a part of me. It's probably that way with a lot of Baby Boomers.

I wasn't an Ali fanatic. He wasn't my favorite fighter. But beginning with his gold medal victory at the 1960 Olympics, Ali was a constant source of humor and hubris, a provocateur who sold tickets and made everybody pay attention whether they wanted to or not.

My first brush with him came unexpectedly. In late December 1963, my family piled into father's Plymouth and headed to Miami Beach for Christmas holiday. Sun, sand and swimming was on everybody's itinerary, but I had a secret agenda that had nothing to do with mistletoe and reindeers.

I'd read in the newspaper that Luis Rodriguez was going to fight Wilbert McClure at the Miami Beach Auditorium during our stay. This would be my chance to actually attend a fight—a prospect that had me far more excited than any of the giftwrapped boxes in the trunk of our car.

My cousin and I bought two tickets in the balcony and were watching the preliminaries when a commotion erupted somewhere on the lower level. Even though there was a fight going on in the ring, people were leaving their seats and rushing toward the source of the hubbub.

My first thought was that a brawl had broken out among some of the fans, not an uncommon occurrence at a prizefight. But when I leaned over the rail and stretched my neck to see what was going on, I got my first look at Cassius Clay in the flesh.

The "Louisville Lip" was standing with his back against the wall, waving a fistful of money over his head and offering to take bets from anybody who wanted to back prohibitive favorite Sonny Liston in their upcoming fight.

Clay (who was a few months away from first becoming Cassius X and then Muhammad Ali) had that familiar mock-angry look on his face as he alternately harangued and cajoled his audience. There was lots of laughter and playful exchange of insults, but I didn't see anyone reaching for their wallets.

A few months later, a friend of mine was reaching for his wallet so often he ran out of money. And it was my fault.

I told my buddy Marty that he could clean up on the Liston-Clay fight by betting big on favorite, sucking in the other kids by giving them 7-1 odds on Liston. I assured him Sonny would break Clay in two and he believed me.

I think Marty ended up paying out around 60 bucks when Liston stayed on his stool at the end of the seventh round. He wanted me to pay half the debt but settled for a quart of cheap vodka.

When Ali stood tall and refused to take that fatal step forward and join the military, I hung a large photo of him on my studio wall and wrote "a better man than most" on it. I was also eligible for the Draft, and I didn't have "nothing against no Viet Cong" either. But most of all, I didn't want to die.

Of course, I knew Ali had done something that I wasn't brave enough to do, but I didn't care. After all, we can't all be heroes. He made me proud to be a boxing fan.

Maybe that's part of the reason I bought a ticket to his embarrassing choreographed "computer fight" with Rocky Marciano—a way to help Ali when he had no other way of making a buck. Curiosity played a role, too.

I walked into the lobby of the movie house where it was playing in Philadelphia and there was Ali, who was living right across the Ben Franklin Bridge in Cherry Hill at the time. He was surrounded by fans and a semicircle of scowling men, identically dressed in black suits, white shirts and black bowties. He signed my ticket stub, and I've cursed myself hundreds of times for losing it.

The so-called fight was worse than I thought it would be. Ali was out of shape with unsightly love handles hanging over his trunks. Marciano was wearing an unconvincing toupee. And when Marciano, his face slathered with fake blood, knocked out Ali in the 13th round, Ali stood up in the back of the theater and yelled, "That computer must have been made in Mississippi!"

It bought the house down. Ali's words emphasized what a farce it was, which somehow made it even less relevant than it already was and took away much of the sting.

Nothing appeased the capacity closed-circuit crowd at the old Philadelphia Arena the night of March 3, 1971, when Joe Frazier won a 15-round decision in one of the iconic fights of the 20th century. Even though the decision was fair, fans in Frazier's hometown went ballistic. They booed and jeered, threw chairs, and anybody foolish enough to say they thought Frazier won were likely to lose their teeth.

That's the sort of passion and blind loyalty Ali generated. He wasn't just a pretty face who could box. He was a leader, a favorite son and, at that time, a king without a crown.

Frazier won the battle, but Ali would win the war, taking his career to yet another level with the "Rumble in the Jungle" and the "Thrilla in Manila." By then, Ali was the most famous man in the world but also one of the most accessible. His fans went along for the ride, and for a while it seemed like it would never end. But it did.

It should have ended with Howard Cosell reciting Bob Dylan's *Forever Young,* as Ali coasted home to a clear-cut decision over Leon Spinks, the night in New Orleans when he won the heavy-weight championship for a third time. At the time, I sat with tears welling up in my eyes, as the pair of old campaigners shared their final magic moment together.

But life is not a storybook. Cosell quit; Ali and Spinks fought on. It did neither of them any good. But they were fighters and fighters fight for as long as they can. It's who they are.

Even as Ali's illness deepened and parts of him floated away, he was always with us, the spark still glowed within.

Now that familiar touchstone we've relied on for so long is gone —and the world is emptier for it. But nowhere near as empty as it would be if Ali had never lived.

ALI'S FITTING FAREWELL

THE WAY TO HONOR ALI IS TO BE ALI

ORIGINALLY PUBLISHED BY ESPN.COM, JUNE 11, 2017

THE COPS HAD BLOCKED off the Route 65 ramp to all vehicles, but people scrambled up the steep grass embankment, some dragging toddlers by the arm, to find a spot where they could see Muhammad Ali one last time. Ali's funeral motorcade would be passing soon, and it was the only spot in the neighborhood where you could get a good look.

The locals came out in the tens of thousands, all along the 19-mile route to the KFC Yum Center where the memorial service was held. But this was no solemn cortege. It was instead, as it said in the official program, a celebration of life.

Some people held homemade signs, some placed flowers on the car. Chants of "Ali! Ali!" broke out spontaneously. Kids ran after the car, just like those old photos of Ali in Zaire, except the kids in Louisville had shoes. They were all too young to have seen Ali fight, but they knew who he was, and they knew he was one of their own.

A few blocks before the Yum Center, vendors were selling Ali T-shirts (I counted at least eight different styles) along with photos, paintings and a big campaign-style button.

The FBI had done its bomb sweep already and a festive atmosphere prevailed.

Rows of TV cameras lined the sidewalk, while early arrivers sought relief from the sun under the trees. Every lamppost had a banner with "Louisville Honors Muhammad Ali" written on it. It seemed more like a crowd waiting for a concert or a sporting event. Even the cops seemed mellow.

Attire was eclectic: from shorts and T-shirt to tuxedos and elegant gowns. One lithe young woman was wearing a leopard-skin print miniskirt with a matching top. Everybody was talking about Ali, and many seemed to have a personal connection. It reminded me of a reggae concert in Wilmington, Delaware I once attended, where half the people claimed to be related to Bob Marley.

"I'm Ali's first cousin," said Eric Kinslow. "My dad and Ali's dad were brothers. I went to his first fight in Louisville, against Tunney Hunsaker. We had a flower shop business, and Ali's dad did all our sign painting. I used to see Muhammad all the time. He was sincere when he spoke and believed what he said. He was very spiritual."

"My mom went to school with Ali," said Terry Holder. "My brothers hung with him. Ali was here in Louisville when they changed the name of Walnut Street to Muhammad Ali Boulevard in his honor. We heard he was at the laundry, so we went and saw him. He already had Parkinson's disease, so I bent over and whispered in his ear, 'You're still the greatest,' and he whispered back, 'I sure am.'"

It would be next to impossible to find anybody standing outside the Yum Center on Friday who would disagree. Ali belongs to the world, but Louisville had him first—and now last.

The interfaith ceremony was as poignant as it was long, the venue packed with 15,000 people, all of whom loved the fallen champion in some way or another.

The theme of all the speeches was pretty much the same, just delivered in different words and in different styles. Maybe the fiery

Rabbi Michael Lerner said it best: "Ali was our heart, and that heart still beats. The way to honor Ali is to be Ali."

Latonya Butler, who was wearing a yellow Ali T-shirt her boyfriend had made, would surely agree. "I'm hoping this today will bring some love and calmness to the city," she said. "There has been a lot of killing."

Yes, there has. And not just in Lexington. It's happening all over the world. If love is a cure, there sure was a lot of for Ali in Lexington this week. But what we sometimes forget is that Ali is revered throughout the world. He was mourned and celebrated by our friends and foes alike. There's a lesson there somewhere.

Ali hasn't spoken to us in words in many years. But he still stirred something inside us. Maybe it just the memory of the way he used to be. Maybe it's because we've come to understand his silence was a message in itself. Maybe he's said it all before.

Outside the Yum Center a warm and persuasive voice repeated (on a continual loop) Ali's six core principles: confidence, conviction, dedication, giving, respect and spirituality. The volume was so low, it was almost like a subliminal message. It was the first thing you heard when you entered the building and the last thing you heard when you left.

How strange that a boxer, a man who rose to fame by hurting other men, has been transformed into a symbol of peace. Had he been a preacher, his silver tongue and pretty face may have made him rich, but a boxer is something different.

A boxer is the other side of the coin, the darkness without which there would be no light. Somehow, Ali managed to become both.

MODERN SUPERSTARS

WHO IS FLOYD MAYWEATHER?

HE TURNED HEEL AND BECAME THE RICHEST
BOXER OF ALL TIME

ORIGINALLY PUBLISHED BY ESPN.COM, JULY 18, 2017

THERE HAVE BEEN certain boxers throughout history who have come to epitomize the eras in which they fought, their personas and fighting styles in sync with the prevailing cultural norms.

It's an elusive and rare quality that can't be manufactured. The role chooses the fighter, not the other way around.

These are fighters who have transcended the sport and become part of a broader narrative, totems of the way we were and what we have become.

Our current standard-bearer is Floyd Mayweather—and regardless of whether you're a fan or not, he's exactly what we deserve.

There is an elite group of fighters who are reflections of the ethos in which they boxed—iconic names such as John L. Sullivan, Jack Dempsey, Joe Louis, Muhammad Ali, Sugar Ray Leonard, and Mike Tyson, each an avatar of the time and place he represents.

It's hard to say for sure what boxing fans of the Gilded Age would have thought of Mayweather. Their hero was Sullivan, whose squared-up stance and handlebar mustache embodied the public's notion of what the heavyweight champion of the world should be.

Like Mayweather, Sullivan was a loudmouth and an unrepentant self-promoter. Beyond that, they have little in common. Mayweather, for instance, takes meticulous care of his body, while Sully had a gluttonous appetite for food and booze that rivaled his pal "Diamond Jim" Brady.

But it wouldn't have been Mayweather's calorie count or his work ethic that would have disqualified him from being the main man during the final two decades of the 19th century. The way he fights would have held him back.

No matter how masterful, there was little interest in a defensive specialist during the gas-lit fin de siècle. They wanted blood, and more often than not, they got it.

Some elite fighters who personified the times in which they fought carried a heavier burden than others. Louis, the first black heavyweight champion since Jack Johnson, was the bridge between Jim Crow and greater acceptance of black fighters. His knockout of Hitler-backed Max Schmeling on the eve of World War II opened the eyes and hearts of many white Americans.

Sullivan, Dempsey, Louis, Ali, Leonard and Tyson were all distinctive in their own ways, exciting fighters who stoked boxing's popularity with the power of firsts and the strength of their personalities.

Mayweather is unique in that he's the only boring fighter to become a multimillionaire. Boring inside the ring that is. Outside of it, he's a TMZ delight, a social media menace and the central figure in the greatest marketing campaign the sporting world has ever seen.

Very similar to the way Ali copied Gorgeous George's over-the-top showmanship, Mayweather pulled off an amazing switcheroo by using another of wrestling's oldest promotional gimmicks: He turned heel and became the richest boxer of all time.

It wasn't difficult. The bratty side was always part of him; he just amped it up to a point to where even he probably isn't sure which one is really him, "Money Mayweather" or the sunny-faced prodigy who came home from the 1996 Olympic Games with a bronze medal and a pocket full of dreams.

Neither Mayweather's jail sentence for domestic violence nor his one-sided mismatches seemed to have hurt his overall popularity. He's selling an opulent lifestyle and undefeated record, assets that remain regardless of whether he's knocking out Victor Ortiz with a cheap shot or coasting to an easy decision over Robert Guerrero.

That changed after his much-ballyhooed May 2015 showdown with Manny Pacquiao, which smashed all previous pay-per-view records only to deliver a ghastly pedestrian affair devoid of highlights. Mayweather's shoulder roll still looked pretty, but the multipunch combinations and lightning attacks are a thing of the past.

His supposed farewell fight, against Andre Berto in September 2015, performed poorly both at the box office and on pay-per-view. It was a clear sign that even Mayweather's most ardent supporters had grown weary of one-sided affairs in which the man they paid to see couldn't be bothered to step on the gas and finish his outclassed opponents.

Tempered genius is like watered-down wine, good for a buzz but not sufficient to get you where you want to go.

Mayweather is 40 now. It has been a long time since he broke Genaro Hernandez, shredded Angel Manfredy and decimated Diego Corrales. We are left with a novelty match against MMA star Conor McGregor that promises much but will most likely deliver little in the way of competitive action.

Perhaps it's only fitting that Mayweather's last stand pits him against McGregor in a scenario that resembles a reality-TV storyline, an appropriate farewell for a brilliant fighter who turned the most lucrative part of his career into a cult of personality.

Novelty fights, however, are like donkey baseball, a bizarre derivation that is good for a few laughs but will never replace the real thing.

The search for a fighter to embody the next era is already underway. Even though boxing will ultimately make the final decision, it's safe to say Mayweather's dazzling turn at the helm is coming to a close.

———

EPILOGUE: On August 26, 2017, Mayweather stopped McGregor in the 10th round. The fight was a farce but sold 4.3 million pay-per-view buys. It was the second-largest PPV in history, behind Mayweather-Pacquiao, which sold 4.6 million buys. As of this writing, Mayweather has not had a boxing match since.

SKYDIVING WITHOUT A PARACHUTE

THE ARTURO GATTI-MICKY WARD TRILOGY

ORIGINALLY PUBLISHED IN *THE RING*, AUGUST 2020

AN UNCLE of a high school friend was a daredevil called Johnny Blackjack. That wasn't his real name of course; it was the name he used when he rode a motorcycle on the Wall of Death at carnivals, competed in barrel-jumping contests and drag races. He died trying to drive a dragster powered by an Allison aircraft engine.

I think of Blackjack sometimes when I watch boxers pounding away at each other's head with wild abandon. You see, when they found Uncle Johnny's helmet, what was assumed his head was still inside, transformed into what looked like barbecued Jell-O.

Blackjack crossed my mind a few times covering the magnificent Arturo Gatti-Micky Ward trilogy. All boxers are members in good standing of the daredevil's club, but these two guys are the type of fighters Johnny would have been, had he picked up the gloves instead of a crash helmet.

The style in which a boxer fights is more about who he is than what he can do. Ward and Gatti were both punchers at heart, but more than that they were extreme risk-takers, fighter willing to push themselves past the point of no return.

All boxers are at least a little crazy or they wouldn't be boxer. That's a given. But what Gatti and Ward did was punch themselves into another dimension where nothing mattered but the fight. The combatants are not really in control after a certain point; the fight itself takes on a life of its own.

You have to wonder what sort of person gleefully swaps punches with little or no regard for their personal safety. Every man or woman who steps into a boxing ring is brave, even the least among them, but fighters like Ward and Gatti go beyond bravery and into a frenzy bordering on insanity.

Studies have found that most high risk-takers have similar personality traits related to sensation-seeking, aggression, and sociability. However, while Gatti and Ward became great friends, outside of a boxing context their personalities were as different as the old, 2,000-seat Sunnyside Gardens in Queens and the T-Mobile Arena in Las Vegas.

Gatti behaved like a hell-raising teenager, full of pranks and living life as recklessly as he fought. He once turned up at a post-fight party dripping blood from an eye cut. To hell with the hospital; Arturo wanted to party. He drank more than he should, hung out at strip clubs, and was embroiled in a couple of alcohol-fueled incidents involving the police. But you couldn't help but love him.

At a private photo shoot a few days before one of his fights in Atlantic City, Gatti regaled a small group of people in the room with the story of how he got the scar on his back. It was street fight over a woman and the other guy had a knife. Arturo demonstrated how he ducked under his foe's attempt to slash his face and came up with a punch knocked the guy cold. Gatti didn't duck quite low enough and suffered a gash on his back.

It's difficult to imagine phlegmatic Ward getting into a street fight over a woman. When asked if his family was as wacky as portrayed in his biopic, *The Fighter*, he laughed and said they were actually worse. Micky is the most levelheaded of the bunch. He's as blue collar as it gets, the kind of man who worked on a road-paving crew while waiting for his hand to heal following a boxing-related injury.

Ward wasn't always a stalker looking to land the left hook to the liver. Well into his career, he had one of those "click moments" that changed everything.

"The funny thing is, if you look at tapes of me when I was younger, I was more of a dancer," Ward wrote in his autobiography, *The Warrior's Heart*. "I didn't become the fighter people recognize today until I was in my late 20s, early 30s. For the longest time I didn't have confidence that I could take a punch, and when I realized I could, everything changed. That cut to the core of being a fighter: When you stand in there and get hit, and you don't go down, and you don't get your brain scrambled, it's an amazing feeling."

Some things stick in your memory forever, like hitting your first homerun in Little League. Ward-Gatti I, May 19, 2002, at Mohegan Sun in Uncasville, Connecticut, was another. A damn good fight was expected going in, but what we got was a masterpiece.

Something happened after the fight I have never experienced before or since. When the post-fight press conference was over, quite a few of the writers wandered back into the empty arena and hung around the ring. It was as if they were reluctant to leave the site of the miraculous event they had witnessed and wanted to linger in the euphoria that had cast a spell over even the most cynical among us.

"It was humbling to watch something like that," said HBO analyst Larry Merchant. "They gave so much of themselves, it's as if they were skydiving without a parachute."

Ward's 10-round majority decision victory was the highlight of his career and led to two more lucrative bouts with Gatti. The second and third fights were at Atlantic City's Boardwalk Hall, which has twice as many seats as the Mohegan Sun. The cover of *The Ring* previewing the second fight was the result of a last-minute brain-wave by photographer Tom Casino—both Ward and Gatti were slug-gers, so why not pose them with Louisville Slugger baseball bats? Everybody thought it was a good idea, and managing editor Eric Raskin dashed off to the nearest sporting goods store to buy the bats.

It turned out to be more than just a cover photo when the image was reproduced on T-shirts.

Gatti won the second and third fights by 10-round unanimous decision. The second held six months after the first, was outstanding but not as good as the first. The rubber match, on June 7, 2003, was, however, another mindblower, and like the first, the third bout was selected as *The Ring*'s Fight of the Year.

Ward, who was guaranteed $750,000 for the third Gatti fight, was already beginning to feel the effects of his career, so he retired. Gatti fought on, winning the vacant WBC junior welterweight title with a 12-round unanimous decision over previously undefeated Gianluca Branco. He made two successful defenses, but by then, his body had had enough, even if Arturo hadn't. He was stopped in three of his final four bouts, the last of which came in July 2007.

Gatti played a prominent role in keeping big-time boxing alive in Atlantic City. The second Ward fight was the first of nine straight appearances in the saltwater taffy capital of the world. The atmosphere inside the Boardwalk Hall when Gatti fought was incredible, and when he made his ring walk the noise reverberated through your body as if you were a human tuning fork.

"It's fair to say that we promoted nine sellouts in a row with Arturo in Atlantic City," said Kathy Duva, CEO of Main Events. "The ticket prices varied depending on the level of opposition. So while the dollar figure for each gate was different, to the best of my recollection, we sold every ticket every time. It was a remarkable run. And we all had so much fun. I will never forget it. The excitement of that time was so exhilarating. It is and always will be among the highlights of my life."

Boxing rarely provides a happy ending, and so it was for Gatti and Ward. Gatti died, July 11, 2009, under mysterious circumstances while on holiday with his wife, Amanda Rodrigues, in Ipojuca, a seaside resort in Brazil. His legend lives on in the hearts of boxing fans and a plaque on the wall at the International Boxing Hall of Fame, where he was posthumously inducted in 2013.

Ward, who still lives in his hometown of Lowell, Massachusetts, suffers from chronic traumatic encephalopathy (CTE), the consequences of taking so many blows to the head.

"The stuff I go through every day, worrying about if I'm going to get a headache and how bad it's going to be, kind of like, consumes you," Ward told the *Boston Herald*. "It's terrible. It makes you nauseous. It's like a thump in the back of my head. You just feel drained all day."

Ward, 54, has pledged to donate his brain to Boston University upon his death, for research purposes. Hopefully, it will be in better condition than Johnny Blackjack's. Micky is a treasure.

Taken as a whole, the melodrama that was the Gatti-Ward trilogy could very well provide fodder for Euripides, Sophocles and their brethren, the guys who left the toga parties long enough to write Greek tragedies. Surely Shakespeare could do it justice. How about an opera?

There was something grand about it beyond three great fights. It was boxing's version of a passion play, complete with suffering and sacrifice. There will be no resurrection for the boxers, just for the sport they loved.

OSCAR DE LA HOYA

BOXER AS TEEN IDOL

Originally published in *The Ring*, October 1998.

It was almost midnight when a car screeched to a halt in the middle of the block in downtown El Paso, Texas. The door flew open, and out jumped a pretty young woman, a look of ecstasy on her face. "Oscar, Oscar," she yelled, abandoning the vehicle in her rush to join a group of about 50 other shrieking women clustered around a large white bus decorated with images of Oscar De La Hoya.

The Oscarmobile had just backed into the service entrance of the Camino Real Hotel, where HBO was throwing a party to celebrate his knockout of Patrick Charpentier in the evening. Oscarmania had reached Beatlesque proportions, creating a series of surreal scenes in which De La Hoya was treated more like a rock star than a fighter.

Several days before the fight, in excess of 1,000 fans, most of them female, packed the Carolina Recreation Center gym to witness a supposedly secret workout. More than 600 people attended a prefight press conference the next day. Among them was Sadie Pedraza, a senior at Socorro High School, who was lucky enough to sneak a kiss while presenting De La Hoya a bag of food from Chico's Tacos, an El Paso landmark.

Pedraza, who said that Oscar's lips were "really soft," was the envy of the approximately 1,500 swooning admirers waiting outside for a glimpse of their hearts desire. "Oscar, I want to have your baby," yelled one woman. "Oscar, I won't ask for child support," screamed another.

The scene at the weigh-in was almost as chaotic. The ever-present gaggle of girls was waiting in the parking lot of the El Paso Hilton, and police had to shoo them to one side so that the Oscarmobile could roll into the lot. Throughout it all, De La Hoya behaved like the perfect Prince Charming, flashing his million-dollar smile and spending much time as possible mingling with his fans and signing autographs. He was obviously having the time of his life. Who wouldn't be?

The phenomenon of boxer as teen idol is unprecedented. True, fighters have always attracted more members of the opposite sex than the average guy, but not even a pretty-boy superstar such as Sugar Ray Leonard reached the status currently enjoyed by De La Hoya. Leonard was married during the peak of his popularity, and that spoiled the sort of fantasy that impels teenage girls put on their best little black dresses and compete with hundreds, sometimes thousands, of other girls for their hero's attention. Moreover, Leonard's charm seemed programed at times, while the "Golden Boy" comes across as entirely natural when interacting with the public.

"He's so sincere, such a nice guy," said Miss El Paso 1996, Michelle Rios, on hand for the weigh-in to give De La Hoya and Charpentier each a bunch of red roses. "You could see in his eyes that he was kind of tired, but he still took time to talk with people. He's cute, but he's also down to earth. I think that's the reason he's so popular."

Even Muhammad Ali wasn't the greatest in this department. Although the idol of millions and extremely popular with women, he was also controversial, hated by large segments of the population during the early part of his career. By the time Ali was a beloved figure, he was too old to be a teenage heartthrob. De La Hoya is 25 and comes without such baggage; he is gracious in victory, and except for a few ill-chosen remarks about black fighters, politically correct at all times.

During fight week in El Paso, it was virtually impossible to avoid the omnipresent image of De La Hoya. Larger-than-life photograph of him posing provocatively with his shirt unbuttoned, a dreamy look on his handsome face, were everywhere. Duck into a bar for a cool brew and there's Oscar picture, reminding you *"Respecto y Control"* is paramount when consuming alcoholic beverages. Turn on the evening news for the latest De La Hoya update, and you discover that even the weather had been Oscarized with small photos of the WBC welterweight titleholder next to the forecast for fight night. Boxer as logo?

El Paso's love affair began in 1996 when he visited the city during a promotional tour for the first Julio César Chávez match, but few would have guessed that by time he returned his popularity would have grown to such gigantic proportions. More than 30,000 tickets were sold the first day they went on sale, and by the time De La Hoya climbed into the ring at the Sun Bowl (home of the University of Texas El Paso's Fightin' Miners) 45,329 fans had paid anywhere from $31 to $329 to see the Golden Boy shine. And when you consider the fact that hardly anybody gave the challenger a chance, those figures were even more starling. Even with such a limited opponent, the crowd would have been even larger if the local cable TV company had not lifted the blackout.

No one was more aware of the impact the massive event would have on De La Hoya's career than Bjorn Rebney, a Los Angeles-based attorney who has handled De La Hoya's marketing since October 1994. Rebney also represents Ray Leonard and has worked with San Francisco 49ers, Steve Young and Hakeem Olajuwon in the past. He sees what took place in El Paso as a "great snapshot of what's good about boxing, an event that transcends the sport."

Oscarmania didn't happen overnight. Nor did it happen by accident. To increase his client's fan base, Rebney has gone beyond the vehicles normally associated with boxing. And now the groundwork is paying off.

"You might think we'd shoot for *Sports Illustrated*, the boxing magazines, or ESPN," said Rebney. "But we want to create cross-cultures and cross-gender appeal, so we also place Oscar in *Bazaar* and *Cosmopolitan*, magazines with younger demographics."

De La Hoya has already earned millions in endorsements, and new deals with Levi and EA Sports—manufacturers of "Knockout," a new boxing video game due to hit the market in September—will bring millions more. According to Rebney, the biggest benefit of sports marketing isn't the money the fighter receives from the clients he represents.

"The real benefit comes when he fights," Rebney said. "The exposure wins over casual sports fans, which in turn increases the pay-per-view buy rate. That gives the fighters leverage when negotiating purses and means more dollars when Oscar steps into the ring."

Does this mean that now De La Hoya can fill football stadiums fighting no-hopers like Charpentier, we'll have to get used to a steady diet of mismatches? Thankfully, the answer is no. Boxing fans aren't the only ones who want to see De La Hoya fight Felix Trinidad. Team De La Hoya, Bob Arum, and Rebney are all eager for a superfight and the super payday that will accompany it. A bout with Trinidad and the ensuing hoopla would also be another step toward the next—and the most elite—marketing plateau.

"There's never been, and probably never will be, another like Michael Jordan. What he has done is unheard of," Rebney said, discussing the relatively small pantheon of athletes who have become marketing icons. "Tiger Woods is big, but he doesn't generate the kind of enthusiasm that Oscar does. One or two huge fights and Oscar will be there.

Of course, the continued growth of Oscarmania is predicated on De La Hoya continuing to win. Arum is so confident of his star's superiority, he offered Trinidad and Ike Quartey a crack at the Golden Boy, no strings attached. "I don't want any options," Arum said at the post fight press conference in El Paso, while promising Trinidad and Quartey more money than they've ever earned before.

Nobody is saying what happened in El Paso signifies that De La

Hoya is just as big throughout the country as he is in that West Texas city across the Rio Grande from Juárez, Mexico. Even though he was embraced by the entire city, the fact that a sizable percentage of the population is Hispanic was meaningful. It also helps that there are no major league sports franchises, and the community is hungry for big-time entertainment.

Even so, it was quite a sight to see so many thousands at a boxing match, many of them demographically desirable (read young and reasonably affluent), sort of consumers corporate America adores. Only two fights in the past 20 years have drawn larger crowds than De La Hoya-Charpentier in the United States. One was Ali-Leon Spinks II (a legend's last hurrah) in 1978, the other Pernell Whitaker-Julio César Chávez (a genuine superfight) in '93.

It's going to take some time and a few more fights before we know to what extent Oscarmania flourishes. But there's something about the scene in El Paso the second week of June that was reminiscent of a certain concert four lads from Liverpool gave at Shea Stadium in 1965.

Boxer as teen idol will undoubtedly rankle some purists, but even the most conservative fans have to love the way De La Hoya turns an assassin when the opening bell rings. And if thousands of women screaming his name during fights is the price we have to pay to watch this this unique fighter test his talent against the best of the rest, so be it. If one thing rang true in El Paso, it was that De La Hoya is the immediate future of boxing, a guy who can not only carry the sport on his back, but maybe even take it places it has never been before.

———

EPILOGUE: De La Hoya fought on until he was TKO'd on December 6, 2008 by Manny Pacquiao. Oscar won world titles in six weight classes and had an overall pro record of 39-6, 30 KOs. He is currently Chairman and CEO of Golden Boy Promotions.

BERNARD HOPKINS

A LEGEND IN OUR MIDST

ORIGINALLY PUBLISHED IN *THE RING*, VOLUME II, 2004

GENIUS AT WORK is seldom spectacular. Regardless of whether it's Einstein at the chalkboard working out his theory of relativity, or Michelangelo on his scaffold painting the Sistine Chapel, it's the results that take your breath away. And so it was when Bernard Hopkins created his latest masterpiece, a knockout victory of Oscar De La Hoya that appeared somewhat prosaic in progress but ultimately turned into his magnum opus—and certainly left De La Hoya breathless.

In the final analysis, it doesn't matter whether or not Hopkins' one-punch destruction of "The Golden Boy" elevates the middleweight champion in the minds of pay-per-view patrons, because as Hopkins said in the aftermath of his division-record 19th successful title defense, "Money you make, and the money you lose. But history you can't erase. That lives on after I'm dead. That's important to Bernard Hopkins."

There's no doubt that history will be kind to Hopkins, a true believer in the power of professionalism and perseverance who has placed himself among the all-time greats of the middleweight division. Today, he stands shoulder to shoulder with Stanley Ketchel, Harry Greb, Ray Robinson, Carlos Monzón, and Marvin Hagler, the iconic boxers who have made the 160-pound class second only to the heavyweight in terms of popularity and prestige.

If Hopkins' knockout of Felix Trinidad started him up the ladder leading to the middleweight Mount Rushmore, the De La Hoya victory was the rock carvers' cue to start sculpting his face in stone. Pretty he is not, but make no mistake, a true legend walks among us. Those who still don't comprehend that fact should be counted among those who think there is no sun on a cloudy day.

It is true, however, that you have to understand the nuances of the sweet science to fully appreciate Hopkins' artistry. He does not swing for the fences like Mike Tyson, bedazzle like Roy Jones, or bleed like Arturo Gatti.

What Hopkins does is as complicated as the inner workings of a computer, but at the same time as basic as digging a ditch. It's a craft honed by countless hours in the toughest gyms in Philadelphia, where a few wise old heads still impart the wisdom handed down from when it took more than a $25 license and towel over your shoulder to call yourself a trainer.

That Hopkins graduated summa cum laude from these inner-city sweatshops come as no surprise to those who have followed his career. But as technically brilliant as he clearly is, it was not skill alone that enabled him to endure the bitter fruit harvested the first decade of his pro career.

His character, as strong and finely tuned as his body, kept him focused when it often seemed the entire boxing industry was conspiring against him. Weaker men would have given up or capitulated to the powers that be. But Hopkins never wavered, never swerved from his chosen path, and never ditched his principles in favor of a fast buck, even when it seemed the roadblocks appeared insurmountable.

True, there were times when Hopkins tripped over his own paranoid-tinged stubbornness, but now, in the golden glow of his latest triumph, even the most egregious misstep seems minor compared to gigantic leap he's taken from penitentiary to the pinnacle of his profession. And when Hopkins entered the MGM Grand Garden Arena to the sound of *My Way*, the sentiment suited him just as much as it did Sinatra.

De La Hoya thought he was going to be fighting the middleweight champion of the world, a tough enough task for a fighter who turned pro as a 133-pounder, even one as gifted as Oscar. But it wasn't just an accomplished and dedicated champion he was confronting; he was also up against the journey that had led Hopkins to that moment. It was an odyssey that had taken him to the heart of darkness and back again, forcing him to battle the boxing establishment just as hard as he did his opponents, fending off detractors at every turn.

"The Golden Boy" never had to wash pots and pans to survive, or practically beg to have his image on the cover of a boxing magazine. De La Hoya never had to defend his title on ESPN for $100,000 or find a storefront lawyer to defend him against a high-priced team of attorneys.

Granted, none of that would have mattered if Hopkins didn't have the fighting ability to go along with it. The combination of the life experiences that have forged him and his impeccable craftsmanship created the most formidable middleweight since Marvin Hagler.

When the De La Hoya fight was announced, it was difficult to find anyone outside the challenger camp who thought he was going to win, but as the fight approached, there was growing support for De La Hoya. Some of that was due to the six-pack that had replaced the paunch Oscar sported for his close shave against Felix Sturm in June. Even so, Hopkins entered the ring a minus-220 favorite, which means punters had to bet $220 on the champ to win $100.

The first was quintessential feel 'em out round. It looked like some sort exotic mating ritual, one advancing and then quickly withdrawing if the other so much as batted and eyelid.

For the first six rounds, it seemed that those who bet De La Hoya had an outside chance of cashing in. But when Hopkins' dominance became more apparent in the seventh and eighth rounds, those riding the long shot must have felt like Stewart Elliot at the 2004 Belmont. When trainer Bouie Fisher told him to "pick it up," Hopkins cranked up the intensity and overtook his rival before they entered the home-stretch.

There was delicious irony in the finishing blow that cut down De La Hoya at the 1:38 mark of the ninth round. The left hook to the liver has long been considered the signature punch of fighters of Mexican heritage, so perhaps it's understandable if De La Hoya and his trainer, Floyd Mayweather Sr., had forgotten that Philadelphia also have a tradition of throwing the left hook.

"We've been teaching that punch for years," said Hopkins' trainer, Bouie Fisher, of the act of planting a punch on that ultra-vulnerable area between the top of the hip and the bottom of the ribcage.

The end came with such suddenness that many among the capacity crowd of 16,112 didn't realize at first what had happened. But there was no missing the unprecedented sight of De La Hoya writhing in agony on the canvas as referee Kenny Bayless counted him out.

It was, as Kevin Iole of the *Las Vegas Review-Journal* wrote, "an old-school punch from an old-school fighter," as emblematic of Hopkins as it ever was of Rubén Olivares, Mexico's finest proponent of the punch.

Less than an hour after Hopkins fulfilled his promise of becoming the first to stop De La Hoya, media matchmakers were eager to bulldoze the career-long middleweight into a match with light heavyweight champion Antonio Tarver.

"I'm not a light heavyweight," Hopkins said. "Do I want to put myself at great risk to do something like that? I've got to think hard about that. I do want big fights, but I'm going to be smart about it."

Hopkins' number-one priority now is to tally his 20th defense of the middleweight title. Regardless of who is in the opposite corner when Hopkins' attempts to extend his defense record, it will be a crucial test of "The Executioner's" drawing power. On the plus side, the De La Hoya fight was Hopkins' first million buys pay-per-view.

Unfortunately, a quick scan of *The Ring*'s top ten 160-pounders fails to unearth a contender who would generate anything close to the $10 million payday he earned against De La Hoya.

Exactly how far Hopkins' own star has risen following his kayo of De La Hoya remains to be seen, but he did garner a guest spot on *The Tonight Show with Jay Leno* the Monday after the fight. Such appearances have become something of a rite of passage for boxers edging their way into the mainstream.

Hopkins should certainly be able to get some mileage out of the fact that he's almost 40 and still the best fighter, pound-for-pound, on the planet. He's never going to be as cuddly as George Foreman, or as pretty as Ray Leonard, but in his own way he can be very engaging. Hopkins is a publicity hound, the sort of quote machine journalist love, and always generous with fans.

Bernard is smart man. He knows he's never going to have the mass adulation De La Hoya enjoys, and perhaps that's how it should be. De La Hoya will always be more of a star than a fighter, while Hopkins will always be more of a fighter a star. And once the opening bell rings, that's what really counts.

———

EPILOGUE: Hopkins made his 20th successful middleweight title defense in February 2005, winning a unanimous decision over Howard Eastman. Hopkins lost the championship to Jermain Taylor via controversial decision in July 2005, but in June 2006 annexed the light heavyweight championship with a unanimous decision over Tarver.

Hopkins won and lost the light heavyweight title three more time before retiring, following a knockout loss to Joe Smith Jr. in December 2016. His April 2014 decision over Beibut Shumenov at the age of 49 made him the oldest boxer in history to win a major title. Hopkins, a stockholder in Golden Boy Promotions, continues to work for GBP as publicist, broadcaster, and goodwill ambassador.

MARCO ANTONIO BARRERA

OVERTHROWS THE PRINCE IN A BID TO BECOME KING OF MEXICO

ORIGINALLY PUBLISHED IN *THE RING*, AUGUST 2001

IT WAS AROUND 11 a.m. on Sunday, and Marco Antonio Barrera was on his way to a well-deserved breakfast. He seemed strangely anonymous as he walked through a maze of slot machines and blackjack tables at the MGM Grand, where the night before he'd won the richest featherweight prizefight in history. No fanfare proceeded him, and although he stopped to pose for a photograph with a fan, for the most part Barrera went unnoticed, just a slender figure in a track suit, accompanied by a few friends and family members.

When he got to the Studio Café, Barrera, a genuine man of the people, stood in line with everybody else and patiently waited his turn to be seated. You couldn't imagine "Prince" Naseem Hamed, even in the aftermath of Barrera's victory the previous evening, doing likewise, which says a lot about the core difference between the vanquished prince and the new king.

It's easy to understand why the citizens of his native Mexico have fallen in love with Barrera. Theirs is a culture that still considers modesty and a down-to-earth demeanor attributes rather than detriments, a culture where fighters' fists are still more impor-

39

tant than his mouth. And now that he's beaten Hamed, Barrera might be ready to assume a title far more important than any belt bestowed by a governing body.

Boxing fans never tired of waiting "the new" somebody or another, and love to speculate about the next Ali, Robinson, or Marciano. We're so hungry for another taste of greatness past, so eager to drape a new hero with the mantle of his predecessor, half the time we don't even wait until the original has retired before looking for his replacement.

The more protracted the decline, the more likely an old hero will still be taking punches when the hunt for his equivalent begins, which is certainly the case in this instance. After all, we've been searching for a new Julio César Chávez since Frankie Randall handed the man generally recognized as the greatest Mexican boxer of all time his first pro defeat back in 1994.

Although "J.C. Superstar" is currently retired, he hung around long enough to see several of his potential successors come and go. Among the false messiahs who have vied for the position heretofore were Miguel Angel Gonzalez, Erik Morales, and Barrera himself, who sputtered after a splendid run of 43 straight wins to start his pro career.

Gonzales was at his best at lightweight, where he was never beaten and successfully defended the WBC title 10 times. "El Mago" was a strong candidate until he moved up to junior welterweight and lost to Oscar De La Hoya. Who knows what would have happened if he hadn't grown out of the 135-pound division.

Morales, who seemed so promising until fairly recently, is still technically undefeated, but it's difficult to find anybody outside of his camp who thinks he really deserved the decision when he hooked up with Barrera in *The Ring*'s 2000 Fight of the Year.

To make matters worse, Morales needed the help of friendly Vegas judges to win the WBC featherweight title from Guty Espadas in his most recent start. Morales may prove us wrong yet, but right now he no longer seems destined for the god-like status enjoyed by the once "Lion of Culiacan."

It was, of course, Barrera's magnificent battle with Morales that reestablished the former's prominence after several years on the periphery. When an immediate rematch wasn't forthcoming, Barrera seemed to slide backward. He won his next three fights but didn't look impressive. There was talk to the effect that the war with Morales had taken all the fight out of Barrera. Maybe that's what Hamed and his brother/manager Riath figured when they agreed to fight Barrera.

Going in, the majority opinion was that Hamed's punch, considered, pound-for-pound, among the sport's most potent, would be too much for Barrera to handle. Then there was Naz's unique style, a hybrid of unorthodox moves and innate brilliance. It had driven many competent fighters to the point of utter confusion before they were summarily dismissed by one or to two of Hamed's bombs. Only four of Naseem's 35 precious victims lasted long enough to hear the final bell, and the Englishman promised to make Barrera number 36.

"I'm in there to get the back of your head dirty," Hamed told Barrera. "I'm coming there to knock you out."

The soft-spoken Barrera was no match for the bombastic Brit in a war of words, and besides, talking trash has never been his style. Beneath his reserved demeanor he is a man of both passion and sensitivity.

As a personality, it's unlikely that Barrera will ever be as charismatic as gregarious Chávez or cheeky Hamed. He's also less likely to be found pounding down Coronas with the boys at corner cantina. As boxers, however, Chávez and Barrera share a common heritage as graduates of the old school of boxing, steeped in the traditional techniques of their trade.

Like practically all Mexicans fighters, Barrera has a grinding offense, featuring a paralyzing left hook to the liver. But as he clearly demonstrated in the Hamed bout, he's also become a disciplined boxer, a valuable asset lacked by many Mexican boxers.

It is this very versatility that could be the key to Barrera becoming a special fighter. The greatest irony was not that he outboxed Hamed, but that he did it with traditional boxing methodology

Naz never bothered to master. In the process, he turned Hamed's world inside out, and for the first time in his career, the Prince could neither hit his opponent cleanly nor avoid punches coming in his direction. It must have been a painful revelation.

An indication of Barrera's growing popularity was the thousands of Mexicans and Mexican-Americans among the crowd of 12,847 in attendance. They were among the first to arrive fight night, filling the cheap ($75) seats with clusters of happy, chanting, flag-waving fans, eager to pit their vocal cords against the equally vociferous English contingent on hand to root for Hamed. Together, they created a marvelous atmosphere that almost compensated for the fact that it was too one-sided to be a good fight.

Things began to go wrong for Hamed even before the fight started. First, he couldn't find a pair of gloves that fit correctly, and then he was doused by a cupful of unidentified liquid as he alighted from the hoop-like device that carried him from the top of the MGM Grand Garden to the floor on the arena.

The first round set the precedent for most of what followed, as Hamed, eager to deliver the knockout he promised, took the fight to Barrera. Virtually all of his offerings either fell short or were blocked, and Barrera countered with accurate lefts to the head, several of which buckled Hamed's knees and drew gasps from the thousands of Brits who had journeyed to Las Vegas to support their countryman.

Hamed, already frustrated by his inability to hit Barrera, initiated a bit of rough stuff in the second, and both fell to the ring floor in an untidy tangle. Naz's nose started bleeding in the third round and a left hook rocked him in the fourth.

Things continued to worsen for Hamed as the fight progressed. A counter right shook him in the eighth and forced to him to momentarily grab the top rope for support. Knowing he needed a knockout to win, Hamed gamely trade with Barrera in the 10th and managed to have his best round of the fight. Barrera quickly reestablished authority in the next round by landing stinging combinations to the head.

Barrera added the final insult in the 12th round, first battering Hamed into the ropes, and then bulldogging him headfirst into a turnbuckle pad. Referee Joe Cortez docked Barrera a point for the blatant infraction, but by then a decision victory was well beyond Hamed's reach.

The unanimous decision went to Barrera by scores of 116-111 and 115-112 (twice).

"He won the fight clearly in my mind," said a gracious Hamed, whose distress was soothed to a degree by his $6.5-million payday "Credit is due to him; he was better than me tonight."

"It was a very hard fight," said Barrera, who took home a career-high $1.9 million. "He's used to fighting Mexican fighters who don't know tactics. Today, I beat him at his own game."

"I've never seen that much excitement for two featherweights," said HBO Sports/TVKO Senior Vice President Mark Taffet, who estimated that when all the numbers are crunched, the pay-per-view would do close to 250,000 buys and break the $10-million ceiling. "It's completely unheard of in this business for featherweights to generate so much money."

Barrera, with his victory over Hamed and de facto win over Morales, already has a leg up in any series involving this trio, and also seems to be taking strides toward gaining Chavez-like prestige.

"Barrera was headed that way," said Don Chargin, the Hall of Fame promoter who has worked with practically all the major Mexican stars during his lengthy career. "Now he's beaten Hamed there's no way of telling how far he can go, especially with the confidence it gave him.

Chargin is not alone in his assessment.

"Chávez is gone, so the Mexican boxing community is waiting for a new hero," said Roberto Raijar, a veteran California journalist with his finger of the pulse of the Latino boxing market. "So, yes, Barrera could be on the same level as Chávez used to be, but it depends on how long he lasts. This is boxing, after all, you never know what is going to happen."

A certain Anglo-Arab Prince, recently demoted to commoner, would undoubtedly agree.

————

EPILOGUE: While Barrera remained popular throughout the remainder of his career, he didn't become the "new Chávez." He did, however, win a return bout with Morales in June 2001 by unanimous decision, and also won the rubber match by majority decision in November 2004 (also The Ring's Fight of the Year). In between, Barrera was stopped by Manny Pacquiao in November 2003. He also lost a rematch to Pacquiao by unanimous decision in October 2006. After the second Pacquiao fight, Barrera began to fade and retired after his final bout in February 2011. He was inducted into the International Boxing Hall of Fame in 2017.

Hamed had one more fight, winning a unanimous decision over Manuel Calvo in London on May 18, 2002, and then retired. He was inducted into the International Boxing Hall of Fame in 2015.

ROY JONES'S ONE-MAN SHOW

UPSTAGED BY THE ROCKETTES AND WHITNEY HOUSTON

ORIGINALLY PUBLISHED IN *THE RING*, MAY 2000.

THE STAGE WAS SET, literally, for Roy Jones to light up Manhattan with the brilliance of his art. He was headlining the first-ever fight card at the legendary Radio City Music Hall, in front of HBO's cameras and a sold-out celebrity-packed house. But instead of a virtuoso performance by boxing's pound-for-pound best, Jones gave us another tease—enough to suggest greatness, but not enough to confirm it.

That has become Jones' pattern of late. His fights have been more or less one-man shows. The opponent is almost inconsequential, a foil for Jones to torment on his way to another handsome payday. It was, as David Telesco suspected, no accident that the challenger was nowhere to be found on the towering mural of Jones that adorned the front of the theater. Even though this was an athletic event, nobody was selling the fight; Jones was the only attraction.

While the absence of competition is unhealthy for any sport, there have always been certain fighters who could, for a spell, carry the game on the strength of their singular genius. But to make it work, that special fighter has to dominate weak competition the way

Joe Louis, Ray Robinson, Marvin Hagler, and Mike Tyson did in their primes. Simply put, that means knockouts. Sure, Muhammad Ali sold some of his lesser fights strictly on the power of his personality, but Jones is not Ali, and neither is anybody else.

After the fight, Jones revealed he had fractured his left wrist 3½ weeks before the fight.

"Everybody told me to cancel the fight," said Jones, who also claimed he hid it from the New York State Athletic Commission. "My dad even said, 'Don't take the fight that way.' I said, 'Dad, God gives you an opportunity [to fight at Radio City Music Hall] once in a lifetime, and this is my opportunity. I have to take it.' I refused to pull out because that's not me."

His sentiment is easy to understand, especially in light of the fact that Jones must have known he could beat Telesco one-handed—if indeed that is what he was. There were a couple of left hooks to Telesco's ribcage that hurt him more than any of the right hands that landed upstairs, and, in retrospect, you couldn't help wonder exactly how serious the injury was.

Some would argue that if handicapped, Jones only bolstered his claim to greatness by winning every round against a big, strong adversary with two good hands. But if Jones came into the ring damage goods, nobody really got what they paid for, and once again, when boxing was in the mainstream spotlight, the fight itself was nothing special.

The production values, however, were first-rate, and if there was ever an excuse for such over-the-top razzmatazz, boxing's debut at the showbiz shrine was it. Jones joined the high-kicking Rockettes on stage for a musical number about an hour before his fight, Whitney Houston sang "America the Beautiful," and rappers Method Man and Redman joined Jones in his ring walk.

Ironically, it was the dazzling quality of the trappings that emphasized the ultimately tedious nature of the fight. It was as if Whitney had sung well but had a sore throat and never reached for those high notes and nuances that make her rendition of any song special. You can't help wonder how many newcomers, attracted to the fight by hype, went home asking, "Is that all there is?"

Several things quickly became apparent as soon as the fight began. Telesco was clearly the biggest and strongest-looking opponent Jones has faced as a light heavyweight. He was also quick enough on his feet to make Jones miss a number of lunging power shots he launched in the first two rounds. Even when Jones landed a lead right, Telesco was usually pulling away, taking much of the sting out of the blow.

It was also it quickly became self-evident that the challenger was not going to take too many chances. Reverse was his gear of choice, and this, plus his size, durability, and lively legs allowed him to stay the course.

If Telesco came close to winning a round, it was the sixth. He bulled Jones into the ropes, dug to the body, but failed to inflict any serious damage. His attack soon petered out, and midway into the next round booing began to emanate from the crowd of 5,932.

Telesco, with abrasions around both eyes, made his only sustained attack in the eighth, pinning Jones on the ropes and hacking away the best he could. Judging by the way Jones flared back with superior punches, you have to figure the champion only allowed to get himself in such a position because of the countering opportunities it offered.

In the 10th, Jones delivered his punch of the night, a compact left hook that whizzed under Telesco's extended right arm and slammed into his ribcage with tremendous force. It was the challenger's biggest crisis of the fight, but he showed commendable grit by refusing to fold and punched back just enough just enough to make it through the round.

Unlike his other recent performances, Jones didn't coast the last few rounds, and stayed on the offensive. It looked like he really would have liked to put Telesco away and provide a fitting climax to the proceedings but couldn't quite pull it off.

"I would have knocked him out if I had both hands," Jones said after winning a unanimous decision by scores of 120-106 and 120-108 (twice).

Most likely, Jones was correct, but the hand wasn't the only issue. Due to the fact that Jones is blessed with astonishing speed and coordination, he has developed a unique style of his own. Apparently, he never felt the need to master some of the traditional technique other boxers use to finish a wounded foe such as Telesco.

"It very much has to do with attitude," said HBO boxing analyst Larry Merchant. "Jones, who calls himself a great athlete who just happens to be a boxer, rarely feels the need to stop a guy. His critics claim he lacks passion, but nobody can be as good at what he does without passion. The problem is that he rarely displays that passion."

IBF middleweight titleholder Bernard Hopkins, who was at the fight to lobby for a rematch with Jones, has his own spin on what took place in the Telesco fight.

"Roy Jones does what Roy Jones does," Hopkins told the *Philadelphia Daily New*s. "He outboxes guys. It was easy. Telesco showed a lot of heart, but he was outclassed and outskilled. If you can't force Roy to fight, really fight, he's not going to do more than he has to."

"When we talk about the great light heavyweights of the past, only Archie Moore and Bob Foster were knockout punchers, had what I call paralyzing power," Merchant said. "Most of the others— Gene Tunney, Ezzard Charles, Billy Conn, Harold Johnson, and maybe Michael Spinks—were not punchers of that sort. They had a lot of decisions on their records, and a lot of their knockouts came early in their careers against lesser opponents.

"At the end of the day, Jones is an extraordinary talent, and we must appreciate him while we can. The next guys down the road could make him look even better than he appears now."

Still, Merchant is the first to agree that style matters very much in boxing, and he can't but wonder how strong Jones's influence will be on the future of the sport.

"Look back 100 years, and see how different boxing was back then," he said. "Boxing as we know probably started with Tunney. Is

Roy Jones the prototype for the kind of fighter we'll be seeing 50 years from now? Or is he one of a kind?"

Naturally, those with a taste for more tradition boxing fare fervently hope it's the latter. A great athlete who happens to be a boxer can only carry the sport so far. What the sweet science needs to take it into the next century is a boxer who happens to be a great athlete. For many, Jones's big night in the Big Apple only deepened the suspicion that he's probably not the one for the job.

———

EPILOGUE: Jones won his next eight bouts, but was knocked out by Antonio Tarver in May 2004, and when Glen Johnson knocked him out again four months later, Jones's career as an elite boxer was over. He kept fighting until February 2018, usually competing against second and third-third rate adversaries.

TERENCE CRAWFORD

BORN TO BOX

ORIGINALLY PUBLISHED ON ESPN, APRIL 19, 2019

IT's strange how some memories fade away like forgotten ghosts and others seem eternally lodged in the hippocampus. That would certainly account for Terence "Bud" Crawford's vivid recollection of his first trip to a boxing gym almost 25 years ago, when he was 7. He didn't realize it at the time, but he had found his calling.

There was a faint trace of youthful joy in Crawford's voice when he recalled the momentous day he first entered the C.W. Boxing Club in Omaha, Nebraska.

"I just wanted to hit the speed bag and spar," Crawford said of his first visit. "When kids talk to me about boxing, the first thing they ask is, 'Can you do that ball?' That's what they call the speed bag. It was the first thing I wanted to do, and then I wanted to spar because I was always fighting. After about two weeks, they let me spar my cousin and we really went at it."

Back then, Crawford was a skinny kid with a bad temper who loved to scrap so much he was kicked off the football team for fighting.

"If it didn't have anything to do with fighting, it wasn't fun,"

Crawford once told Tony Boone of the *Omaha World Herald*. "That's what I like to do, fight."

Maybe that shouldn't be too surprising. Crawford's father and grandfather were amateur boxers, as were two of his uncles. It's in his blood.

There are plenty of kids who give boxing a try, particularly those hoping to punch their way out of poverty. Some stick with it and others don't, but very few have accomplished as much as Crawford. There's something extra inside him, something that has infused his life and fueled his passion.

"I fight so hard because I've been scared since a child," reads a post on Crawford's Twitter account from a year ago.

Not many boxers would make a public confession like that, but Crawford is comfortable enough in his own skin to be candid. He has the casual self-assurance of somebody who knows who he is and what he can do.

Success and the money it brings don't appear to have affected him in any fundamental way. Crawford still likes to fight as much as he did the first day he arrived at the C.W. Boxing Club. But things might have turned out differently if trainer Midge Minor hadn't taken a liking to him because he had a "fighter's attitude."

With Crawford's father away in the U.S. Navy much of the time, Minor became Terence's surrogate father. The teenage years were particularly challenging. Fearing he would lose him to the streets, Minor would pick up Crawford after school and show him boxing videos until it was time to go to the gym.

There are a lot of wise old heads in boxing gyms, hoping to turn kids' lives around, and Minor is one of them. He was there when Crawford needed him and helped fashion the angry child into arguably today's finest prizefighter.

Since turning pro in March 2008, Crawford has accomplished things he could only dream of as a kid. He's undefeated (34-0, 25 KOs), has won titles in three weight classes and is currently No. 2 in ESPN's pound-for-pound ranking. In 2018, he won an ESPY for Fighter of the Year.

Crawford, who will make a second defense of his WBO world welterweight title against former junior welterweight champion Amir Khan on Saturday night at Madison Square Garden in New York, remains a zealot married to his craft. Ten years into his professional career, the 31-year-old still has an agile mind and a natural cruel streak that's totally old school.

Remember those images of Marvin Hagler running through the snow in Cape Cod, ice on his beard, wind and snowflakes blowing in his face? Crawford has that same kind of intensity. There was a similar shot taken of him recently while out for a frosty run down a snowy road.

Crawford seemingly can't get enough. His frequent presence at fights has not gone unnoticed. Television broadcasters often mention it when the camera scans the audience for celebrities. But Crawford is not there to be seen. He's there to watch the fights and maybe learn a thing or two.

"I'm a fan of the sport," Crawford said. "A lot of times I get to the fights real early and watch all the fights. I also like to see the top fighters in the world, see how they break down their opponents, what they do in certain circumstances. I look for anything where I can get an edge."

Roy Jones Jr., Floyd Mayweather and Pernell Whitaker were Crawford's early muses. These days he's often ringside to support Top Rank stablemates such as Steve Nelson, Jamal Herring, Shakur Stevenson and Ismail Muwendo. Crawford is particularly enthusiastic about ESPN.com's 2018 Prospect of the Year, Teofimo Lopez, another Top Rank boxer, about whom Crawford says, "He's got everything he needs to become boxing's next superstar."

He sees more of those young fighters in action than those he's preparing to fight himself. Somewhat surprisingly for a guy who examines boxing and boxers the way a theoretical physicist studies quantum mechanics and black holes, Crawford is not big on watching videos of his opponents.

"I don't for the simple fact that he's not going to fight me like he fights everybody else," Crawford said. "I make sure I'm at my best on fight night, so I'll be ready for whatever."

We've heard the same thing come out of the mouths of dozens of boxers, with mixed results. Crawford, however, has the smarts and ability to consistently pull it off.

He's a master of the mid-fight adjustments. It's as if he has an invisible toolkit from which he can produce whatever move or punch he needs on a split-second's notice.

There were moments of uncertainty on his way to a ninth-round TKO of Yuriorkis Gamboa in June 2014, but there hasn't been a single instance when Crawford looked in serious danger of losing a fight.

He is already good enough and accomplished enough to be a mainstream star. But it doesn't always work that way. At the moment, Crawford is stuck somewhere between underappreciated virtuoso and household name.

Crawford's plight is reminiscent of Hagler's protracted slog to success. After laboring far too long just below the surface of cross-over popularity, Hagler's breakthrough came in the wake of his iconic knockout of Thomas Hearns. But it came too late. Two more fights and Marvelous Marvin was gone, retired, never to fight again.

Crawford has yet to find his Hearns, and it's unlikely that he will when he takes on Khan (33-4, 20 KOs).

Still, win or lose, Khan always puts on a good show. He's a good puncher and has the guts to go after Crawford, which could very well result in a violent finish, most likely in Crawford's favor.

The way it looks now, Crawford will likely get his due incrementally, with a definitive victory over Khan another step in that direction.

Crawford's numbers continue to rise. There were 13,328 fans in attendance at Omaha's CHI Health Center to watch his TKO of José Benavidez Jr. on October 13.

The Khan fight is on pay-per-view, which will provide a more accurate indicator of Crawford's popularity. TV fans didn't have to pay a premium to watch Crawford's three previous fights.

It will be Crawford's third match as a welterweight, a talent-packed division where opportunities to find an opponent capable of providing a signature win are far greater.

Crawford and his girlfriend, Alindra Person, are raising three sons and two daughters. These days you're much more likely to find Crawford taking his son to a youth wrestling match than shooting craps on the corner.

Crawford is not a scared child anymore, but the memory of how it felt lingers, reinforcing his commitment to his trade and his family. He doesn't want his children growing up around gang violence the way he did.

Whether he was born to fight or circumstances made him a fighter is a distinction that no longer matters. What's important is that Crawford held his destiny tight to himself and never lost his love of fighting. It's always been what he does best.

———

EPILOGUE: Crawford remained undefeated, stopping Kahn in the 6th round of a one-sided match. The impressive victory, however, didn't perform well on PPV, garnering only 150,000 buys. He has made three more successful titled defenses since the Kahn fight, all by way of knockout.

THE GENIUS OF HI-TECH LOMACHENKO

HIS ATTACK IS LIKE JAZZ

ORIGINALLY PUBLISHED BY ESPN.COM, DECEMBER 9, 2017

THE HOTEL WAS full of hard-looking men in black leather jackets and pouty women wearing slinky outfits. Not the friendliest looking lot, but if you knew the magic word, instant camaraderie and safe passage to your room was assured.

Somebody shouted "Lomachenko," and the tough guys looked up as one, pumped their fists in the air and replied in kind at the top of their voice, "LO-MA-CHEN-KO!"

Boxing is like that, a zone of tolerance where people of different cultures, united in their love of the sport, sometimes come together in rough-hewn camaraderie. Sometimes is the key word here, but when it works out that way, it's also a place where stereotypes are confounded, and commonality overcomes dissimilarities.

The folks at the hotel weren't gangsters and their molls. They were the same Ukrainian fans that stuffed the 3,000-seat casino showroom at the MGM National Harbor in Maryland to watch Vasyl "Hi-Tech" Lomachenko stop Jason Sosa earlier in the evening. They chanted and sang as their countryman took apart brave Sosa, providing a wall of noise worthy of a thundering regiment of cavalry.

There was an air of festive inevitability about the fight. It has been that way for a long time. When you've lost only twice in 407 pro and amateur fights, people get used to you winning. It's expected.

Although Sosa fought the best he could and lasted nine rounds, he was not considered a serious threat to beat Lomachenko. Neither was Miguel Marriaga, who was stopped in seven rounds in Lomachenko's most recent fight.

But those were just claw sharpening exercises. The play dates are over. Lomachenko's junior lightweight title fight with Guillermo "El Chacal" Rigondeaux on Saturday at Madison Square Garden Theater is the real thing.

Like Lomachenko, Rigondeaux (17-0, 11 KOs) is a special fighter, a product of Cuba's celebrated amateur program and winner of more than 450 amateur bouts, including gold medals at both the 2000 and 2004 Olympics. He defected from his homeland in 2009, turned pro the same year and won his first major title in his ninth pro bout.

But more than anything else, Rigondeaux is, by far, the best opponent of Lomachenko's pro career, and vice versa. In terms of pedigree and combined talent, it would be difficult to make another fight of equal merit.

Why, then, is the fight taking place in the Madison Square Garden Theater and not the main arena, which holds almost four times as many people?

You could say that Lomachenko and Rigondeaux's popularity hasn't yet caught up with their capacity for greatness. But pedigree and talent alone are seldom enough to fill the big room. There has to be a connection beyond excellence. Boxing is tribal. Our guy verses the other guy.

The Ukrainians at Lomachenko-Sosa were not there chiefly because Lomachenko (9-1, 7 KOs) is such a fantastic fighter, though it certainly ups the ante. They were there because he's one of them —their guy.

But how does their guy become our guy or, better yet, everybody's guy?

An aesthetically pleasing style is a common thread. Without that fun-to-watch foundation, the rest doesn't matter that much. Personality is also critical. If an audience can relate to a fighter because of who is, as well as how he fights, it can create a bond beyond borders and native tongues.

Few geographical gatecrashers have done it better than Roberto Duran, Alexis Arguello and Julio César Chávez—a Panamanian, a Nicaraguan and a Mexican, respectively. One of the keys to their success with U.S. fans was that each had compelling qualities that helped forge instantly recognizable identities, brands that matched their fighting styles.

Duran, the snarling ruffian with mad skills who fought with measured savagery; Arguello, the charming "El Caballero," who turned into an assassin once the bell rang; and Chávez , the reincarnation of the stoic Aztec warrior—noble, proud and lethal.

They were avatars of warrior archetypes to which all cultures could relate. No wonder we didn't care where they came from or where they hung their hat.

The most recent example of the phenomenon is Manny Pacquiao, one of the most extraordinary rags-to-riches stories in sports history. The Filipino fighter conquered the world with extreme violence and a boyish smile, an irresistible combination that made him an international celebrity and multimillionaire.

In some ways, Lomachenko, 22, resembles Pacquiao: Constantly moving, attacking from unexpected angles and almost always punching in combination. Going for the knockout every time out.

But while primetime Pacquiao was all about raw aggression and reckless abandon, Lomachenko's attack is like jazz, a creative discipline with infinite variations.

The 29-year-old Ukrainian's fusion of ingenious footwork and offensive virtuosity is hypnotic. He feints like a fencing master and pivots as if ball bearings are attached to the bottom of his boxing boots—constantly stepping around opponents, changing direction in order to attack from a variety of angles, swiveling one way to unload and then another to escape.

Rigondeaux is a much harder sell.

"The Cuban style is different," Bob Arum told *Boxing News*, the British weekly, as his promotion approached. "They pile up points, then they stink you out till the end of the fight because all they care about is winning the fight on points."

It's hard to argue with Arum's assessment. Watching Rigondeaux when he doesn't feel like fighting is a shoot-me-now situation. Boxing fans have long memories, and those painfully lackluster showings made Rigondeaux look like a wallflower in a twerking contest.

The curious part is that when Rigondeaux is in a feisty mood, the results have often been highlight-reel material. The man can take you out with one shot.

Vegas odds-makers have made Rigondeaux a +300 underdog, but if there's a 130-pounder that can outfox Lomachenko, it's Guillermo. Jackals are often depicted as clever sorcerers in myths and legends, but this "Chacal" will need more than sleight of hand on Saturday. He must enter the ring with teeth bared, ready to bite.

Some say that Lomachenko is good enough to make Rigondeaux fight, giving him no choice but to engage. It's like what Thomas Hearns said when asked why he slugged with Marvin Hagler instead of boxing: "The reason I started out slugging is because I had to."

Lomachenko-Rigondeaux is for the connoisseurs and fight geeks, but it's also the next step in search for a new hero. It would be unrealistic of Arum, or anybody else for that matter, to think of Lomachenko as a replacement for Pacquiao. Pac-Man was a once-in-a-lifetime phenomenon. We won't see the likes of him again.

Nonetheless, Lomachenko is well positioned to be the next man up. First, however, there's an engagement with a Senor Jackal, who has ideas of his own. The drift of time seems to be in Lomachenko's favor, but Rigondeaux is not your ordinary B-side.

Expectations for Lomachenko are high. He's got to win this one if he wants to keep up with forerunners like Duran, Arguello and Chávez. The guys in the black leather jackets will always be there. They are of the same blood. But they're not enough.

What Lomachenko needs now is everybody else. A spectacular performance Saturday would be a perfect invitation.

———

EPILOGUE: Lomachenko stopped Rigondeaux in the sixth round and has since tallied eight more victories before suffering his first defeat, losing a 12-round decision to Teofimo Lopez. Sidelined during the Covid-19 pandemic, Lomachenko returned to action and tallied two comeback victories.

A WALK ON THE
DARK SIDE

THE MAN WHO WANTED TO BE SOMEBODY

THE LIFE AND DEATH OF SONNY BANKS

ORIGINALLY PUBLISHED IN *RINGSIDE SEAT*, WINTER, 2021

SONNY BANKS WAS on the ropes under attack when he threw the best punch of his life, a left hook of geometric perfection that put Cassius Clay on his ass. It happened in the first round, a moment frozen in time, a few seconds of glory that defined a man's life.

"Cassius went down with his eyes closed," wrote Angelo Dundee in his book, *My View From The Corner*. "But, when his butt hit the floor, they opened and lit up."

How different things would have been if Clay had not gotten up, but he did, and Banks's bid for boxing immortality slipped away, bit by bit, with every punch Clay landed.

Clay was an Olympic champion backed by a syndicate of rich white guys out of Louisville, a unique talent that would soon rule the boxing world as Muhammad Ali. He was supposed to win, and win he did when referee Ruby Goldstein stopped the fight 26 seconds into the fourth round. It was a good call. Banks was still dizzy from the punishment he had taken in the third round when he answered the bell for the fourth.

Neither Clay nor Banks was originally scheduled to fight the main event at Madison Square Garden the night of February 10, 1962. But when Eddie Machen pulled out of his heavyweight bout with Cleveland Williams with an injury, MSG matchmaker Teddy Brenner made some calls, and Clay and Banks took the fight on a week's notice.

Other than their profession, Clay and Banks shared little in common. It was a loquacious extrovert, who was becoming more famous with each passing fight, against a polite young man from rural Mississippi who was as green as he was enthusiastic, and virtually unknown outside of Detroit boxing circles.

Whether they realized it or not, a national TV audience and a small crowd at the Garden witnessed a slice of history—the first knockdown Clay suffered as a professional, an incident that grew larger in significance as time marched on to a James Brown beat and Ali became arguably the most iconic person of the 20th century.

Machen's injury was the first domino to fall, setting in motion a series of events eventually leading to tragedy, always an unwelcome reminder of what's really at stake.

———

Lucien "Sonny" Banks Jr. was born on June 29, 1940, in Birmingham Ridge, Lee County, Mississippi, a farming community about halfway between Tupelo and Saltillo. Sonny was the second youngest in a family of four brothers and two sisters raised by Lucien and Lillian Banks. They lived in a part of Birmingham Ridge known as the College Hill Community. Located on a red-dirt road, the tiny hamlet consisted of a general store, gas station, a Baptist Church and a collection of clapboard houses.

Banks did well in school, both in the classroom and on the football field. He carried himself with dignity and was unfailingly polite, the sort of guy who stood out for more than his athletic physique. For as long as he could remember, Sonny wanted to be somebody— somebody that mattered beyond the ordinary day-to-day struggles of life.

There were few options for a young black man living in Mississippi during the 1950s, especially with the police and Ku Klux Klan working as one. Banks and Emmett Till would have been around the same age when Till was murdered in 1955 in Money, Mississippi.

Banks quit school in 1958 and joined the tail end of the Great Black Migration (1917-1970), traveling north in search of work and a better life. Getting a job in the big city was just a start as far as Sonny was concerned. He wanted to fulfill his potential but wasn't sure how until boxing came into his life.

Sonny's brother, Jim Banks, who followed him to Detroit, said, "Lucien got interested in boxing from watching *Wide World of Sports* on TV. One day, he just went to the gym and started training."

According to Banks, the catalyst was the sounds coming out of a boxing gym he passed while walking down a street in Detroit. "I went inside to see what it was all about, and I was fascinated. The next day I went out and bought some boxing gear and that was it."

Theodore McWhorter, described by columnist Lyall Smith as a "spidery little man," had been around Motor City boxing since before Berry Gordy was a baby. According to Smith, McWhorter "organized a group of sportsmen-businessmen in the hope of uncovering, training, and promoting a new face who can knock the stuffing out of all the other faces belonging to heavyweight boxers around the world."

McWhorter figured Banks was as good candidate as any and started calling him the "best since [Joe] Louis," saying Sonny "could whip any of 'em right now except the top four."

Ted Ewald and Burns Stanley fell for the pitch and agreed to sponsor and manage the strapping lad from Mississippi. As a wealthy sportsman, Ewald came from a prominent Grosse Point family; Burns Stanley was a Harvard-educated tax attorney. My guess is that they were from the Roger Mayweather "don't-know-shit-about-boxing" country club set.

Both families befriended Banks, especially the kids, or as Ewald put it, Sonny "was on chummy terms with my children." It was Stanley, a member of the company's legal staff, who helped Banks obtain a job at the Ford plant.

"I was probably closer to Sonny than anyone except his mother and family," said Stanley. "With him, fighting was the answer to a driving ambition to achieve recognition and perhaps make a lot of money. What he saw for himself without boxing was a life in the foundry. He wanted something better."

Without benefit of single amateur fight, Banks turned pro May 19, 1960, winning a four-round decision over Ernie Berthet Jr. at the Graystone Ballroom, a historic Detroit venue on Woodland Avenue. In its heyday, the trendy nightspot, which opened in 1922, hosted jazz greats such as Bix Beiderbecke, Duke Ellington, Billie Holiday, Count Basie, and Glenn Miller. By the time Banks fought 12 of his 25 pro fights there, the once glamorous ballroom that had advertised "room for 3,000, 4,000 if you dance closely," was in decline.

Banks, who stood 6' 2" and weighed anywhere from 189 to 205 pounds during his career, was far from impressive against Berthet. It was a clumsy, mauling affair with Banks prevailing mainly on the basis of his strength and determination.

"That showed me something," Banks said. "I never believed you could be so good in the gym and so bad in the ring."

He won his next four fights by knockout, but in his sixth bout, Joe Shelton clobbered him when Banks turned his head toward his corner to look for instructions. The "next Joe Louis" was obviously as raw as sushi with a steep learning curve ahead of him.

After losing a decision to Chuck Garrett in his seventh match, Banks rebounded with five straight knockouts before getting stopped by Clay. Banks was no dummy; he knew he'd been fooling himself but wasn't about to quit.

"All those early knockouts were the worst thing for me," he said after losing to Clay. "They made me think I was all that good. But I'm learning. Every fight I'm learning."

Banks's education included a knocked loss to Young Jack Johnson in his next bout, but then he won eight of his next nine against marginally better opponents. He also avenged his only loss during the streak by knocking out previously undefeated Lee Batts.

Banks was coming along nicely but slowly, and still needed a lot more seasoning when his management shifted into kamikaze mode. Any chance of continuing to improve disappeared when Banks was matched with lethal-punching Cleveland Williams on July 21, 1964. Going from 13-11-3 (12) Don Warner to 61-5-1 (50) Cleveland was beyond stupid.

Ewald plastered huge posters of Banks knocking down Clay all over Williams's hometown of Houston, which undoubtedly helped attract a paying crowd of approximately 9,000. But slick marketing doesn't help after the bell rings. Banks had no more of a chance than one of those posters in a Texas hailstorm.

I hit Sonny with some of the hardest punches I've ever thrown," said Williams after stopping Banks in the sixth round. "They should have stopped it in the fifth round. I thought I was going to kill him. Why would they send him out for the sixth round, when he was battered like that? I'll never understand managers who care so little for their fighters."

The Texas boxing commission recommended to the Michigan commission that Banks be suspended for six months. Ewald, who would later become part owner of the Detroit Pistons, filed an appeal, but was denied at a hearing.

What the hell was Ewald thinking? Why would he want to endanger the health of a man he claimed was a "fine person" who he "often had at his home for dinner?"

Perhaps it was ignorance. The damage head blows cause was not as well understood in 1964 as today. The term Chronic Traumatic Encephalopathy (CTE) hadn't even been coined, but two world champions, welterweight Benny "Kid" Paret and featherweight Davey Moore, died of brain injuries suffered in the ring during Banks's career.

Maybe it was an attempt to cash out and recover as much of the $20,000 Ewald and Stanley claim to have invested in Banks before it was too late. It's a fairly common practice in the boxing industry, but if true in this case it certainly casts Ewald and Stanley in darker light. How much did they really care about the young man upon who they had showered their largess?

The reverse could also have been the case. Banks hadn't fought in 10 months, and probably needed the money. He could have become restless working at the foundry, eager to keep trying before his hopes and dreams slipped away entirely. He was also thinking of getting married, but realized he wasn't yet in a position to support a family.

In an effort to gain insight into the situation, I reached out to Ewald's son, Teddy Ewald III, who knew about Banks but said he was too young at the time to remember anything. He suggested speaking with his sister, Wendy, who could probably help, but she declined to be interviewed

———

There were only around 1,200 paying customers at the 7,000-seat Philadelphia Arena on May 10, 1965. There was no television, no radio, just the print media. The stories they wrote and the photos they took are the closest most of us will come to knowing what it was like the night Sonny Banks took the blows that killed him.

The final domino fell with a sickening thud in the ninth round. Sonny was on his back, his legs bent, his left arm spread-eagle, his right by his side, and his head resting on the canvas. It appeared as if he was looking up at the lights that illuminated the ring. But he was not. His eyes were closed.

Local heavyweight Leotis Martin suddenly stopped celebrating his hard-won victory and the crowd that had been delirious a few minutes prior grew quiet. Rich Westcott, sports columnist for the *Delaware County Daily Times*, captured the moment and the emotions the fight invoked as well as anybody.

"A few minutes earlier, it had been a terrific fight. The pace was furious, and the sparse crowd roared its approval as the two hard-hitting heavyweights exchanged assaults with unrestricted violence," wrote Westcott. "It was awesome. Sitting under the bright lights at ringside—pelted by drops of sweat from the fighters—you marveled at the brutality of it all."

Boxing fan J.R. Jowett, who later became a respected boxing writer, was a paying customer at the Martin-Banks match, which took place almost 60 years ago. He's probably among the few attendees still alive.

"Banks came to win, not just be an opponent," said Jowett. "He was not just an opponent taking a hopeless beating. It was a rugged and punishing fight. Sonny was giving Leotis all he wanted. Banks was taking the fight to Martin, and Leotis was kind of playing possum and looking for mistakes and counters, which is how he fought.

"The fight ended in a split second; it wasn't that Banks was hurt and Martin had to finish him off. Banks went down like a man on the gallows. Leotis' right hand anchor punch was probably one of the best anybody ever had.

"A cloud fell over the crowd like it usually does when a guy doesn't get up. I remember the announcer exhorting people to move away and 'give him air.' And some asshole yelled out, 'Why don't you lay him out in Fairmount Park?' Funny how you remember things like that."

Banks had suffered brainstem damage and a subdural hematoma. He was taken to Presbyterian Hospital where neurosurgeon Dr. Robert S. Andre performed emergency surgery. Sonny died May 13, three days after the fight. He was 24 years old. His brother, Jim, and Ewald were by his side.

Whether it was a touch of class, worry about selling tickets so soon after a Ring death, or both, Philly promoter Lou Lucchese postponed a card featuring Kitten Hayward vs. Vince Shomo scheduled for the following Friday.

———

Banks was buried on May 17, 1965, at the Westlawn Cemetery in Wayne, Michigan, Among the estimated 200 mourners were his family, boxers Henry Hank, Ron Harris, Marty Marshall, and Johnny Summerlin, who also trained Banks. Former boxing commissioner Frank Cavanaugh attended, along with Ewald and Stanley. The service was held at King Solomon Baptist Church, which had a boxing gym on the second floor where many Detroit boxers trained.

Joe Louis's sister, Eulalia Barrow, seemed to know what most folks at the graveside were thinking when she said, "You know that about 15 years ago I could be sitting where Sonny's family sits. What has happened to this young man could have happened to my brother, Joe."

For me it's Sonny's own words that resonate the strongest down through the decades, words that ring true because they echo the sentiments of so many boxers that came before and after him.

"I want to be somebody," he said, "but I'm nobody and have no chance of being anybody until I get in the ring."

When remembered today, if remembered at all, it is usually because Banks was the first to knock down Muhammad Ali. Only three other boxers—Henry Cooper, Joe Frazier, and Chuck Wepner—did likewise during Ali's 61-bout career. But Sonny Banks was the first, and that can never be taken away from him. It made him some-body, even though he never realized it.

THE PHILADELPHIA "DEATH SQUAD"

AN UNPARALLELED SERIES OF BOGUS LOSSES

ORIGINALLY PUBLISHED IN *THE RING*, SEPTEMBER 1980.

"They would call you on the phone and say, 'You're fighting tonight.' I would say, 'no,' and they would say, 'The money is good.' At the time, I had no money. They say, 'All you have to do is go out, throw a couple, take a shot—not a solid shot or nothing—and get out.'

"I really wasn't hurt. I knew I could have beaten these guys I fought, but I was told I had to let them win. By then, I was so far into it, I would give up the easy win instead of fighting four hard rounds and take a chance of getting cut. I knew I had to lose anyway."

—Confession of a "Philadelphia Death Squad" Member

IF YOU THOUGHT THAT SET-UPS, dives and fix fights went out with the era of B-movies, take a closer look at the preliminary bouts the next time you go to the fights. The ancient art of going into the tank is alive, and if not exactly well, certainly thriving.

73

Boxing has always carried its own onus. The possibility of a fix is a cross the game must bear.

Philadelphia, a city rich in boxing heritage, boasting champions from "Philadelphia" Jack O'Brien to Matthew Saad Muhammad, is currently the focal point of a scandal of the seamiest sort. A ragtag band of Philly-based fighters, if you dare call them that, have been involved in an unparalleled series of bogus knockout losses.

It is impossible to say where it all began. Cynics will say that Abel was in the bag long before his loss to Cain, but that is an old story. Around Philadelphia, in more recent years, it was not an unusual sight to see Johnny Barr Sr. toweling off a diver after a quick dip. Among the local in-crowd, these chronic losers were jokingly referred to as "Johnny Barr Specials."

Not surprisingly, considering the scum polluting boxing's waters, Barr's ready-made-to-order service became very popular. Soon this roving band of tank artists visited venues throughout Connecticut, New York, New Jersey, Maryland, and Virginia, as well as Pennsylvania.

This sort of thing is nothing new to boxing, nor is it practiced exclusively along the Northeastern corridor of United States. But in Philly, they do it to the max.

If it can be said that behind every great man there is a woman, then it also can be said that behind every great fighter there are a lot of palookas. Records padded with non-entities are common among champions.

Losing fighters come in all shapes, colors and sizes, just like the winners. Overall, the losers can be categorized into groups: bums and stiffs. There is a major difference between the two. Bums, regardless of how dismal their win-loss record, give an honest effort and often lasts the distance. Stiffs invariably get blasted out, one way or another.

There is also a fine distinction between a set-up and a dive. The set-up is little more than a gross mismatch—the opponent so outclassed that victory for the favored boxer is virtually assured. This sort of bout can kill. A dive, however, is relatively safe, but also a form of fraud.

To understand the reason for stiffs, it's imperative to comprehend that a promoter's process of building a ticket seller is a precarious one. Unfortunately, the best fighters don't always make the best box-office attractions.

Promoters try to protect their products by minimizing their chances of losing, hopefully maintaining a semblance of competition along the way. It is at this level that the stiff gets most of, though not all, of his work.

It could be argued that the first stiff and first substitute came through the door wearing the same pair of pants. It is boxing's unique utilization of the last-minute sub that gives the stiff his opportunity. Honest matchmakers—and they do exist—usually pick bums to nurture their fledglings.

J Russell Peltz, until recently director of boxing at the Spectrum, has a reputation for putting together decent fights. Nevertheless, there has been an occasional splash on his cards.

"I have no excuse," Peltz said. "Sometimes you get stuck at the last minute, and you want the show to go on. I usually tell the commissioner to keep an eye on these guys."

Lazy matchmakers often prefer to make one simple phone call and order the entire losing side of their undercard to go—send two lightweights, a middleweight and a heavy, easy on the hot sauce.

How much blame can't be placed at the promoters' doorstep? Plenty!

"Booking agents don't get calls for winners," said fight broker Gary Hegyi, who has dealt with a few Death Squad members in his time. "They get calls for losers."

The economic law of supply and demand is at work here, and promoters usually get what they asked for.

So blatant have been the antics of the Death Squad that the mind boggles at the audacity of it all. As a safeguard, most athletic commissions suspend a boxer for 30 days or more following a knockout loss. This causes few, if any, hassles for our resourceful band of travelling losers.

Take middleweight Malik Muhammad, for example. He was starched in one round by Henry Bunch on January 16, 1980, in Washington D.C. (Matt Williams, promoter). Three days later, Muhammad was iced by John Molander in Hempstead, New York (Jimmy Winters, promoter). He is not alone. Darnell Smith was kayoed by Miguel Sanchez in White Plains on October 10, 1979 (Lou and Richie Falcigno, co-promoters). Eight days later, he was flattened in Philly by Tyrone Moore (Butch Lewis, promoter). Mike Grant was stopped in West New York, New Jersey on November 28, 1979 (Al Certo, promoter), only to be stretched again on December 4 in Upper Darby (Russell Peltz, promoter). And the beat—and beatings—goes on, and on, and on.The ever-popular name switch has become a favorite gambit used to circumvent the suspension lists mailed out by commissions. So many fictitious names are use that it is almost impossible to accurately ascertain just how large the Death Squad really is.The strange example of Derrick Wheeler illustrates just how ingenious the Death Squad can be. In a case of "Will the Real Derrick Wheeler Please Fall Down," Wheeler's birth certificate was used by his cousin to obtain a New York State boxing license. After losing (via knockout, of course) under Wheeler's name, his cousin continued his losing ways under his own name. Wheeler's name however was picked up by various other tankers and used repeatedly. The real Derrick Wheeler has never even been in the ring.

Death Squad member Bob Saxton has been accused of also fighting under the rather uncreative alias of John Saxton, a charge he bitterly denies. "I am Bobby Saxton. They're trying to say I am the other Saxton. I'm not him." Let's hope Saxton is telling the truth. If not, it means that during a bleak stretch in 1979, he was knocked out three times in less than two months. Not the best tonic for one's health.

Two other members of the Death Squad agreed to talk to *The Ring*, but only if their identities be kept secret. They also refused to be photographed. The quote at the beginning of this piece tells their basic method of operation. For the most part, they are teenagers, hungry for a dollar and willing to take a risk to get it. Other serious charges were made. One squad member alleged he was offered an extra $50 to fall down in the fourth round after winning the first three. He also claimed to have complied and been rewarded accordingly.

Earlier this year, *Philadelphia Daily News* columnist Stan Hochman wrote a five-part exposé entitled, "Boxing—A Killer Sport." Considerable space was afforded Barr and his accomplices.

Barr offered Hochman his standard line: "Promoters would call and say 'We've got an average kid. Bring something ordinary.' I take an ordinary kid and then I see their guy. He's had a lot of fights. I say 'Is this what you call an ordinary kid?' And then he beats my kid. I haven't done anything."

The heat has been on since then, and Barr has passed the baton and gym keys onto his son, Johnny Junior. The younger Barr used to be the star of his father's stable until a detached retina forced him to the other side of the ropes.

Another of Barr's helpers was Robert Taylor. Figuring that he was on to a good thing, Taylor went into the business himself. He took over management of several of Barr's so-called boxers and recruited others, mostly corner boys from the notorious Columbia Avenue strip.

During a short but active career, Taylor succeeded in getting himself suspended in both Pennsylvania and New Jersey. Robert Lee, New Jersey's deputy commissioner, put it this way: "I felt that, if the man had such disregard for the rules or regulations of this commission, I would rather not having manage in the state of New Jersey."

New Jersey is also now enforcing the rule that says that all visiting boxers must have a valid license from their home state, a step in the right direction.

State athletic commissions were supposedly created to police the sport, protect boxers and make sure the paying public is not ripped off. It is at best a confusing picture, looking like a jigsaw puzzle put together by a drunken carpenter.

Attaching a diver's purse is an effective after-the-fact method of discouraging such hanky-panky. Virginia commissioner Bill Brennan followed this course after four Death Squad members took the plunge in Richmond on November 29, 1979.

"This was the most sickening thing you've ever saw," Brennan said. "A blind man could have seen it."

Alvin Bracey, Bobby Watson, Al Smith and Carl Cherry were named by Brennan as the culprits. But don't bet the rent money those were their real names. In this game of musical stiffs, the only people who know for sure aren't talking.

Consistency is a big problem with commissions. New York was the first state to install a computer to compile records. They invited other states to plug in for a $200 fee. Sounds like a reasonable idea, but according to commission spokesman, Rose Lewis, they still haven't hired anyone to program the damn thing.

Pennsylvania's lame-duck commissioner Howard McCall blames lack of staff and funding for the failure of his office to police and patrol the Death Squad. "Right now, there are too many outlaw gyms. Guys open a place, stick a ring in there, a few bags, and haul kids in. The commission is supposed to control training facilities, but all we've got is two full-time people."

What may seem at first glance to be only a small-time racket (the average purse for such performances is about $200) is a serious problem for boxing. The cash customer is being cheated, and so are the genuine pros. A conservative estimate of bouts featuring Death Squad members in 1979 is well over 100. Those are 100 paydays missed by hungry, legitimate fighters.

Another excellent deterrent is loud complaints from disgruntled boxing patrons. This requires a little education. How do you spot a stiff? Any boxer entering the ring in black socks and sneakers is immediately suspect. Fans seeing anything suspicious should scream bloody murder. Let us not forget that most commission posts are political appointments.

The rosin dust kicked up by the Philly Death Squad has spurred more action against questionable knockouts that anything in decades.

In that respect, it has been a good thing. The reins have been significantly tightened. The Death Squad, in its original form, is no more. Too many are hip to Barr, Taylor and company. They have been forced into the background, victims of their own bold impudence. Unfortunately, other flesh peddlers have come forth to take their place. The Death Squad in some form will continue to roll, and the next splash you hear may come, once again, from the shores of the Schuylkill River in Philadelphia.

———

EPILOGUE: Since the Professional Boxing Safety Act became law in 1997, boxers are required to have a Professional Boxers Federal Identification Card. The card has a license number and photograph of the boxer that has to be presented at the weigh-in. This has made significant inroads toward solving the problem but has not completely eliminated fixed fights.

Bob Lee, who was quoted in this article, was found guilty of money laundering and tax evasion in 2000. He was fined, sentenced to 22 months in prison and banned from boxing for the rest of his life.

A TOUCH OF LARCENY

BOXING'S OPEN SECRET

ORIGINALLY PUBLISHED IN *RINGSIDE SEAT*, WINTER, 2017

BOXING IS TRAPPED in a Sisyphean cycle of ups and downs. The Gennady Golovkin-Canelo Alvarez fight was only the latest boulder to come rolling back down the hill and flatten the sport. The best middleweight championship fight was brought low by a scorecard so bizarre, it seemed to confirm our worst suspicions.

But what are our worst suspicions, anyway? That boxing is corrupt? That's not a suspicion, folks, it's a fact. Boxing is and always will be an outlaw sport, which is a significant part of its appeal. Why do you think the fixed fight is de rigueur in virtually every boxing movie? Boxing and corruption go together like garter belts and stockings. It's okay if a little larceny is part of the package —as long as your favorite isn't the one getting the shaft.

For many people, the gross vagaries of boxing are a total turnoff, but how do you account for the millions who love it? Why endure the agony for an occasional brush with ecstasy? The truth is that what Pierce Egan christened: the "sweet science of bruising" is highly addictive. Not like heroin, crystal meth, or booze. The delivery system is entirely different. Nobody shoots boxing into their veins, snorts it up their nose, or pours it down their throat.

Boxing's delivery modus operandi is through the senses, especially sight, sound and smell. Most likely, dopamine has something to do with it. This neurotransmitter has many functions, one of which plays a major role in reward-motivation behavior. You might not think about it in those terms, but you know it when you feel it—an euphoric rush that verges on an out-of-body experience.

But it's more than that. Hardcore boxing fans are part of an underground community, what Egan called the "knowing cove." Members recognize a set-up or mismatch when they see it, understand that promoters are basically salesmen out to make a buck, and know that judges' pencils are not always guided by what is taking place inside the ring.

The thing that most boxing detractors don't understand is that boxing junkies are willing to tolerate a helluva lot of bad in search of the good. Yes, they moan and groan about the quality of the fights, deride boxers they believe are ducking dangerous opponents, and seethe at pay-per-view fees. After a particularly egregious decision or some other travesty, they frequently swear they've quit boxing for good. But a few days later, they find themselves back on-line searching for obscure results from a club show in Bulgaria.

These are the people who keep boxing going even at the worst of times. They tell one another they're hooked and laugh about it, but it's true. In that respect, being a boxing fan is a little bit like joining the Mob. Once you're in, you can't get out.

There are no detox clinics for boxing junkies. They have to tough it out through all the disappointments and betrayals that are endemic in this atavistic blood ritual. There is no alternative but to ride out the whirlwind until something better comes along.

Such was the case in the aftermath of Golovkin-Canelo. The rivalry made the fight such an anticipated event, it was even more heated after it was over. Golovkin's supporters were positive that the draw verdict was a rip-off, and Canelo's fans insisted their man won fair and square. In a close fight, both boxers always think they've won, and it's the same with their followers.

The reaction is reminiscent of political debates. It doesn't matter what the candidates say, hardly anybody will switch allegiances because they've already made up their minds before the first word is spoken.

That being said, not even the most devoted Canelo fans could justify Adelaide Byrd's dumbfounding score of 118-110 in favor of the Mexican boxer. Because her eight-point spread was the only vote for Canelo in the split draw, it stood out like the gold teeth in Jack Johnson's mouth.

Byrd began her judging career in Philadelphia when she was Adelaide Triplett, married to former pro turned trainer, Dwight Triplett. At the time, she was judging club fights at the Blue Horizon, so her frequently inexplicable scorecards didn't attract much attention. But when she resurfaced in Las Vegas working progressively important fights, it was unsettling to say the least.

It didn't help when Nevada State Athletic Commission Executive Director Bob Bennett defended Byrd in the immediate aftermath of GGG-Canelo by saying, "She's an outstanding judge who had one bad night."

That's total bullshit. Byrd has had numerous howlers, including having Amir Khan ahead when Canelo knocked out the Englishman in the sixth round of a one-sided fight in May 2016. The next month, Top Rank CEO Bob Arum asked the commission to remove Byrd from the Vasyl Lomachenko-Nicholas Walters fight, only to have his request denied.

"(Bennett) had to know that she had some very questionable scorecards in the past," Arum told the *Las Vegas Review-Journal.* "He had to know because we told him."

Is Byrd simply incapable of understanding what is taking place inside a boxing ring or is something more sinister in play? Due to the subjective nature of scoring a fight, proving a professional boxing match was fixed in that manner is extremely difficult. The burden of proof is on the accuser and circumstantial evidence would not be sufficient.

That doesn't stop us from speculating, based on the acknowledged fact that corruption has been an integral part of boxing since men first came to scratch in the 18th century.

An early villain was Norwich butcher Jack Slack, a nasty piece of work credited with introducing the "chopper," the equivalent of today's rabbit punch. According to historian Bob Mee, Slack was a "swaggering, shiftless bully" who "thought nothing of involving himself in fixed fights." In the vernacular of the times, he not only "tossed" fights but also organized "cross affairs of the knuckles" involving other fighters.

The public lost interest and faith in prizefighting during Slack's decade-long, scandal-riddled reign as England's bare-knuckle champion. It might have died along with him in 1778 if it hadn't been for Tom Johnson, an honest and skilled fighter widely credited with saving the sport. The boulder was on the way to the top of the hill again but would inevitably come barreling back down as the cycle continued to spin, sometimes slowly, sometimes with disconcerting speed.

Slack was a freelance villain, but organized crime got its hooks into boxing early on, and it would be naïve to believe it is no longer involved.

When Sonny Liston applied for a New York boxing license in 1962, he told Commission Chairman Major General Melvin L. Krulewitch that he had untangled himself from all ties to organized crime. Krulewitch didn't buy it. He told Liston "The wrong people do not disengage easily" and sent him packing.

Whether or not Krulewitch did the correct thing denying Liston a license is debatable, but the old Marine had the "do not disengage easily" part right. For example, when Frank "Blinky" Palermo, fight-fixer and partner of Mafioso Frankie Carbo, was released from prison in 1969, he was right back in the boxing business, using a wholesale fish business as a front.

The ignoble art of fight fixing has changed over the centuries, not in purpose but in practice. Although not extinct, taking a dive for money has fallen out of favor, especially at the seven-figure level. Bribing a fighter to fall down who is making millions would be so costly there'd be no profit in it. Besides, there are much cheaper ways.

ESPN's Teddy Atlas was on point when he erupted in one of his rabid diatribes following the Golovkin-Canelo fight. The preferred approach today is through administrative channels, which are the local boxing commissions, aided and abetted by the various alphabet cartels. Those two entities select the referees and judges, and the promoter pays them—a system ripe for abuse.

Money is not the only enticement used to persuade officials to lean one way or another. Like fighters taking dives, cash (while still king) is no longer the norm. It's the plum assignments and all-expenses-paid trips overseas that influence certain arbitrators, either overtly or subconsciously. Regardless, they know which way the wind is blowing, and the powerbrokers know which officials are susceptible. Most of the time nobody needs to say anything. The right people know the drill. And while there are many principled officials working fights, it only takes one appalling scorecard out of three to cause a stink.

While stronger methods are occasionally utilized, the ploy of placing the appropriate judge in the right spot at the right time has worked well. Of course, a knockout usually eliminates any score-card hanky-panky, which is one of the reasons knockouts are so popular with the paying public. Boxing in Nevada is particularly susceptible to scams of this type because the state is controlled by the gaming industry, which depends on gambling and tourism to prosper. If one fighter has a massive fan base and his opponent's is relatively small, which one do you think the Las Vegas establishment wants to win?

Prizefighting is the exception to the "a house divided against itself cannot stand" tenet. It has been its own enemy since the start but is still standing, albeit on wobbly legs from time to time.

The fact that boxing is still popular enough to generate massive amounts of money in the face of more than two centuries of turmoil is confirmation of its improbable staying power.

Perhaps we are genetically hardwired to crave vicarious violence. A mountain of anecdotal evidence would suggest so. Popular entertainment from zombie apocalypse to digital Armageddon feeds this need for gratuitous carnage with fantasy. Boxing cuts much closer to the bone, exposing the spectators to the real thing.

MMA and other forms of combat sports are similar, but boxing is a higher calling, an exceedingly stylized martial art capable of creating both savage beauty and poetic brutality with just one punch.

It's been said that nothing can be bad for boxing because boxing itself is bad. That's an exaggeration to prove a point, but it speaks to the futility of expecting it to change. Boxing heaven is beyond our reach because it does not exist. Instead, think of it as the charming black sheep of the sports family, the one we love, not only despite its faults, but also because of them.

———

EPILOGUE: Alvarez won a 12-round majority decision in a rematch on September 12, 2018. It was another well-fought close fight. Golovkin has since won four fights and wants another crack at Alvarez. Canelo has won seven fights since the return bout, but suffered his second loss of his career when he moved up to light heavyweight and dropped a unanimous decision to WBA titleholder Dmitry Bivol on May 7, 2022. Canelo said he wants a third GGG bout before a rematch with Bivol.

RETHINKING BOXING'S PERFORMANCE-ENHANCING DRUG CONUNDRUM

TESTING IS LIKE A DOG CHASING ITS OWN TAIL

ORIGINALLY PUBLISHED BY ESPN.COM, APRIL 3, 2013

I CAN REMEMBER BOBBY CZYZ, who was moonlighting as a color commentator at the time, holding forth at great length on the subject of steroids during a Fox Network production meeting for a 1996 fight card.

He seemed to know an awful lot about them at a time when performing-enhancing drugs (PEDs) were seldom discussed in boxing circles. Czyz, who was scheduled to fight Evander Holyfield in a few months and suspected Evander was juicing, joked that he wouldn't be surprised if Holyfield's head exploded before he had a chance to knock it off. Everybody else laughed and looked sheepish. Holyfield had been rumored to be a PED user, and years later, his name was linked to an investigation of illegal steroid distribution networks, although nothing was ever proved.

But that wasn't the reason steroid abuse were the hot topic that weekend. South African heavyweight Frans Botha had tested positive following a split decision over Axel Schulz the previous December. The result was changed to a no-contest, and the IBF's announcement as to whether it would strip Botha and vacate the title

87

was imminent. Fox needed to know the outcome before the show started, and I was tasked with the unenviable job of pestering then-IBF president Bob Lee until I got an answer. As it turned out, the IBF did strip Botha and vacate the title, and I managed to deliver the news in time for the broadcast. For me, however, the fights were secondary. The big takeaway that weekend was the unsettling realization that boxing had entered a new age: the PEDs era.

Almost two decades later, PEDs are dominating boxing's news cycle with uncomfortable frequency, and despite increased testing, a growing number of busts, steeper penalties and a disapproving public, more and more fighters are apparently using them.

"I think that PED use is rampant among fighters," said Dr. Margaret Goodman, neurologist, former ringside physician and president and chairwoman of the Voluntary Anti-Doping Agency (VADA). "We are only finding the tip of the iceberg due to archaic profiles and announced testing. I can't give a percent, but it is high. It has become an easy quick fix for many—especially as athletes know they are rarely checked. And when they are checked, the ones caught are typically those that didn't stop the substance in time or received poor advice on use."

Although it's true that some commissions do not test at all for PEDs and many that do test for them use inadequate procedures, fighters keep turning up dirty anyway. Consequently, there is a clamor for more and better testing. More suspensions. Higher fines. More lifetime bans. In other words, it's a fight to the finish with the outcome and benefit to boxing being problematical at best. Is this really the only solution?

Historically, prohibition hasn't worked, regardless of the substance being prohibited. It didn't work with alcohol, it didn't work with drugs, and in all likelihood, it won't work with PEDs. If you think new and improved testing is the answer, I believe you're fooling yourself. Just as Internet hackers always manage to find a way around the most advanced computer-security technology, PED gurus will find ways to beat new detection methods, including unannounced random testing. Look at how many years Lance Armstrong beat random testing. In the long run, testing is like a dog chasing its own tail: Round and round you go, getting nowhere fast.

The current testing model also can be inconclusive, as the recent boondoggle involving the Lamont Peterson-Kendall Holt fight plainly demonstrated. At first, there was an erroneous report that Peterson—who had been busted for having traces of synthetic testosterone in his system during his December 2011 victory over Amir Khan—had again been caught using a banned substance. As it turned out, neither Peterson nor Holt had failed his drug test. According to the Washington D.C. commission, one of the boxers, presumably Holt, provided an atypical test result, meaning that the amount of the banned substance (in this case HCG, a fertility drug that increases testosterone and facilitates weight loss) wasn't sufficient enough to give the boxer a significant advantage. Perhaps it's time to rethink the entire dilemma.

The health issue is a good place to start. As it stands, the vast majority of fighters will suffer some degree of brain damage regardless of whether their opponents used PEDs. Boxers have endured the consequences of absorbing repeated blows to the head since the birth of bare-knuckle prizefighting in the latter half of the 18th century. Since that time, numerous rule changes have been adopted in an effort to make boxing safer. It has been an ongoing process that continues to evolve, but the sport still takes a terrible toll on its participants, nonetheless.

Actual ring fatalities are comparatively rare (usually fewer than a dozen a year), but the number of boxers who, later in life, suffer concussion-related degenerative disorders of the central nervous system is staggering.

"I think that PED use significantly contributes to the increased risks of brain injury in fighters," Dr. Goodman said. "I am hoping this will be proven one day soon."

But how much does it really matter? Performance-enhancing drugs, such as anabolic steroids and human growth hormone, have been available for only a relatively short period of time compared to the history of boxing. But debilitating injury and death have been a part of the bargain since the start, and in all probability would remain so even if PEDs were eradicated. And as far as fighters doing harm to their own health is concerned, a lot of them wouldn't think twice about the risk if they thought using PEDs could give them an edge. It's the nature of the beast.

The other chief objection to the use of PEDs is that it gives the user an unfair advantage, and if Dr. Goodman's belief that use of PEDs is "rampant among fighters" is correct, the only way a fighter can make sure he or she is not at a disadvantage is to also use PEDs.

Becoming a professional boxer is asking for trouble, but although fighters bear the brunt of the suffering, both combatants and fans share a mindset that relegates thoughts of disaster to a remote corner of their minds.

With the exception of families and friends, how many spectators do you think were worrying about long-term consequences as they watched Mike Alvarado and Brandon Rios tear into each other last Saturday? A reality check is the last thing a fan wants when experiencing the euphoria of witnessing two amazingly courageous fighters sacrificing all in the pursuit of glory. What's more, I don't recall anybody wondering out loud if either or both men were juicing. For 12 spellbinding rounds, nothing mattered but the fight itself.

If, as many have suggested, sports are an escape from the rigors of everyday life, then boxing has to be the ultimate diversion, a world in which fantasy and reality are melded into one by an agreed-upon suspension of disbelief. You could say the same about a lot of sports, but nowhere except boxing are the stakes so high and the desire to see things through an idealistic lens so prevalent.

We don't like to acknowledge boxing's inconvenient truths unless we absolutely have no alternative. It temporarily spoils the illusion and takes away from the pleasure. We work hard at finding ways to rationalize an irrational activity and get defensive when somebody reminds us how heartbreaking the cost can be. But when you get right down to it, boxing is all about hurt and hurting, and like it or not, PEDs are now part of that process.

But don't be so sure that the picture is as one-dimensional and bleak as mainstream thinking would have us believe. Consider for a moment a few scattered lines culled from an article published in the *British Journal of Sports Medicine*: "Performance enhancement is not against the spirit of sport; it is the spirit of sport. To choose to be better is to be human. Athletes should be given this choice. Drugs are against the rules. But we define the rules of sport. If we made drugs legal and freely available, there would be no cheating. We have two choices: to vainly try to turn the clock back, or to rethink who we are and what sport is."

There is something to be said for this outlook, and I believe that legalizing and regulating PEDs would better serve boxing than the current model of endless rounds of testing, banning and controversy. The biggest hurdle to legitimizing use for fighters isn't that PEDs (like all drugs) can be harmful. The foremost problem is that after so much adverse publicity and widespread handwringing, it would be a public relations disaster and possibly marginalize boxing to an even greater extent than it is already.

It's a thorny issue with no perfect answer. Nonetheless, there has to be a better way than the current system, so before dismissing out of hand the concept of decriminalizing PEDs, ask yourself if you're satisfied with the status quo and convinced testing will solve everything. If not, it's time to start thinking about alternatives, even those that fly in the face of conventional wisdom.

————

EPILOGUE: Things have not changed very much since this article was published, and in some ways have gotten worse. Some of the nefarious alphabet cartels now give boxers who flunk PED tests short suspensions and heavy fines, the latter of which does nothing but enhance the so-called sanctioning bodies' coffers.

TARNISHED IDOL

THE MURDER OF TYRONE EVERETT

ORIGINALLY PUBLISHED IN *BOXING BABYLON: BEHIND THE SHADOWY WORLD OF THE PRIZE RING*, CITADEL PRESS BOOKS, 1990.

THE HIGH-POWERED BULLET entered the right nostril, ripped through the brain, exploded out the back of the skull, smashed through the window, and finally came to rest on the sidewalk across the street. A few minutes later, a man and a woman were seen leaving the house. They left behind thirty-eight packets of heroin on the dining room table and the body of boxer Tyrone Everett in the upstairs bedroom.

Six days later, Everett's girlfriend, Carolyn McKendrick, surrendered to the Philadelphia police and was charged with his murder. The man seen leaving the scene of the crime with her was Tyrone Price, a homosexual and admitted drug dealer, who soon became the chief witness for the prosecution.

The story of sex, drugs and violence that unfolded during the trial were to forever sully the memory of Everett. He was an extraordinarily gifted boxer who, only six months earlier, had been robbed of the WBC super featherweight title by a scandalous decision.

Everett was one of five brothers raised by their mother, Doris Everett, in South Philadelphia. Like so many others poor kids, he started boxing for trophies, discovered he was good at it and decided to try to make some money.

His first pro fight, on September 22, 1971, was a four-rounder at the Scranton CYC, a couple of hours north of Philadelphia. Despite the coal country debut, he was almost instantly recognized as a special talent.

A mercury-quick southpaw, Everett developed a darting style that made him almost impossible to hit. He would prance around his opponents, jump inside long enough to land a crisp punch, and then vanish before a retaliatory blow could be launched.

While his style often made for boring, one-sided fights, it's doubtful he lost more than a dozen rounds in thirty-seven professional fights. The only fight he ever lost was a fix.

Though Everett's less-than-macho methods alienated many of Philadelphia's old guard and blue-collar fans, he more than made up for it at the box office by attracting an entirely different demographic. They were generally a younger crowd, dressed in superfly threads and sporting top-heavy Afros.

Everett had a big following among the 20th and Carpenter Street gang, a particularly fierce collection of inner-city kids who waged a successful street war against the Black Mafia for control of drug traffic in the neighborhood where they grew up. He also drew a large contingency of women, who were entranced by his pretty green eyes and well-earned reputation as a ladies' man. Going to see Everett fight became the in thing to do, and thousands turned out to see the tiny dancing master every time he was on the bill.

Everett was, in many ways, a contradiction. He was polite and soft spoken, and during his early success, almost timid among strangers. But as Tyrone's star rose, he began to expose the other side of his personality, the conceited, arrogant side.

There was an undeniable streak of cruelty, most blatantly expressed in his utter contempt in which he held most of his opponents. A good example was his bout with Korean Hyun Chi Kim in July 1975, at the Spectrum.

Despite an inflated ranking, Kim was a limited fighter, vastly inferior to the Philadelphian. Everett administered a lopsided beating but did it from a safe distance until the Korean was exhausted and demoralized. Once he realized his opponent was a sitting duck, the distasteful facet of Everett's makeup asserted itself.

"Everett displayed his perverted sense of class last night by needlessly taunting a beaten, half-blind opponent who might have jumped out of the ring if his handlers hadn't thrown the towel into it," wrote Jack McKinney in the *Philadelphia Daily News*.

"I'm mean, man! Mean," growled Everett, dramatizing his claim with grotesque facial contortions as he popped right hooks against the closed left eye of Hyun Chi Kim, an overrated and under-motivated Korean who didn't understand what Everett was saying.

"So, after twenty-seven wins," wrote McKinney, "Tyrone Everett still leaves a lot of people with the distinct impression that he is a front runner whose courage is directly related to his recognition of his opponent's ineptitude."

Had Everett been an ordinary boxer, both he and his tasteless hot-dogging would have been quickly forgotten. What made him so infuriating to the purest was the fact he was blessed with enormous talent. Among the most frustrated was J Russell Peltz, the Spectrum's youthful Director of Boxing who agonized over Everett's indiscretions while gleefully counting the gate receipts.

They developed a love-hate relationship that was still unresolved at the time of Everett's death. While they openly feuded, and at one point only communicated through Everett's manager, Frank Gelb, they shared a common business interest.

"My wife, Linda, thinks Tyrone was always trying to win my affection and acceptance. And that I would never give it to him," said Peltz. "Maybe she was right. In my opinion, Everett never realized just how good he was. If he had gone all out, he would have knocked out practically every guy he fought."

Regardless of their personal differences, Peltz worked hard, along with Gelb, to secure Everett a title shot he had earned by beating virtually every contender in the 130-pound division.

At the time, the WBC title was held by Alfredo Escalera, a

charismatic performer known for his toothy grin and proclivity for bringing a boa constrictor into the ring. The swashbuckling Puerto Rican was no slouch, but by 1976, Everett was almost unbeatable. After considerable wrangling and postponements, the match was made for November 30 at the Spectrum.

The promotion drew a record-breaking crowd of more than 16,000. For the first twelve rounds, Everett fought his normal cautious fight, outboxing Escalera and scoring with snappy counters. Then in the thirteenth round, a freakish accident tore open a wicked cut on Everett's forehead. Escalera's front teeth smacked into the Philadelphian's brow, severing a vessel and causing blood to spurt in an alarming manner.

Everett responded magnificently, attacking his adversary with more ferocity than he'd ever shown before. It was a revelation, especially to those who had questioned Everett's courage in the past. In what might have been his finest moment in the ring, he blinked away the gore, bit down on his mouthpiece, and went all out.

Ace cutman Eddie Aliano managed to hold together Everett's ripped skin for the final three rounds, but the blood-spattered boxer abandoned his aggressive attitude and reverted back to his usual hit-and-run tactics. Though it was the prudent thing to do and typical of Everett's philosophy, it was also a decision that probably cost him the title—and maybe a whole lot more.

"Escalera's people told me later that if Everett had come forward the last few rounds, he would have won. Escalera was so tired he would never have lasted if Tyrone hadn't started dancing again," said Peltz.

At the sound of the final bell, the crowd, sure the local favorite was the new champion, erupted in a joyous celebration. Jubilation soon turned to anxiety, as the tabulation of the official scorecards was abnormally slow, often a sign that things aren't exactly kosher.

When ring announcer Ed Derian finally read the split decision verdict in favor of Escalera, there was first a stunned silence. It was as if the people couldn't believe what they had heard. Then they got angry—real angry.

With the crowd teetering on the brink of violence, Pennsylvania boxing commissioner Howard McCall grabbed the microphone and told the incensed crowd he was suspending the decision pending an investigation.

It was pure baloney, and McCall knew it. Nevertheless, he desperately wanted to avert a riot. The ploy worked, and the crowd gradually grumbled its way out into the night, convinced Everett had been shafted but hopeful justice would eventually prevail. It didn't.

There was no investigation, and the outrageous decision for Escalera stood. The most shocking aspect of the sordid affair, however, was the fact the pivotal vote for Escalera was cast by Philadelphia judge Lou Tress.

If it went the distance, it was a given that Puerto Rican judge Ismael Fernandez would vote for Escalera regardless of what happened between the ropes, and he did by a 146-143 margin. Mexican referee Ray Solis, the only so-called neutral official, scored the bout 148-146 for Everett. But when Tress cast the deciding 145-143 vote for the defending champion, it not only added insult to injury, it felt like a collective kick in the nuts.

Though Everett had neither sought nor expected any favors from the sad-eyed man in a baggy grey suit, it was assumed Tress, as a Philadelphian, would at least render a fair verdict.

"I remembered standing in the ring before they announced the decision," said Gelb, who is still haunted by nightmares about the infamous decision and its aftermath. "I peeked at the scorecards and then looked around for Tress. He had already left his seat and was on his way out of the arena."

Tress died of cancer not long afterward, but he's remembered as a villainous character by practically everyone who saw the Escalera-Everett travesty.

Rumors persisted that his pencil was guided by factors other than the normal criteria for judging a professional boxing match. Though no charges were ever lodged, many boxing insiders nodded toward "Honest" Bill Daly as the culprit who allegedly made the arrangements for Everett's downfall.

Daly, who has also died since, was an elderly scalawag leftover from the days when convicted felons Frankie Carbo and Blinky Palermo ruled much of boxing. He had retired in Puerto Rico a few years before Everett's challenge and was reputed to have a financial interest in Escalera.

Surprisingly, considering "Squire Bill's" unsavory reputation, not an eyebrow was raised in Everett's camp when the old boy flew into Philly a few days before the fight. It was later learned Tress had a brother who worked at a horserace track in Puerto Rico.

"After the weigh-in, I was sitting in my hotel room relaxing before it was time to go to the fight," said Gelb. "There was a knock at the door, and a well-known fight character came in. Let's just call him my 'mystery guest.' He said, 'Are you okay, Frank?' I told him yes and then he said, 'Are you sure you're okay?'

"I didn't know what he talking about, but a few days after the fight, it hit me. I put two and two together, and another piece of the puzzle fit into place. The mystery guest was an old buddy of Bill Daly's. Maybe if I'd taken the hint, we could have worked out some sort of a deal. Who the hell knows?"

Naturally, the controversial loss to Escalera was a bitter setback for Everett, but he was young, and everybody assumed he would get another chance. The defeat certainly didn't deflate his ego or take the sting out of his tongue.

Peltz remembered when Everett showed up at the Spectrum not long after the debacle to view a videotape of the bout.

"He sat staring at the screen with a blank face for the longest time. He didn't say a word," said Peltz. "Then, around the fifth or sixth round, he got Escalera so off balance, Alfredo's face was in his crotch. 'Look at that, I made him suck my dick.'"

It was Everett's penis that was ultimately complicit in leading him to an early grave. A father of four by the time he died at age twenty-four, some say he considered himself god's gift to women. And there were plenty of pretty young girls who agreed with his assessment.

"He treated me nice," a tearful Sherry Arthur told reporters after learning of Everett's death. "After he won $10,000 at the Spectrum, he bought me a living room set, a bedroom set, a TV and a glass table. I knew he was dating a lot of people, but I never seen any. Women flock around men like that, anyway. But I know he loved me. I'll bet my life on it, and I used to love him, too."

Not all of Everett's female friends shared Ms. Arthur's admirable opinion.

At her trial, Carolyn McKendrick painted a vastly different picture of the handsome young boxer. She maintained she shot him in self-defense and produced hospital records in an attempt to prove past abuse at Everett's hands. According to McKendrick, Everett beat her so frequently, the incidents were too numerous to count. She said the punishment grew progressively worse as her lover's ring opponents gradually got tougher.

"He punched her in the jaw. Her mouth was bleeding," testified Cynthia Laverne Dill of a beating the boxer allegedly gave McKendrick outside an after-hours club the summer before his death.

Robbin Evonne Craddock, a close friend of McKendrick, told the court about another alleged altercation between Everett and Carolyn. Craddock said she was visiting McKendrick when a heated argument erupted.

"I went down to see if I could stop it, and when I got there, she was holding his arm," said Craddock, who was upstairs when things turned nasty. "He jerked his hand back and hit her with his fist. She fell off the couch, but Everett jumped on her and continued to strike her. That's when she threatened him."

According to Craddock's testimony, when Everett refused to leave the house, McKendrick picked up a glass ashtray and threw it at him. The boxer instinctively blocked the missile with his arm the same way he had thousands of punches, and then knocked her to the ground as if she was one of his ring opponents.

Everett was "getting ready to kick her, when he spotted the broken glass from the ashtray and picked up a piece," stated Craddock.

"'I'm going to hurt you where you prize the most, your face,'

Everett threatened, clutching a chunk of broken glass. He jabbed at her, but I pulled him away."

The action was almost as hot-and-heavy in Judge Robert A. Latrone's courtroom. Neither the prosecution nor defense pulled any punches.

"I'm going to level with you," said McKendrick's attorney, Stephen H. Serota at the beginning of the trial. "Carolyn McKendrick shot Tyrone Everett. Make no bones about it. The question is, did she have a good reason."

With minor exceptions, both McKendrick and the prosecution's star witness, Tyrone "Terry" Price, gave the same account of Everett's death. As was his habit, the boxer slept at McKendrick's house at 2710 Federal Street the night before he was shot. McKendrick departed that morning to help her sister get her car repaired. Everett was left alone in the house with Price, a transvestite who appeared in court dressed as a woman.

About twenty minutes after she left, McKendrick returned unexpectedly and discovered her bed in disarray and Everett sweating and flustered. Although Price claimed he never had a sexual relationship with the victim, McKendrick formed the opinion that her boyfriend and Price had engaged in a sexual encounter in her absence. She confronted Everett and demanded to know what had transpired while she had been gone.

"She kept asking [Everett] who had been in that room. He kept laughing," said Price.

As the quarrel escalated, Everett "came at Carolyn with his fists up, and I jumped into the middle of it," said Price. "He didn't hit her. He kept saying he was going to tell her [who had been in the bedroom].

"I'm not going to take another beating from you," McKendrick allegedly told her lover, as she picked up a .30 caliber Ruger Blackhawk from the bedroom bureau.

"That's no plaything," Everett said, still laughing.

McKendrick testified that when Everett raised his hands and moved toward her, she felt threatened. "I fired the gun, turned and ran. As far as I could see, he was still moving forward. I didn't know I'd hit him."

In his closing argument, Serota asked the jury, "Was it reasonable for her to do what she did? Aren't [Everett's fists] weapons?" He went on to describe his client a "love slave" fearful of another beating.

Prosecutor Roger King countered by calling the defendant a "love queen" who murdered Everett in cold blood because she had been spurned in favor of a transvestite.

"Twenty-four years went up in smoke [that] comes out to the muzzle of a seven-inch gun. Was this a justifiable act? I submit no," said King while asking the jury to bring back a verdict of first-degree murder.

After deliberating just two-and-a-half hours, the jury of eight men and four women found McKendrick guilty of third-degree murder. The twenty-three-year-old woman was led away in handcuffs to begin serving her sentence.

Serota was positive his client would have walked if the victim had not been a local celebrity. He filed an appeal on her behalf that was eventually denied. Carolyn spent exactly five years in prison and was then released.

Regardless of the trial's outcome, many questions remain: Was Everett dealing drugs? Was he bisexual? Was Carolyn McKendrick really the one who pulled the trigger?

"Tyrone would never do any drugs himself," said Tyrone's brother Mike Everett, who was also a world-class boxer. "I know my brother, and he couldn't have fought the way he did and take drugs. But he was probably fronting people money to buy drugs. Once you start making a little money, you get greedy and look for ways to invest it and make some more. That's what Carolyn was into. That's the kind of life we were living back then."

If Tyrone was investing part of his boxing purses in drugs, it couldn't have been a very profitable enterprise. At the time of his death, his 1976 yellow Cadillac Coupe was being repossessed and his telephone had been disconnected.

Price also testified that although he'd never been sexually intimate with Everett, at least four homosexual acquaintances had told him they'd had sex with the former number-one contender.

"Tyrone was a ladies' man," said his mother, Doris Everett. "Those rumors were impossible."

"We don't believe all that junk," said neighbor Al Crushman, who was interviewed by the *Philadelphia Daily News* while the McKendrick trial was in progress. "He didn't need to mess with any fags. He had too many women. Even at his funeral, he must have left fifteen girls crying on the corner."

Not everybody close to Everett was so sure.

"I'm not a judge and jury, but you find a lot of stuff on the streets," Everett's trainer Jimmy Arthur told writer Bob Ingram many years after the tragedy.

The question of whether or not McKendrick actually shot Everett is just as titillating as the boxer's sexual propensities, if not more so. McKendrick was no angel. She was on probation for two convictions of firearms and narcotic violations, as well as another bust for receiving stolen property.

"Carolyn was a very classy lady," said Serota, "but she came from people who were the scum of the earth."

Throughout her relationship with Everett, Carolyn was married to Ricardo McKendrick, an authentic tough guy who was sentenced to prison in 1974 for distributing heroin. Ricardo was released shortly before Everett was killed and was rumored to have taken out a contract on the boxer's life.

On June 4, 1977, nine days after the shooting, the *Philadelphia Tribune* published an article by staff reporter Len Lear, which cast serious doubt on the State's case.

"Carolyn McKendrick, who has been charged by police with the slaying of boxer Tyrone Everett, is 'going to take a fall to protect the real killer,' reliable sources told the *Tribune*."

"Not true, just street talk," said Serota many years after McKendrick had been released. "The details of the way it was told, by both Price and Carolyn McKendrick, are too involved. In my opinion, her story fit all the physical evidence. She knew too much.

"Want to know what I think happened? Well, I'll tell you. She came home and Everett was balling a fag. She got bent out of shape and told Everett to get out of the house. She was incensed. He came at her and threatened her. He obviously could have hurt her. You could call it a lovers' spat, I guess. But at that point, I think she just wanted to end the relationship."

In a 1989 interview published in *PhillySport* magazine, both Tyrone's mother and his brother Eddie said they still doubted Carolyn was the shooter. They also hinted that Ricardo McKendrick might have been part of the deadly equation. If they are correct, it's unlikely he was the triggerman.

Boxing trainer George James, who had no reason to lie, claimed he was standing on a corner near the death house talking to Ricardo at the time Everett laughed his final laugh.

"It couldn't have been Rickie," said James. "He was with me when we both heard the shot."

"I know Rickie didn't have nothing to do with it," said Mike Everett. "I don't know why they dragged that boy's name into it. I don't think he had much animosity about her and Tyrone. Carolyn did it because of jealousy or whatever went on behind closed doors.

The truth of what happened to Everett is obscured by time and the conflicting accounts of those involved. But the stories persist. One narrative still heard on the streets tells how a hired gunman was so impressed by Everett's standing in the black community, he refused to go through with the contract and returned his client's the money. Could the contract possibly have been passed to Carolyn?

Years after his brutally abrupt exit, the controversy surrounding the life and death of Tyrone Everett continues. Opinions on both his career and character are as divided as the scorecards that robbed him of the super featherweight championship. In the final analysis, all we really know for sure is that a life was tragically wasted.

It has been suggested that things might have turned out differently if Everett had received a square deal in the Escalera fight. As world champion, Tyrone might have been able to shake the streets from his soul.

Perhaps he'd still be alive if he had thrown caution to the wind and tried to win the title by knockout. Most observers believe such a result was well within his capability. But Everett knew boxing was a dangerous game and always played it safe. It was his life outside of the ring that courted the Reaper.

———

EPILOGUE: There have been no revelations about Everett's murder since this account was originally published. However, since George James is now dead, I will reveal something I never would have during his life. Roughly six months before Everett was killed, James told me he had just visited Ricardo McKendrick at Graterford prison. His mission was to try and persuade McKendrick to drop the contract he'd taken out on Tyrone's life.

A confirmation of sorts concerning the Escalera-Everett fix can also be revealed now that Blinky Palermo is dead. Shortly after the fight, when Peltz spoke to him about what happened. Blinky told him that Lou Tress "could be bought for a cup of coffee."

THERE'S NO HONOR IN A SUCKER PUNCH

BOXING'S CARDINAL SIN

ORIGINALLY PUBLISHED BY ESPN.COM, MAY 24, 2017

ALTHOUGH MANY ARE reluctant to admit it, boxing fans, by and large, are a bloodthirsty lot. How could it be otherwise? Whether by craft or crudity, the objective of the sport is to inflict bodily harm on another human being.

But even in such a brutal undertaking as prizefighting, there are limits— certain actions are considered beyond the pale

The sucker punch is one of them. It's always been that way, even back in the bare-knuckle era, when throwing your opponent to the ground and falling on top of him was permissible. Even kids know a sucker punch is cheating.

An early case of some note took place on a sunny July day in 1835, when William "Bendigo" Thompson squared off with Ben Caunt in a field behind the Appleby House, a secluded roadside tavern near Nottingham, England.

Caunt was much bigger than Thompson, outweighing him by approximately 45 pounds, but Thompson was a superior athlete, quick, agile and, in the parlance of the day, as slippery as goose grease.

Throughout the fight, Thompson connected with bruising punches to Caunt's head and body and then pretended to slip and dropped to one knee, ending the round on his own terms. Going down on purpose was against the rules, but much like today's basketball players angling for a foul shot, it's hard to prove if a fall is real or fake. And Thompson was an early master of the art.

Utterly frustrated by Thompson's evasive tactics and verbal insults, Caunt coldcocked his antagonist during the 30-second rest period at the end of the 22nd round. Thompson was sitting on the knee of one of his cornermen, as was the custom of the day, when "Big Ben" hit him full force, knocking him and the cornerman over backward.

Caunt was immediately disqualified, and Thompson was declared the winner.

Almost two centuries later, the sucker punch remains taboo but is also an integral part of boxing. On March 3, 2018, super middleweight contender Jose Uzcátegui was the unfortunate recipient of a particularly malicious sucker punch, a bare-fist lightning bolt he never saw coming.

It had already been an inauspicious evening for Uzcátegui. A few minutes earlier, he had been disqualified for knocking out Andre Dirrell with a left hook that landed a split second after the bell rang to end the eighth round. It was a borderline call, but referee Bill Clancy awarded the fight to Dirrell, who was deemed unfit to continue.

Uzcátegui was standing in his corner awaiting the official decision when Dirrell's uncle and trainer, Leon Lawson Jr., approached. It appeared that he was going to speak with Uzcátegui 's cornermen, who were standing on the ring apron and leaning over the ropes.

Suddenly, Lawson turned toward Uzcátegui, who was looking in another direction with his hands at his sides, and threw a left hook that landed flush on the side of Uzcátegui's face. It was one of those "no he didn't" moments, followed by outrage at such a cowardly attack.

In the confusion that ensued, Lawson left the ring and slipped out of the building. He has been charged with first-and second-degree assault but remained at large.

Many noted that the incident was eerily similar to James "The Harlem Hammer" Butler's despicable behavior after losing a 10-round decision to Richard Grant in November 2001, a nightmare scenario with ominous overtones.

After the decision was announced, Butler, his gloves already removed, walked toward the winner with his hand extended for what looked like the customary post-fight handshake. But instead of a handshake, Grant was the recipient of a scandalous sucker punch.

Grant collapsed and lay on the ring floor, blood oozing from his mouth. It was a stomach-churning sight, one that accentuated the monstrous nature of Butler's craven attack. The punch had dislocated Grant's jaw and lacerated his tongue.

There was no slipping away for Butler. The show at Manhattan's Roseland Ballroom was a fundraiser for the Twin Towers Fund, and roughly 500 policemen and firemen were in attendance. Butler was arrested as he left the ring, convicted of assault and served four months in Riker's Island.

Tragically, the occurrence foreshadowed an even worse event. After being released from prison, Butler moved to California, where Sam Kellerman, the 29-year-old brother of broadcaster Max Kellerman, allowed the troubled boxer to stay with him on a temporary basis (Max Kellerman now works for ESPN).

In October 2004, Butler murdered Sam Kellerman in the apartment they shared. After he was apprehended, Butler confessed and was sentenced to 29 years behind bars.

Butler is a particularly nasty case, but flaws can be found even at the highest level. Former heavyweight champion Riddick Bowe was the perpetrator of a pair of sucker-punch episodes that took place back-to-back in 1994.

In his first fight after losing the title to Evander Holyfield, Bowe fought Buster Mathis Jr. in Atlantic City. Mathis proved an uncooperative target, but a steady barrage from Bowe convinced Mathis to seek refuge by taking a knee in the fourth round, whereupon Bowe clobbered him with a right to the head that ended the fight.

Referee Arthur Mercante would have been well within his rights to disqualify Bowe, but after huddling with New Jersey commissioner Larry Hazzard, Mercante rule it a no contest. At the time, it was shrugged off as a questionable call. But what happened at a news conference for Bowe's next fight indicated that the Mathis foul might have been more than an isolated, heat-of-battle slipup.

Bowe and Larry Donald were standing at the dais, neither looking aggressive, when suddenly Bowe bounced a combination off Donald's face. To make matters worse, Donald's hands were behind his back when Bowe chose to let him have it.

Bowe won a unanimous decision, but after the fight, he was served legal papers in connection with a civil suit filed against him in Los Angeles Superior Court.

In similar high-profile incidents, Marco Antonio Barrera sucker punched Erik Morales at a news conference before their second fight, in June 2002, and Bernard Hopkins smacked Winky Wright at the weigh-in for their July 2007 bout. It's not as rare an occurrence as you might think.

The motivation for these breaches of protocol falls into numerous categories of various culpability. Some, as with Uzcátegui's final punch against Dirrell, are just a matter of timing, usually with no premeditation involved.

Frustration, however, is often a major factor. It certainly was for Ben Caunt and many who followed in his footsteps.

Prefight tension and a bitter rivalry momentarily pushed Barrera over the edge. Bowe's ego was having trouble coming to grips with being a former champion, and it brought out the nasty side of his character.

Then there are the fake rumbles, staged to attract customers. But that's the showbiz side of boxing.

To better understand the roots of the phenomena and why the sucker punch is one of boxing's cardinal sins, we have to go back to the beginning, back before Caunt and Thompson battled behind the Appleby House.

The rise of prizefighting in England, a country imbued with a martial tradition, began in the first decade of the 18th century. Originally, it was seen by many as a better way of settling disputes than deadly duels with a sword or pistol, and as such, it had a code of conduct.

Even among the lower classes that populated boxing's ranks and made up the largest part of its audience, there was an instinctive sense of fair play. Yes, it was a vicious and often illegal business, but cheating was frowned upon, and not only because large amounts of money were wagered on the outcome.

When boxers say it's not about the money, they are lying. It's always about the money. Every time. But there's something else, too —something money can't buy.

From the journeyman's pride in going the distance to a world champion holding a belt above his or her head, it's about self-respect and knowing you've given your best and fought with honor.

That might sound corny, but it's true. Ask any fighter who has thrown his last punch and spent his last dollar. What they did in the ring will always be who they are.

That will never change. Boxing has to celebrate bravery and pride in an honest effort. For that is, after all, what gives the sport a measure of nobility. And there's no nobility in a sucker punch.

———

EPILOGUE: Leon Lawson Jr. eventually surrendered to the police and was charged with first-degree felonious assault. However, a Prince George County District judge dismissed those charges and charged Lawson with single count of misdemeanor assault.

WHY BOXING FANS RIOT

A CLOSER LOOK AT BAD BEHAVIOR

ORIGINALLY PUBLISHED IN *RINGSIDE SEAT* NUMBER 10, SPRING 2020

EMPTY BOTTLES CAME out of the darkness and into the light seconds before exploding on the concrete floor, sending shards of glass spraying in all directions. A few bottles at first, the bombardment quickly escalated as more fans in the balcony were caught up in the moment.

The boxers and the referee quickly exited the ring and fans sitting within range scampered for cover. I found myself crouched beside my second-row aisle seat, about 25 feet from the ring, mesmerized by what was happening.

Potential danger wasn't a consideration. I had purchased a ringside seat and wanted to experience the insurrection up close, partly for the thrill and partly because I was too stupid to be afraid. I was not alone in this madness.

Philadelphia Inquirer boxing writer Gene Courtney was the only member of the press still ringside. He had an early deadline and was furiously pounding the keys of his typewriter, a cigarette dangling from his lips, while his wife held a folding chair over his head.

As usual, alcohol was the catalyst. The hurled bottles had been at least partway filled when they entered the building. There wasn't any frisking back then. If you had a ticket and were sober enough to walk, you got in. Fittingly, the bombardment ended when the insurgents ran out of ammunition.

The hostile outburst was triggered by a bad decision that went against the B-side boxer Ruben de Jesus who gave an excellent account of himself against local ticker seller Augie Pantellas. When Pantellas won a 10-round split decision something snapped. Sometimes it doesn't take much.

Even though de Jesus was from New York, a lot of the folks in the cheap seats probably identified with him. They, too, were underdogs, hard-working people who never seemed to get ahead of the bills. Their man had just fought the fight of his life, only to get hosed by two piss-ant judges. It was a protest against the boxing establishment, a message from the powerless to the powerful.

My baptism by fire was wonderfully madcap and just scary enough to give it an edge. Even now, wherever some crazy shit breaks out, I flash back to that March 1970 night at the old Philadelphia Arena—my touchstone when things get deliciously lawless.

They seldom show disturbances on TV, but you can always tell when something is going down by the way people turn away from the ring and look elsewhere. My father always chuckled when it happened and made the same corny old joke about the fight in the stands being better than the one in the ring.

Unscheduled disturbances are part of boxing—a curious byproduct like cauliflower ears and shoving matches at weigh-ins. But that's my opinion. I think it's fair to say that most people believe any disruptive behavior, large or small, brings discredit to the sport, poses a danger to public welfare, and is bad for business.

I won't argue the first two points, but I'm not too sure about the third.

It's been almost 50 years since that unforgettable night at the Philadelphia Arena, but unruly behavior has shown no sign of going away. Security is tighter now, which has significantly reduced the number of weapons in the arena. But there's no way, short of mass sedation, that could stop human beings from losing their cool.

A recent reminder came on January 11, 2020, when light heavyweights Joe Smith Jr. and Jesse Hart fought at the Hard Rock Hotel and Casino in Atlantic City. There were no incoming projectiles, but chaos ensued anyway when Smith, the union laborer from Long Island who retired Bernard Hopkins, won a split decision.

It had been an entertaining, hard-fought match, but Smith was a worthy winner.

Apparently, not everybody felt the same way. It was Philly verses Long Island, and there was quite a bit of money on the line. The Hard Rock sports book had Hart a 3-1 favorite.

"There was a long delay before they announced the decision," said promoter J Russell Peltz, who was in attendance along with his wife, Linda. "It must have been 10 minutes, maybe 15. That's never a good sign, so we moved to the back."

Fighting in the stands commenced immediately after the decision was announced. It spread like a slow-moving flood, oozing down the risers to the floor and out into the lobby, where spectators formed a semi-circle around the brawlers.

There's often a slapstick quality to these impromptu skirmishes, laced with a dash of peril, a food fight with a cherry bomb in one of the pies.

I gather the melee eventually spilled out onto the boardwalk, reminiscent of old cowboy movies, where a brawl starts in a saloon and ends in the street. Yippee- Ki-Yay, motherfucker!

I didn't hear about anybody going to the hospital or getting arrested. As long as no serious damage was done to the Hard Rock, nobody gave a rat's ass. It was just another night at the fights. The post-fight free-for-all was an added attraction—like fireworks after a baseball game.

Boxing's outlaw status is, if only subliminally, a substantial part of its appeal. Going to the fights isn't the same as going to a concert or a movie. It's not the same as going to a baseball or basketball game. It's all about fighting. Fighting permeates everything. Is it any wonder some of the lubricated punters want to get in on the action?

Disorderly conduct among spectators has been part of pugilism since the birth of modern boxing in 18th century England. During much of the bareknuckle era there was a roped-off inner circle between the spectators and the ring, where men with bullwhips prevented would-be interlopers from interfering with the fight. Ouch!

Even so, it wasn't that unusual for the inner circle to be breached, allowing the rum-filled mob to run amok.

That sort of mayhem wasn't limited to the British Isles. When Englishman James "Deaf 'Un" Burke traveled to New Orleans in 1837 to fight Samuel O'Rourke, he was lucky to escape with his life. Soon after the fight began, O'Rourke's second, Mick Carson, pushed Burke and threatened to "slit his gizzard." The Deaf 'Un replied with a punch.

"This was the signal for a general scrimmage in which the Irishmen joined O'Rourke, attacking Burke and his friends with fists and sticks," reported the *Charleston Courier*. "Burke was followed by a crowd of Irishmen with shillelaghs, dray-pins, whips and other weapons. A well-wisher, seeing him pass, handed [Burke] a bowie knife, and another gave him a horse, on which he escaped."

There's some question as to what happened to the man who gave the Deaf 'Un a horse. Some accounts say he was beaten to death by the mob, others that he was seriously beaten but survived.

These days, boxing likes to present a high-tech corporate image, and who can blame it, but it is just veneer. There's more money and more lawyers today, but boxing hasn't fundamentally changed. Neither have the fans, which means we should expect a spot of bother every now and then. It's part of the deal.

When the shit gets real and violence spreads beyond the ring, traditional wisdom says the safest place is under the ring, and that's likely true. But how many people can fit under there, anyway?

As in so many things, location is everything. There's usually some part of the arena where no fighting is going on. Head for it you can, but if you find yourself in the middle of a boxing riot (any riot, actually) with nowhere to run, your only choices are duck-and-cover or start swinging.

That's what happened to more than few innocent bystanders when Oleg Maskaev fought Hasim Rahman at Atlantic City's Convention Hall in November 1999. In the eighth round of the main event, all 234 pounds of Rahman suddenly came crashing through the ropes and out of the ring, compliments of a Maskaev right hand.

Rahman landed on the ringside table, knocked it over, barely missed HBO's Jim Lampley, and slid headfirst onto the floor. A TV monitor that was sitting on the table also hit the deck, but not before bouncing off the back of Rahman's legs. He was done for the night.

The instant Rahman went through the ropes, two things happened almost simultaneously. Somebody hurled a chair, blindsiding referee Steve Smoger, who was hit on the back of the head. Concurrently, a group of Rahman supporters rushed the ring, trampling anybody in their way.

It was on. In a matter of seconds, practically everybody on that side of the ring was caught up in the turmoil. And it wasn't a "Hey, man, there's a beverage here" situation.

Spectators fought each other and security guards for approximately 10 minutes with little regard for the Marquis of Queensberry rules. Flurries of folding chairs flew through the air, looking like giant Frisbees as they whizzed past. Police had to be called in from the street to put a stop to it.

"There is something organic about it. There's the contagion theory," said Jason Lanter, a psychology professor at Kutztown University. "We know people do things in crowds they would not do alone. They think they're anonymous. People make poor decisions in crowds."

Moreover, neuroscientists have discovered that the medial prefrontal cortex, which plays a major role in self-reflection, is more dormant during group action. This allows people in crowds to act in ways they ordinarily wouldn't.

Another factor is tribalism, a strong loyalty to one's own tribe, party, or group, which was essential to the early survival of the human species. But there's a catch. Tribalism can also foster an amity-enmity complex, where those who belong to the in-group are tolerated, while others are part of an out-group and subjects of hostility.

Boxing is supposed to be controlled violence, and for the most part boxers work within the current interpretation of the rules. Sure, all fighters cheat a bit, some a lot, but disqualifications are a comparatively small percentage of overall results. Usually, it's the audience that goes bonkers.

Such behavior is what's known in academic circles as "destructive energy." Watching an exciting sporting event both builds up and relieves destructive energy. Providing this is achieved vicariously, it's a good way to alleviate stress. Nonetheless, it can backfire.

According to the authors of *Violence and Aggression in Sporting Contests*, "For a certain subset of sports fans, witnessing violent sports is not enough to reduce such energy to tolerable levels, and only personally experienced aggressive acts serve to relieve the tension built up before, during, and after an exciting sports event."

Despite all efforts to suppress those darker parts of our nature, boxing fans are still boxing fans, a cult that worships at the altar of violence. Oh, sure, some like it fancy and others like it plain, but in the end it's all the same—a fight.

Like the running of the bulls in Pamplona, sometimes the line between spectators and participants is so blurred it's hard to know the difference.

EXTRAORDINARY
CHARACTERS

BOXING'S BAD GUYS

THE FIGHTERS YOU LOVE TO HATE

ORIGINALLY PUBLISHED IN *RINGSIDE SEAT*, WINTER 2021

"In films the good guy always wins, but this is one bad guy who ain't gonna lose."

—Sonny Liston

SONNY LISTON KNEW the drill as well as anybody. Black hat versus white hat is good for business, an old formula that never gets old. Sonny was born to play the part—a mob-handled black ex-con with a sullen disposition and a 16-wheeler of a left hook. When he tried to change the script after winning the heavyweight championship, he couldn't. Sonny had worn the black hat for so long he would never escape its shadow.

All boxers, including the baddies, have a common root in antiquity—in mankind's search for survival at a time when the bad guys often lived in the neighboring village.

Sports as an allegorical proxy for war is an ancient concept. It does not matter whether it's a team or a one-on-one rivalry, sides will be inevitably drawn and "the other" will become the enemy, ideally only for the length of the contest.

It's the fans that determine who is and who isn't a bad guy. And it's not always something a boxer did that pisses off the devotees—attitude counts a lot. The media can be influential, but the paying public is the ultimate arbiter. It's a consensus of like minds. If enough fans, for whatever reason, consider a fighter a flaming asshole, the jury has spoken.

Certain boxers, such as Jack Johnson, were hated for who they were, not what they did. Being the first black heavyweight champion automatically made him a bad guy (or worse) as far as the United States' white population was concerned. True, he was a badass all right, but clearly not a bad *guy*. In a larger, historical sense, Johnson was a civil rights and boxing pioneer because he had the courage to be his own man.

Muhammad Ali and Floyd Mayweather were both good guys and bad guys at various times during their careers. The shifts in popularity were, in large part, tied to cultural change, but you can't banish this pair to the bad-guy hoosegow. On balance, admiration outweighs the animosity.

So, who are the real bad guys, and what is it about them that gets fans riled up in the first place? Like so much of boxing, it's subjective. There's no bad guy Hall of Fame to guide us, and it doesn't look like they'll be building a Bad Guy Wing in Canastota anytime soon.

In the meantime, just so we're ready if and when the time comes, here are 10 nominees for the inaugural induction.

Note that bad guys' misdeeds vary in kind and seriousness, as do the men. The following rogues' gallery ranges from pathetic losers and criminals to cheaters and the mentally impaired, along with a few relatively sane renegades. If they share anything in common, it's desperation. The difference between them is the way in which their desperation is manifested.

LUIS RESTO

I remember arriving at *The Ring* editorial office the morning after the Luis Resto-Billy Collins junior middleweight fight at the Garden, June 16, 1983. My colleague Ben Sharav was already there, clutching a roll of film he'd taken on his way to work.

Sharav had been at the fight and witnessed the frightful beating Collins had absorbed in person, so the next morning Ben stopped by Billy's hotel room on his way to work. He wanted to check on him, see how he was doing, and maybe take a few photos.

Five of us crowded into the tiny darkroom and watched the images of the boxer's ravaged face emerge in the developing fluid tray. It looked like a ghostly mug shot, and Billy's eyes were like lumps of coal in a snowman's face.

Luis Resto achieved all-time villain status after it was discovered that his trainer, Panama Lewis, removed padding from his gloves prior to Resto's win over Billy Collins in 1983. Due to injuries suffered in the fight, Collins never fought again and died a year later in a car crash some believe was a suicide.

For me he will always be that face in the developing fluid.

ANTONIO MARGARITO

After big fights at the MGM Grand Garden Arena, there's always a crush getting off the escalator that takes you up to the casino level. There's usually a bit of jostling, but nothing serious. But as the escalator rose the night Manny Pacquiao pancaked Ricky Hatton, you could hear angry voices yelling, "cheater, coward, let's get him."

At the top of the escalator was an area sealed off by portable walls, which were rocking back and forth as fans pounded them. It wasn't exactly the villagers storming Dr. Frankenstein's castle, but these people were fired up. On the other side you could glimpse a startled looking Antonio Margarito, the target of their wrath.

Earlier in the year Margarito and his trainer, Javier Capetillo, were busted for trying to load Margarito's gloves with a plaster-like substance before his bout with Shane Mosley. The fight went on and Mosley scored a sixth-round knockout.

Instead of being pummeled by the angry mob at the MGM, when he returned from a year's suspension, Margarito was legally pummeled by Pacquiao and Miguel Cotto, effectively ending the career of "El Tornado de Tijuana."

We are left with a perplexing question: Was the Mosley fight the first time Margarito loaded his gloves? It is widely assumed that he'd been cheating for some time, but without proof it's a lost cause. We do know, however, that he never won a significant fight after being caught.

JAKE LAMOTTA

It rained the morning of June 14, 1960, the day Jake LaMotta testified before a U.S. Senate sub-committee. As he made his way up the steps to the Senate Building, dodging umbrellas and ignoring the press, Jake couldn't stop thinking about the upcoming ordeal.

"The middleweight champion of the world is about to admit to the greatest sin in boxing. What a shit feeling—like going to confession for the first time. I was in a cold sweat," said LaMotta.

It was common knowledge that LaMotta had thrown his November 1947 bout with "Blackjack" Billy Fox so that the mob would arrange a title bout for him. But the sub-committee wanted Jake to testify under oath for the official record.

Jake hated the fact the scandal was front-page news again. For years LaMotta was reviled for throwing the Fox fight, beating his wife, and doing six months on a chain gang for pimping an underage girl. Jake never pretended to be something he wasn't, but occasionally an old sinner is dragged out of purgatory like a hibernating badger and into the light.

When his biopic, *Raging Bull*, was released in 1980, Jake underwent a cultural rebirth as a gritty old pug always good for a laugh. The iconic status of Martin Scorsese's movie helped LaMotta remain a minor celebrity until his death at age 95 in 2017.

Although the stigma of the Fox fight had faded, the fix was prominently featured in every obituary. Jake wouldn't have liked it, but probably would have understood why it had to be that way. It was that rainy morning in D.C.

MIKE TYSON

Of all the things that happened that night at the MGM Grand, the image I recall the most vividly is Mike Tyson climbing up the side of the bleachers, trying to get to the fans throwing stuff at him. He snapped when somebody dumped a beer on his head and started to climb. You could tell by the look on his face he'd rip those people to shreds if he got close enough. A couple of his minders got him down in time and guided him backstage.

Meanwhile, Evander Holyfield was in an ambulance, holding a white towel to his right ear.

The "Bite Fight" alone was enough to put Tyson at the forefront of the era's bad guys. It wasn't an isolated instance. He also habitually punched after the bell, tried to break Kevin McBride and Frans Botha's arms, and bit McBride's nipple.

Despite his numerous transgressions, including being convicted of sexual assault and serving three years in prison, Tyson's die-hard fans never deserted him

It was a case of mass infatuation. During his early years, millions of people fell in love watching Tyson snuff out sacrificial victims on TV, images they hold dear and are reluctant to give up. Tyson was simultaneously the baddest of the bad guys and the most popular fighter in the world, which says as much about us as it does "Iron Mike."

Tyson, now 55, has become a blissed-out friend to the world, fronting a cannabis empire that includes a 420-acre ranch and resort in the Mojave Desert.

Mike's exhibition with Roy Jones was a mid-life crisis that became a pay-per-view hit. Snoop Dog's unforgettable quote, "This is like two of my uncles fighting at the BBQ," says it all. The bad guy has mellowed, and Tyson is at peace.

"Pass the Dutchie 'pon the left-hand side."

FRITZIE ZIVIC

For decades, the gold standard for dirty fighters was welter-weight champion (1941-1942) Fritzie Zivic, a rule breaker extraordinaire. He was known as a "gentlemanly dirty fighter" because he apologized after every foul, but kept giving the other guy the business, anyway. His motto was "Always work the ref's blind side."

According to Pittsburgh Boxing's Facebook page, "Zivic took pride in his evil reputation; it was a part of his identity. He definitely looked the part, with his flat nose, mischievous smirk and wide-eyed stare. But playing the bad guy role was strictly for the ring. Fritzie was unquestionably a nice guy outside the ropes, with a quick wit and an ability to connect with the common folk that made him popular with the Pittsburgh fight crowd."

"[The public] put a label on me as a dirty fighter, but I never lost a fight on a foul in my life," said Zivic during an interview with author Peter Heller. "I'd give 'em the head, choke 'em, hit 'em in the balls, but never in my life used my thumb because I wanted no one to use it on me."

Nonetheless, Al "Bummy" Davis claimed it was a thumb to the eye that sparked the memorable freak-out when he fought Zivic at Madison Square Garden in November 1940. Davis didn't wait for the apology. He slammed approximately 10 punches into Fritzie's balls. When referee Billy Cavanaugh disqualified Davis at 2:34 of the second round, Bummy kicked him in the groin.

At that point, what did he have to lose?

ANDREW GOLOTA

Has anyone figured out yet what the hell was the matter with Golota? His back-to-back disqualification losses to former heavyweight champion Riddick Bowe in fights Golota was winning never made sense. Sometimes a boxer on the brink of defeat will try to stave it off by hitting his opponent in the nuts, but on the way to victory? Twice! That's crazy.

My best guess is the "Foul Pole" suffered from a serious personality disorder, featuring paranoid panic attacks and self-destructive behavior, or maybe he was already suffering from CTE caused by blows to the head. The third and most unlikely explanation is that he had to throw the fights for whatever reason and wanted to show what he could really do before fouling out. It sounds far-fetched, I know, but it wouldn't be the first time. The Greenpoint Crew, an infamous Polish crime organization, was active in Golota's hometown of Chicago at the time.

There were also troubles outside the ring. In 2002, Golota was arrested in Juliet, Illinois for impersonating a police officer. When Chicago police went to Golota's house in 2006 to investigate a sexual assault of which the boxer was accused, they discovered more than a dozen illegal weapons.

When asked about his fouls and DQs during a late-career come-back, Golota said, "I'm clean fighter now. I take shower twice a day." Unlike a lot of his punches, his deadpan delivery was spot on.

ADRIAN BRONER

Broner stood before Judge Nancy Margaret Russo in an Ohio courtroom looking like a dude who hadn't been home for a week and was worried his wife had thrown all his belongings out the window. He held his hands out appealingly and talked in circles, but Judge Russo was having none of his bullshit.

Broner had repeatedly failed to show up for previous court dates and still hadn't provided documentation as to why he could not pay a judgment of almost $800,000 to a woman plaintiff, after pleading guilty to assault and unlawful restraint.

Judge Russo jailed Broner for contempt of court, and he was

taken away in handcuffs, a rumpled, overweight sad sack who had thrown away the prime of his career.

Broner was insufferable from the start—a Floyd Mayweather wannabe who was so starved for attention he posted a video of himself wiping his ass with $100 bills in the bathroom of a Popeyes franchise.

At his best, Adrien was fast and flashy, a spiteful puncher with a slick defense—a blue-chipper who got away with being a total douche while he was winning. But he was never the same after Marcos Maidana mugged him, December 14, 2013, down San Antonio way.

It was difficult to know what to think when Broner posted a video talking about suicide. Was it a cry for help or just another attention grab? From the outside looking in, he seems lost in an artificial world of his own making and is afraid there will be nothing left if he steps back into reality.

RICARDO MAYORGA

For a few years the mad man from Managua was King of the Bad Guys. He fought with feral aggression, a street fighter in boxing gloves, moving to a helter-skelter beat.

He was a beer-guzzling, cigarette-smoking, swaggering braggart who flaunted convention, grossed out his rivals, and seemed capable of running amok at the slightest provocation. In other words, he was magnificent.

When Mayorga stopped welterweight champion Vernon Forrest in the third round to unify the 147-pound title in January 2003, he swooped in like a buccaneer boarding a galleon. Before Forrest knew what had hit him, it was all over, and Mayorga was the new champ.

After beating Forrest by majority decision in the rematch, Mayorga was featured on the cover of December 2003 issue of *The Ring*, a cigarette in his mouth, his face a stony mask. He's looking over his shoulder as if he's worried somebody or something was gaining on him. And there was.

Mayorga lost the title to Cory Spinks via a controversial, majority decision. He had a good win now and then after that, but became a high-end B-side, knockout victim to the stars. Felix Trinidad, Oscar De La Hoya, Shane Mosley, Miguel Cotto, and others stopped him.

Even after he'd flamed out, Mayorga came to fight and tried to win, but usually went down swinging. There's honor in that.

Ricardo hid behind his fury, his safe place where nothing could hurt him. But anger alone is a thin diet and has been of little help since he retired from the ring in April 2019. With the assistance of the WBC, Mayorga entered a drug and alcohol rehab in August 2020. Fellow countryman and two division former titleholder Rosendo Alvarez is helping care for him.

HARRY GREB

Legendary middleweight champion Harry Greb has long been portrayed as a crazy man, a dirty fighter and drunken philanderer. Then there's the oft-told tale of Harry getting blowjobs in the dressing room before fights. Some say the rumor has been debunked, which is probably correct, but I reserve the right to hold out hope that it actually happened, at least once or twice. Stephen Compton, author of *The Life and Times of Harry Greb*, believes the "Pittsburgh Windmill" was partly the victim of the yellow journalism that flourished in the 1920s.

"One can trace the beginning of Greb's bad boy image to just before the second bout with Gene Tunney," said Compton. "Tunney dumped his former manager Doc Bagley and signed up with Billy Gibson because of Gibson's clout both politically and with newspapermen. They began a concerted publicity campaign to discredit Greb's win over Tunney and framed him as a dirty fighter."

In 1946, James Fair published a largely bogus Greb biography called *Give Him To The Angels*. "[Fair] portrayed him as a wild, drunken womanizer who once bit off an opponent's nose during a fight," said Compton. "Fair's book was eventually pulled from circulation, but he continued to get paid to publish salacious fictional articles about Greb for years, and those same stories were picked up by a new generation of writers and taken as gospel inaccurately.

"The truth, I think, is somewhere in between. Greb certainly participated in some legitimately wild events. He fit well into the Roaring Twenties. But several of those events were exaggerated. The bulk of them coming so close together, late in Greb's career at a time when he was most visible, has colored his life inaccurately."

But what about the blowjobs? I've heard the same anecdote about singer Al Jolson. Somebody needs to get to the bottom of this.

MYSTERIOUS BILLY SMITH

No list of bad guys would be complete without the man who earned the nickname "The Dirtiest Fighter Who Ever Lived" by being disqualified 13 times. Born in Nova Scotia, Smith did most of his fighting in the United States, claiming the vacant welterweight title by knocking out Danny Needham in 1892. He held the title until Tommy Ryan took it away with a 20-round decision in 1894.

Smith, whose repertoire of fouls included head butts, elbows, knees, and biting, was frequently his own worst enemy. For example, in January 1900, Smith knocked down Rube Ferns 15 times—that's right 15 times—only to be disqualified in the 21st round.

In December 1911, the *Sacramento Union* reported that Smith had been fatally wounded when a jealous ex-husband shot him three times. Turned out the newspaper underestimated Smith's recuperative powers. The old reprobate survived his wounds and lived until October 1937.

———

Kids don't take up boxing because they dream of being the next Elbows McFadden, a fighter who wielded his cubiti like battleaxes. In their hearts, they all want to be champion. There probably wouldn't be boxing if they didn't. Most young boxers are dreamers by nature, which is one of the reasons the sport survives. But it's inevitable that some hopefuls will become bad guys. It's the law of averages.

Boxing creates and magnifies the bad guy archetype, a volatile but necessary ingredient in the pugilistic cocktail. We would be lost without them. Imagine Sherlock Holmes minus Professor Moriarty or Doctor Jekyll with no Mr. Hyde? Joe Louis without Max Schmeling?

So, here's a toast to the bad guys. Like Tony Montana said, we need them so we can point our "fuckin' fingers and say, 'That's the bad guy.'"

ONE OF A KIND

YOU'LL NEVER SEE ANOTHER LIKE LEON SPINKS

ORIGINALLY PUBLISHED IN *RINGSIDE SEAT*, WINTER 2021.

LEON SPINKS, who died February 5 at the age 67, had personality that stood out like a diamond in a pawnshop window. He was raw and honest and made people laugh without even trying. He was fierce in the boxing ring and cuddly the rest of the time, a man who lived life minus a steering wheel.

His younger brother, Michael, was thoughtful and spoke softly, George Harrison to Leon's Ringo Starr. What they shared beyond brotherly love was boxing, the vehicle that made them Olympic gold medalists and world champions.

Michael was moved carefully as a pro, while Leon was on a faster track. Still, it seemed ludicrous when Leon, after only seven professional fights, was given a title shot against Muhammad Ali. What were they trying to do? Ruin the guy?

It was more a matter of protecting Ali. At 36, he was on the homestretch and coming off a taxing fight with Earnie Shavers. He needed a challenger who would put up a good fight but have virtually no chance of winning. It couldn't be just any of old pug. To maximize revenue, a recognizable face had to be in the other corner.

Leon ticked all the boxes. Except for Sugar Ray Leonard, he was the best known of the five American boxers who won gold medals at the Montreal Games. He radiated a zany, almost childlike behavior that made people chuckle at his antics over their morning coffee and newspaper.

All the same, the first Ali-Spinks was a hard sell.

"NBC and ABC wouldn't bid on it, so CBS took it," wrote columnist Paul Benson. "Stung by the fans' disinterest and perhaps feeling gloomy about his mounting financial problems, Ali took to uncharacteristic public sulking, declaring that he would do no interviews. 'I'm just tired of the press, and I'm tired of people,' he said— perhaps the most surprising words he ever uttered."

In hindsight, it appears obvious. Ali, just four fights away from the finish line, was poorly conditioned and world-weary. Even so, when Spinks won a 15-round decision victory in March 1978, it was considered one of the biggest upsets in heavyweight championship history.

People were astonished that the neophyte from St. Louis's notorious Pruitt-Igoe housing project could vanquish arguably the greatest heavyweight champion of all time.

Looking back, it's difficult to know whether winning the heavyweight championship was the best thing that ever happened to Leon or the worst. The seven months he held the title was pretty much one long celebration. Spinks was headed for an Andy Ruiz Jr.-style rematch.

"I started living a wild life… women, drugs, all that stuff. I did a lot of things wrong. It's like I had no responsibility at all," Leon told The *Chicago Tribune*'s Sam Smith.

Before Leon was done, all that stuff included being arrested for driving the wrong way on a one-way street without a license, crashing his two-day old Corvette, and a week later running it through a fence. Speeding tickets fell like confetti. Everything was a blur.

"I was going through life so fast that I never thought what it was about, what I wanted to do with my life," he told Smith.

The media couldn't get enough if him. There were photos of Leon posing on the hood of a Rolls Royce and another of him taking a bath, wearing a cowboy hat and smoking a cigar. Thing got even rowdier when Mr. T joined the team.

There was no problem selling the rematch with Ali. A crowd of 63,350 packed the Superdome in New Orleans and ABC paid $3.5 million for the broadcast rights. Approximately 90 million viewers watched in the United States and an estimated 2 billion worldwide.

In turned out to be the final victory of Ali's legendary career. He boxed carefully and won a unanimous 15-round decision. Leon's cut was $3.75 million, but he claims he never saw a penny.

Leon fought on until December 1995, going 19-16-2 in his final 37 bouts, including a cruiserweight title fight with Dwight Muhammad Qawi and a crack at heavyweight champ Larry Holmes. Leon lost both inside the distance.

As one might have expected, he fell on hard times after his career ended, the millions of dollars Leon had earned in the ring gone. He was reportedly homeless at one point, living in a shelter. He worked at McDonalds and the YMCA in Columbus, Nebraska. At other times, he was a greeter at Mike Ditka's Chicago restaurant.

He stepped back into the spotlight when his son, Cory Spinks, won the welterweight championship in December 2003. That night in Atlantic City, when Cory took the WBC, WBA and IBF belts from Ricardo Mayorga, Leon's famous gap-tooth grin was shining brighter than it had in years.

He became a regular guest during Induction Weekend at the International Boxing Hall of Fame (IBHOF), where he was a fan favorite, seemingly at peace after going through some dark times.

For me, there's still a nagging question: Was Leon ever really happy? Was his public persona a mask he wore to ward off the memories of his tormented childhood?

John Crittenden, who grew up on the same block as the Spinks brothers, told John Florio and Ouisie Shanpiro, co-authors of *One Punch from the Promised Land*, that "Leon was a quiet kid. He kept to himself. He was bullied a lot. He wouldn't stand up for himself.

He shied away from everybody. We really did bully him and Michael. They wouldn't fight. They cried and ran home."

The harassment stopped when Leon and Michael joined the hard-core DeSoto Rec Center and learned to box, but perhaps Leon carried that hurt with him throughout his life. Perhaps the beaming smile and party-hardy lifestyle was an effort to compensate for the pain of a deprived childhood. It's not uncommon, you know.

He never really like being called "Neon" Leon, but after a while learned to go along with it and laugh like everybody. It's strange how fragile a fighting man's feelings can be.

Conversely, after escaping Pruitt-Igoe, Michael lived a relatively tranquil life away from the ring. He accomplished far more than Leon, winning the light heavyweight championship, holding it for years and then beating Larry Holmes for the lineal heavyweight title.

Michael, of course, was a better fighter. It usually comes down to that in the end.

But we'll never know for sure what Leon would have achieved if he could have found a way to slow the powerful forces of commerce that ate him up as fast as it could, worried he'd beat them to it. He was tough and brave, and not without talent, willing to fight anyone regardless of whether he was in shape or not—a real fighter.

Leon was the flavor of the year in 1978, his face on the cover of *Sports Illustrated*, his victory the winner of a trio of *Ring* magazine awards: Fight of the Year, Upset of the Year, and Progress of the Year. There was no way he could top that. He had peaked in his eighth pro bout.

The rest of Leon's career was mainly about hanging on and paying the bills, and there's nothing wrong with that. There were some decent wins over guys like Bernardo Mercado and Alfredo Evangelista along the way, but the years went by, the losses piled up, and he finally retired in December 1995 with an overall record of 26-17-3 (14).

Those are the unremarkable stats of a remarkable fighter. The truth doesn't reside in the numbers; it's about what he did in the most important fight of his life, about how a scared kid who used to have his lunch stolen became heavyweight champion of the world. As much for who he was as for what he did, Leon is the Spinks brother the general public remembers, the one who looked like a vampire when he took out his bridgework. Michael is the brother whose name they sometimes forget.

I doubt it bothers Michael. He's always looked up to his big brother and wanted to be just like him. He couldn't, of course. There is only one Leon Spinks, and now he's gone.

REQUIEM FOR A KITTEN

REMEMBERING STANLEY HAYWARD

Originally published in *Boxing News,* August 26, 2021

EVERYBODY LOVED STANLEY "KITTEN" Hayward, as much for his personality as his fighting prowess. When he died on August 10 at age 82, the Philadelphia boxing community mourned not only the loss of an outstanding boxer and link to the past, but also the passing of a remarkable man who brought a smile to the face of virtually everyone he met.

Hayward was a free spirit, a charmer who embraced life and wasn't afraid to grab it with both hands and see where it took him. Boxing was part of that but far from the whole. Women and horse racing were his passions and partying his pastime. Much of the time training wasn't even a consideration.

"I run all night and sleep all day," was how he put it.

Kitten had a warm glow of humanity running through him and a roguish affability. He had a knack of making people feel comfortable around him. He joked with the men, flirted with the women, and seemingly never ran out of something to say.

Hayward, who turned pro on September 24, 1959, reached his fighting peak between September 1963 and December 1965, that's when he beat the intimidating sextet of Percy Manning, Dick Turner, Curtis Cokes, Vince Shomo, Tito Marshall and Bennie Briscoe. All, except Shomo, were in or close to their primes.

"The type of fighter I was, I took punches to make a fight. I was a fighter's fighter," Hayward told Tris Dixon, author of *The Road to Nowhere*. "You couldn't come to a fight of mine and sit down because there was always going to be action. That's how Philly fighters work."

So how did this out-of-shape playboy susceptible to eye cuts manage to achieve so much inside the ring?

Natural ability played a role and so did the skills learned by sparring with Philly's finest. He was a slick aggressive fighter with a dancer's sense of balance. His punches hurt, and he was a good finisher, but the foundation of his success was his heart. Kitten was willing to bleed for victory, take risks and get off the floor.

"I not only learned to fight," Hayward said. "I learned to entertain."

His nationally televised fight with future world welterweight champion Cokes at the Blue Horizon, May 1, 1964, is a cult classic. Hayward was knocked down and hurt in the second round but rallied to stop Cokes in the fourth. It is considered by some to be the best fight ever held at the fabled venue.

A Pyrrhic victory over Briscoe in December '65 pushed Hayward near the top of the welterweight ratings, where he sputtered to a halt and lay idle the next 10 months like a battleship in dry-dock. He wanted Cokes again, who was by then the WBA welterweight champion, but got Gypsy Joe Harris instead.

"Who does [manager George Katz] have me fight without a tune-up? Only the hottest kid in the division," Hayward told writer Dan Haney in 2012. "Man, [Harris] was beating on me until I managed to drop him. But he gets up and starts whupping on me some more. The fight was stopped on cuts, and I was just as upset with George for sticking me in there unprepared. We parted ways shortly after that."

Hayward remained an attraction, fighting Emile Griffith twice, winning the first in October 1968 and losing the second in May

1969. In between those two bouts, Hayward lost a 15-round decision to Freddie Little for the vacant WBC and WBA super welterweight tiles. The money was decent but nothing special. Still, the $50,000 purse Kitten got for the second Griffith fight was the most he ever made.

Paris had fallen in love with Kitten in 1967, when he knocked down Frenchman Jean Josselin twice but had to settle for a rip-off draw. Hayward returned to Europe in 1970, fighting three times in Paris and once in Rome. While his record was a meager 1-2-1, he scored well outside of the ring, and not just with the ladies. He became friends with Yul Brynner and Omar Sharif, which led to a bit part in a spaghetti western and a leading role in Danish porno. Kitten was having way too much fun to worry about training.

When he returned home in 1971 sporting a French accent, nobody seemed to know if it was real, a prank, or maybe just an affectation. However, there was no doubt about the first-round knockout Kitten suffered at the hands of Eugene "Cyclone" Hart in his first Philadelphia appearance since October 1968. In any event, the left hooks Hart landed seemed to knock out the accent as well as Kitten.

Hayward had four wins and three losses in his final seven bouts. His last, on March 27, 1977, was a sad affair held at a Firehouse Hall in Bristol, Pennsylvania, where Larry "Tumbler" Davis stopped him in the fourth round. It was hard to watch.

Kitten's saving grace was that he never changed and emerged from a 48-fight career (32-12-4 with 18 inside the distance) the same elegantly dressed bon vivant he'd always been. He became a tipstaff with the Philadelphia Court System, where he worked for more than 30 years, an achievement of which he was rightly proud.

Kitten has often been described as being larger than life, but maybe that's selling him short. In a way, he seemed to embody all that life has to offer, a universal man who just so happened to box.

SPARRING WITH EAKINS

THE OUTLAW GENIUS WHO PAINTED BOXERS

ORIGINALLY PUBLISHED IN *RINGSIDE SEAT,* FALL/WINTER 2019

"Respectability in art is appalling."

— *Thomas Eakins*

IN ORDER TO be accepted as a student as the Pennsylvania Academy of Fine Arts (PAFA), applicants must submit a portfolio of their work. Among my offerings was a crude painting of Dick Tiger fighting Gene Fullmer, copied from a *Boxing Illustrated* cover. Much to my surprise, I was accepted.

The Academy was the first art school in the United States, founded by Charles Willson Peal and others in 1807, a venerable institution housed in a magnificent Victorian building designed by Frank Furness and George Hewitt. It is now a National Historic Landmark.

Many famous artists have studied there, including filmmaker and multi- media artist David Lynch, of *Twin Peaks* and *Mulholland Dr.* fame. He left in 1963, and I arrived in 1964. It wasn't much of trade-off. Compared to Lynch, you could fit my artistic talent into a cocaine spoon.

There was only one guy among the hundreds of students with whom I occasionally talked boxing. He was quite a bit older than most of us, smoked Pall Malls, and looked more like a factory worker than art student.

On rare nights when I stayed late after school, somebody would usually ask if I was going to the fights. They knew about my guilty pleasure, and most seemed repulsed and curious in equal measure. But they didn't judge. Art students are generally a tolerant lot, crazy but tolerant.

I would ride the El from Center City Philly to 46th and Market, a block away from the Philadelphia Arena, a rundown relic, built in 1920, that was once the jewel of the city's entertainment venues. There were folks selling bean pies, incense, and copies of *Muhammad Speaks* along the way. The TV studio that hosted *American Bandstand* was on the same block, always shuttered and locked, well before fight time.

I couldn't afford to attend as often as I would have liked, but I managed to see Gypsy Joe Harris fight a couple of times while attending PAFA. He was on the verge of stardom at the time, already recognized as a unique talent. His career was short, but at his best Gypsy Joe was boxing's Miles Davis, an improvisational genius—the likes of which I've never seen before or since.

My knowledge of art history was rudimental when I enrolled at PAFA, but I knew Thomas Eakins was a big deal, a celebrated artist whose legacy was forever intertwined with the Academy's. He'd been dead for more than a century by then, but people there sometimes talked about him as if he were still alive. Despite all the animosity between the school and the artist during his lifetime, the Academy was eager to embrace him and his work.

Reproductions of his paintings of scullers on the Schuylkill River were the first to catch my eye. Next was a grand revelation: Eakins painted boxers.

Maybe the Eakins-boxing connection nudged PAFA's selection

committee in my direction when they saw my amateurish attempt to duplicate a magazine cover. I can't think of any other reason they allowed me to set foot in the joint.

In his time, Eakins had been a student, a professor and eventually the director of PAFA. He was an innovator, on the cutting edge of representative painting, ahead of his time in both his own work and controversial teaching techniques. He was the bad boy of art who looked up the skirt of Victorian morality and saw she wasn't wearing underpants.

Eakins's bohemian lifestyle went against the grain of the snooty moneyed class. He was accused of being a homosexual, seducing two nieces (one of whom committed suicide) and having a ménage á trois with his wife, Susan, and his childhood friend, Addie Williams

Eakins's most malicious detractor was his brother-in-law, Frank Stevens, who accused him of bestiality, but provided no proof.

Who knows what's true and what's not? Does it even matter? Artists living eccentric and often selfish lives are pretty much the norm. The truth is that in the long run, it's the art that really matters, not the person who created it. Like boxers, artist sacrifice body and soul in pursuit of their aspirations. They couldn't stop if they wanted to.

Eakins was famously forced to resign from the Academy in 1886 because he removed the loincloth of a male model in a class that included female students. It was the first thing you heard about him at PAFA, which was usually delivered with a salacious grin. He was our very own antihero.

Being booted out of the Academy was a stunning blow for Eakins, cutting off a regular salary and access to the patronage of affluent society. Critics, keen to curry favor with the art establishment, either ignored or denigrated his work.

Disappointed but unbowed, Eakins pressed on with his work and, as the end of the 19th century drew near, he returned to the subject of the male figure, which included his boxing painting.

"Thomas Eakins was quite open about his interest in prizefights, and, with his friend, sportswriter Clarence Cranmer, regularly attended the amphitheater of the Philadelphia Arena, which was on the other side of Broad Street from the Pennsylvania Academy of the Fine Arts," writes Kasia Boddy in her comprehensive tome, *Boxing: A Cultural History.*

It was, of course, an earlier manifestation of the Philadelphia Arena, at a different location, than the one where I first saw Gypsy Joe. Although Eakins and I were born more than a hundred years apart, I sometimes wonder what it would have been like to sit next to him at a fight.

Sidney D. Kirkpatrick, author of *The Revenge of Thomas Eakins*, wrote that according to Cranmer, "Eakins attended nearly three hundred fights by the end of the century, and he grew to be such a perceptive spectator that Cranmer did not hesitate to ask his opinion of a fighter's ability."

"The charged atmosphere of the arena inspired Eakins's final series of paintings of athletes," wrote Alice A. Carter in her book, *The Essential Thomas Eakins.* "These complex canvases tested Eakins's knowledge of anatomy and perspective and demanded his full concentration."

Eakins created three major boxing paintings in 1898 and 1899. He approached the subject from a different point of view than George Bellows, America's other great boxing painter, who depicted fighters in action.

"Eakins was uninterested in painting boxers exchanging blows," wrote Boddy. "His paintings explore the moments within a fight when the action stops (*Taking the Count* and *Between Rounds*) and the moment when it's all over (*Salutat*)."

Two of the paintings, *Between Rounds* and *Salutat*, are considered among Eakins's best works. Both feature local featherweight "Turkey Point" Billy Smith, who, along with other boxers, Eakins befriended.

Between Rounds, which hangs in the Philadelphia Museum of Art, has always been my favorite. Smith is seated on his stool, leaning back against the corner post, his gloved hands holding the top rope, as Bill McCarney, Smith's second, fans him with a towel.

The man leaning over the ropes is Ellwood McCloskey, his manager. The ring lights guide the eye down from the towel to the illuminated boxer, then on to the white collar and cuffs of the timekeeper, finally coming to rest on the man's polished black shoes. Four men suspended in time, connected by light.

In the darkened area beyond the ring stands a policeman and further back is an elevated press box, where several reporters are scribbling notes. Up in the balcony, fans can be seen peering down, waiting for the next round to start. A white-bearded gentleman in the front row is probably poet Walt Whitman, whose portrait Eakins painted in 1888.

The setting is a Gilded Age rendering of the Blue Horizon, Philadelphia's iconic 20th century boxing venue. I can almost imagine sitting in the balcony with the poet and rest of the rouges' gallery, hollering encouragement and advice—the way I did in the years before the decorum required of the media muffled the fun.

Salutat features Smith, his right arm raised in victory, facing the cheering spectators, including Cranmer (waving his hat) and the artist's father (on the far right). Eakins carved the words *dextra victrice conclamentes salutat* (the right hand of the victor salutes those acclaiming him) into the original frame.

"While [Smith's] chiseled white body evokes classical sculpture, his tanned face and hands remind us that he is a working-class American boy," wrote Boddy. "The victorious boxer's body, and in particular his musculature, is highlighted by bright electrical light, but the painting seems equally interested in celebrating his intimate involvement with the spectators.

"Although a contemporary reviewer complained that these men are brought 'so far forward as to give the impression that both victor and audience might shake hands,' this seems to be one of the painting's greatest strengths."

This rings true to anybody who has attended a boxing match. Idolatry often overrides societal norms. Fans reach out to touch fighters during their ring walk and leave their seats to congratulate or console them afterward. Actor Dustin Hoffman recalled seeing an ecstatic fan "wiping all he could of the sweat from the boxer's body onto himself."

Salutat was Eakins's final boxing painting. As usual, the critics picked it apart, but boxers loved his work. "Mr. Eakins, to me, was a gentleman and an artist, and the realist of realists," wrote "Turkey Point" Smith, after he retired from boxing.

Eakins, age 71, died on June 25, 1916, at his home at 1729 Mount Vernon Street.

"He was a silent man, not sad exactly, but disappointed—he had some blows. There was a sadness underneath; he had not been able to do what he wanted to do," said his widow Susan in 1933.

It was more than 50 years after his death that Eakins's unique contribution was fully appreciated. He would be flabbergasted to learn that in 2006, his *The Gross Clinic*, a portrait of Dr. Samuel S. Gross performing surgery, sold for $68 million dollars.

"Today, the sound and the fury that surrounded Thomas Eakins is forgotten," wrote Carter, "and his legacy is just what he would have hoped for had he dared to hope in those final years: a priceless heritage of luminous canvases celebrated for their uncompromising honesty, skill, originality, and beauty."

———

I left the Academy knowing that I had no future as a painter but continued to hang out with my art school friends. Broke and crashing on other people's couches, I found part-time work posing for students at PAFA.

The female models posed naked, while the men were allowed to wear jock straps. I'm delighted to report that no instructor ever removed mine so that the female students could see the Full Monty. After all, it's pretty drafty in those studios.

BEHIND THE SCENES

TEN PERCENT OFF THE TOP

THE MISADVENTURES OF A FRONT MAN

ORIGINALLY PUBLISHED IN *RINGSIDE SEAT*, SUMMER, 2021

I LEFT Madison Square Garden before the main event started and headed for the parking lot, depriving myself of the only opportunity I would ever have to see Muhammad Ali fight live—against Earnie Shavers, no less. But I surrendered to an uncontrollable urge to leave, and the only thing I knew for sure was that I had to put some miles between boxing and me before sunrise.

The opening bell must have rung by the time I exited the Lincoln Tunnel on the Jersey side and gunned the car into the early morning gloom. I was not angry or upset, just tired. I wanted to go home and sleep. Tomorrow would be soon enough to think.

That night marked the beginning of the end of an adventure into territory for which I was unsuited and ill prepared, a stranger in a strange land. Circumstances persuaded me to step out of my comfort zone, and I did, willingly diving into a parallel world where it's virtually impossible to fly above the fray. Long term it wasn't for me, but I have no regrets. The best part of slipping into darkness is the stories.

———

The deal went down at the Pup Tiki on Philly's Walnut Street, one of those kitschy Polynesian-themed joints that were popular in the 1970s. There were three of us, promoter J Russell Peltz, trainer Leon Tabbs and myself, hashing out the details of a transaction that would make me manager of junior lightweight Jerome Artis.

I sat there sucking up a rum drink called Missionary's Downfall, as Russell explained the terms of the arrangement: I would be Artis's manager and Peltz (the Spectrum's Director of Boxing) would promote him. We'd take 10 percent off the top and split it fifty-fifty between us. How Jerome and Leon divvied up the other ninety percent was their business.

We had similar contracts with welterweight Alfonso Hayman, junior middleweight Fred Jenkins, welterweight Leroy Jefferson and later, junior lightweight Wade Hinnant.

It seemed like a sweetheart deal. I would be managing boxers backed by the biggest promoter in town. There would a few bucks coming my way and a new measure of respect. I was suddenly a guy with connections. I had been a boxing fan since I was in short pants and *The Ring* magazine's Philadelphia correspondent for around three years. I knew my shit. Well, I thought I did.

I was a front man, the managerial face, the guy who officially held the contracts on the Fab Five, but I wasn't the money, power or brains. My job was to shepherd my little stable the best I knew how.

———

Jimmy Arthur had a second-floor gym at 17th and Reed, where Alfonso Hayman trained, and I loitered. It was a dusty, barebones affair, brought to life during training hours like a movie set, when the lights go on and the director yells "action."

Arthur was born James Arthur Washington, and after a brief pro career as Jimmy Arthur, he became a trainer, but kept his fighting name. Most everyone called him Art, anyway. He was a slim, wiry man who ran with his boxers and kept a half a pint in his locker. He was, as Peltz likes to call him, "the greatest trainer you've never heard of."

Hayman was one of those guys who always had a toothpick in his mouth. When he trained, he took it out and carefully, almost reverentially, placed it on a small white towel. His workout routine was uncannily precise, always the same in the same order, except on sparring days. When he was finished, he'd change into his street clothes, put the toothpick back in his mouth and leave. Sometimes he never said a word the whole time.

The first Hayman fight in which I was involved was a 10-rounder at the Spectrum, September 10, 1974, against fellow Philadelphian Mario "The Spider" Saurennann, who unfortunately looked unnervingly like his nickname.

I was surprised and relieved when Hayman won a split decision. He landed some decent punches, but The Spider jabbed the bejesus out of him. Maybe a hard fight was just what he needed because Hayman's next bout was the biggest win of his career, a 10th-round TKO of Johnny Gant, a world-rated welterweight from Washington, D.C.

All right. So far, so good.

Hayman wanted to fight again before a mooted rematch with Gant, and Peltz put him on an upcoming Spectrum card. Then everything changed, especially for me. Alfonso suffered a cut eye sparring, and the fight was cancelled. I was at the gym when he returned from seeing the doctor.

"Sorry about your eye," I said. "Did the doctor say how long he thought it would take to heal?"

"Get the hell out of my face, or I'll kill you," Hayman yelled.

Before I could fully comprehend what was going on, Art stepped between us and gently pushed me in the direction of the stairs. "You better get out of here," he said, and I did, as fast as my sneakered feet would carry me down the sagging wooden stairs and into the street.

———

It was early evening in North Philly, and the street was empty except for an old guy sitting on his stoop, smoking a cigarette. I double-checked to make sure my car door was locked and loped across the road and into the lobby of the 26th Street Rec Center.

The Rec Center is housed in an old redbrick structure built in 1912. Boxing is only one of the many activities available, but like Noah's ark in the deluge, it is boxing that stands out—a shelter from the storm for young men who seek salvation from the streets through the power of their fists. That's the idea, anyway.

I parked my butt on the wood bench that ran along the wall and watched the kids shadowbox and hit the heavy bag. Then I heard a voice that would soon become all too familiar.

"Hi, I hear we're going to be working together." It was Jerome, who had sidled up unnoticed and sat next to me. "You're a hippie, right? I'm sort of a hippie, too."

I was not sure what the term meant to him, but I laughed. Despite his barefaced attempt to ingratiate himself, I liked him right away. That's always the case with people like Jerome. Every successful con artist has to have a likeable personality, and in many ways that's what Jerome was, a conman, but a conman with a difference. He was a gifted boxer, good enough to beat Sugar Ray Leonard for the 125-pound championship at the 1972 National Golden Gloves.

Jerome was a good-looking man with a chameleonic personality, nice to some, nasty with others, whichever worked to his advantage. In boxing circles, he was generally considered an arrogant big mouth, which was a fair assessment. Boasting and trash talk were nowhere as prevalent as today, and Jerome's popinjay persona garnered media attention.

He was also supposed to be just a few credits short of a degree from Temple University. It sounded like a load of horseshit to me, but it got his face in all the papers. Artis's career wasn't what it could have been, but it's safe to say he never lost a press conference.

Artis was an unorthodox defensive boxer, nimble on his feet, adroit at the art of ducking, pivoting, and sidestepping with the brio of a pool shark. He was also one of those boxers who could come off the streets and go eight or 10 rounds with little or no training. Imagine how tempting that would be, especially to someone like Jerome who personified the "million-dollar talent with a dime's worth of dedication" metaphor. The little prick's favorite excuse for not running in the morning was that his hemorrhoids were "acting up."

———

Hayman was a Vietnam combat veteran and probably suffering from posttraumatic stress disorder (PTSD), a genuine desperado subject to angry outburst and reckless behavior. His normally restrained demeanor must have fooled a lot of people, including me.

There were seven months between the first Gant fight and the rematch, which like their first fight took place at the Capital Centre in Landover, Maryland. Gant won a decision in a rather uneventful affair. The real fun began when I went to promoter Eli Hanover's office to get paid.

Hayman was already there and had taken both his share, as well as Russell's and mine. When I appealed to Hanover he said, "What do you think I am, a debt collector?" One glance at Hayman and I knew I had to play it cool, so I shrugged and walked out

———

Arnold Giovanetti lived just off South Broad Street, pretty close to the stadium complex. I paused before ringing the doorbell. I was going to meet a boxer who had threatened to kill me and a guy who allegedly had ties to organized crime. But Giovanetti wanted to buy Hayman's contract and was willing to reimburse us for the money owed from the second Gant fight.

"Come on in," said Giovanetti as he opened the door. "We're in the kitchen."

Hayman was there, along with a huge black guy who sometimes

provided security for boxers. I don't know if they were expecting trouble, but all I wanted was to get the money and split.

Giovanetti had two checks already written, one for Hayman's contract and the other for the money Alfonso owed us. I signed the contract, endorsed the checks, and then traded them for cash. I shook our host's hand and was out the door 15 minutes after I entered.

It was the last time I saw Giovanetti. In August 1977 his Cadillac was found at the Philadelphia airport, but he was never seen or heard from again.

———

In the 1970s Tyrone Everett and middleweight Bennie Briscoe were Philadelphia boxing's biggest attractions. Like Jerome, Everett was a 130-pounder, and it wasn't unusual for Artis (who beat Everett in the amateurs) to fight on the undercard of shows headlined by Everett. The prospect of an Everett-Artis showdown smelled of money and the weasels began to circle. Enter George Sullivan.

This creep ran a security business, renting out bodies to keep order at events. According to *60 Minutes*, which did an expose segment on Sullivan's business practices, some employees were issued fake firearms, a terribly dangerous practice because criminals will assume they are armed.

Artis had sold a piece of himself to Sullivan, and it wasn't long before my new partner tried to break the contract on a technicality. Thanks to some backdated paperwork signed by Jerome a day or so before the hearing, I won the case and the contract remained valid. The fighter was probably playing both ends against the middle, but he knew Russell controlled his immediate future.

What Peltz, Tabbs, and I could not control was Jerome's lifestyle (at one point he had two women pregnant at the same time) and slip-shod approach to training. Who knows why he was the way he was? We just had to deal with it the best we could.

Any chance of an Everett-Artis fight was wrecked when Tyrone's girlfriend put a bullet through his brain on May 26, 1977, but there was still a nice payday coming. By June '77 Artis's record was 16-1-4, (6 KOs), and MSG matchmaker Teddy Brenner figured he would make a suitable tune-up opponent for former WBA featherweight titleholder Alexis Arguello. The purse was $12,500, the equivalent in purchasing power of about $53,300 today.

———

It was early morning and still semi-dark when I pulled into local high school parking lot, down by the athletic field. Jerome got out of the car walked down to the track and began to run. What neither of us noticed was a pup tent set up on the grass. After about three laps, two high school jocks came out of the tent in their underwear and demanded to know what he was doing.

"What the fuck does it look like I'm doing?" Jerome yelled, giving them the finger as he sprinted back to the car.

I've always wondered what those guys were doing in that tent.

Jerome stayed at my apartment for a couple of days before the fight. The fiasco at the high school was as close as he came to doing any roadwork. Jerome spent most of his time in the bathroom, after taking laxatives in order to make weight.

In top shape he might have given Arguello a decent fight, but as it was, he had no chance. Regardless, Artis had to make weight to get paid. That's always the bottom line. He made weight, but that's about all he did.

"I'm sorry, Nigel, but your guy didn't want to fight," said referee Lew Eskin who stopped the fight after Arguello knocked down Artis twice in the second round. He didn't get any argument from me.

———

Hayman's greatest moment came when he was already on the backside of his career. Thomas Hearns had won all 17 of his pro bouts by knockout and was among the hottest prospects in the country when Peltz brought him to Philadelphia to fight Hayman on

April 3, 1979. Hearns won all 10 rounds on every judge's scorecard, but Hayman was still on his feet when the final bell sounded.

Hearns was booed as he left the ring. Hayman got a standing ovation. It was a pure Philadelphia moment, a tribute to a faded fighter who showed the hotshot what it meant to be Philly tough.

————

Hayman robbed a jewelry store (where he worked as a porter) of between $3,000 and $4,000. He surrendered and pleaded guilty, but sentencing was postponed, and he was released on $5,000 bond until after he returned from Italy following a knockout loss to Carlos Santos.

Hayman was back in court on December 24 and became upset when Judge Richard B. Klein raised his bond from $5,000 to $25,000. As Deputy Sheriff Jack Wright began to handcuff him, Hayman punched him in the jaw and pulled a pistol from his pocket.

When Chief Police Inspector George Fencl, who was in court to testify in another case, reached for his gun, Hayman pointed the .357 Magnum at him and said, "Don't try it." He then bolted from the third-floor courtroom and out into the street.

Fencl broadcast Hayman's description over police radios. He was spotted running down Market Street by two police officers who chased him, subdued him, and took him back to court to face additional charges. If Fencl had not been there, Hayman might have made it.

Hayman was eventually released from prison, and in 2017, the old outlaw was inducted into the Pennsylvania Boxing Hall of Fame. I zoomed in on the picture of Alfonso getting his plaque. And there it was, a toothpick in the side of his mouth.

————

Jerome and I remained friends. The last time I saw him was at the Blue Horizon, where he was selling programs for Peltz. Things went well for a few shows, but then he took off with all the program money. It was inevitable.

If Artis did indeed have two sides to his personality, the good eventually gave way to the bad. Alcohol and street drugs hastened his downfall, and there were reports of domestic abuse from a female sportswriter he lived with on and off.

A few years later, I heard that Jerome was HIV positive and had moved to some kind of treatment program upstate. He died in July 1999 at the age of 45. Leon Tabbs told me what happened: Jerome was in court for failure to pay child support, and after telling the judge a pack of lies, he dropped dead on the courtroom floor.

———

I still have to get away from boxing occasionally, but not for the same reason I left the Garden early that night in 1977. There's too much other stuff going on and time is running out. But I always come back to boxing, my faithful companion since childhood. Managing was a crazy idea. I was young and foolish, but isn't that when we live life to the max? If I could go back and change one thing—I would stay for the Ali-Shavers fight.

ANATOMY OF A PROMOTION

THE PLIGHT OF CLUB FIGHTS MINUS TV

ORIGINALLY PUBLISHED IN *THE RING*, AUGUST 1986

PROMOTING club fights can often be exercise in futility. The risks are many and the rewards are few. But if there is one thing universally bemoaned by those of us who love the sweet science, it is the passing of the small, neighborhood fight clubs—the breeding ground for so many great fighters.

This is the story of one such club and the man who is fighting to keep it alive. Someone once said that the difference between failure and success is doing a thing nearly right and doing a thing exactly right. When promoting on the club level, the margin for error is even slimmer.

The first thing I noticed when I got to promoter J Russell Peltz's office was that the staircase was missing. As my eyes adjusted to the dim light, I saw that the entire first floor of the building (Peltz's office occupies the second floor) resembled a construction site. In fact, that is exactly what it was. The home of Peltz Boxing Promotions for the past 16 years had been transformed into a hardhat area.I groped my way up a temporary staircase and found the doorway to the room that has been the virtual heartbeat of Philadelphia boxing for well over a decade. The office was almost in as bad shape as the first floor. There were holes ripped in the ceiling. The soggy and stained floor was so warped from rain damage that it looked like a sea serpent was hiding underneath the rug. All of the photographs and posters had been removed from the walls. Boxes and chairs were stacked, ready to beat a hasty retreat.

Amidst the wreckage of what had once been an immaculate mini-museum of Philadelphia boxing sat Russell, undauntedly pecking at the word processor. Neither sleet, snow nor impending eviction could keep the promoter from his appointed rounds on fight day. Despite an apparent state of siege, it was business as usual at 801 North 27th Street."I didn't think they would evict me so soon," said Peltz with a moan. "We bought a new building two blocks down the street and sold this one. But the tenants in the new place haven't left yet. And the new owners of this building are trying to force me out. They have turned the water and electricity off a couple of times."

Despite the chaotic surroundings, it was all systems go on this particular April morning in 1986, and the first order of business was to check to see if the out-of-town fighters had arrived safely. Manager Ben Getty was supposed to have driven up from Fayetteville, North Carolina, the night before with a couple of opponents. One of them, Cortez Treadwell, was fighting Philly welterweight Hugh "Buttons" Kearney in the main event. Without him, the show was in serious jeopardy, if not completely ruined. A quick call to their hotel confirmed that all was well with the evening's imports and that they would be at the weigh-in at 11 a.m.

———

Things have not always gone so smoothly for Peltz. When he first began promoting in 1969, it was not unheard of for the former sportswriter to scour bars looking for last-minute replacements. Peltz launched his promotional career at the Blue Horizon, outgrew it, and then returned to his roots in March of 1984. Since then, he's promoted a show per month (except August '84) at the North Philly venue.

Boxing in general, and Philadelphia boxing in particular, has changed a lot since 1969. That was back before America's unprecedented success at the 1976 Olympics prompted television to rediscover the Manly Art. When Peltz took the promotional plunge, what was left of the old Philadelphia boxing establishment laughed at him. But boxing's latest "Boy Wonder" had the last laugh, when a record-breaking SRO crowd of 1,606 turned up to see Bennie Briscoe KO Tito Marshall in the first round.

Peltz prospered. His early cards regularly featured the likes of Briscoe, Cyclone Hart, Willie "The Worm" Monroe, Bobby "Boogaloo" Watts, George Benton, Leotis Martin, Jimmy Young, Sammy Goss, and towards the end of this first run at the Blue Horizon, Matthew Saad Muhammad. Fight-starved Philly fans responded enthusiastically to both the matches and Peltz's bargain-basement ticket prices, as low as $3.00 at the beginning.

Peltz's original series of shows at the Blue Horizon provided a springboard for him and many of the fighters. A few years later, a hop, skip and a jump took him from the Horizon to the Philadelphia Arena (an ancient 7,000-seat brickyard left over from the days of Gil Turner and Len Matthews) to the Spectrum, where Peltz took over as director of boxing in 1973.

After a few years of prosperity, the once thriving Spectrum boxing program went belly up. This was largely due to the Spectrum's own cable network's (PRISM) adverse effect on the live gate and the advent of casino boxing in nearby Atlantic City. Peltz continued to promote occasional low-budget cards in various Philadelphia suburbs, but the bulk of his shows were held at the Sands Hotel Casino in Atlantic City.

During his stay at the Sands, Peltz, together with the casino and actor Sylvester Stallone, formed a promotional group known as Sands/Tiger Eye, Ltd. It was under this banner that the Blue Horizon reopened for boxing in March 1984. The plan was to use the Horizon as a sort of farm club, developing talent for bigger cards at the Sands.

The surprising thing about Peltz's return to the venue was the size of the crowds. Although the cards lacked the glamorous names of years gone by, the fans turned out in relatively large numbers to watch local prospects hone their skills. Things rolled along in fine style until the contract between Peltz and the Sands expired in May of this year.

Without the subsidy, Peltz's Blue Horizon promotions would have to survive strictly on the income they generate at the gate, pretty much a mathematical impossibility. Peltz prints 1,200 tickets for each show, but even if he sales every last one of them, the promotion still loses money.

"We are averaging over a thousand fans for each show, but we're still about $2,000 dollars short of breaking even. If I could figure out a way to make up the difference, we could run here forever," Peltz said. "Maybe a sponsor is the answer."

———

A light rain was falling as Peltz and his assistant, Maureen Sacks, zippered themselves into matching black satin Peltz Boxing jackets and climbed into Peltz's Cadillac for the short drive to the Pennsylvania State Office Building, site of the midday weigh-in. "The only thing I've learned about the weather is not to worry about it," Peltz said, casting and wary look at the soggy sky, "because you sure cannot do anything about it."

The weigh-in for a club show seldom features the dramatics that sometimes occur when the sport's big names and egos step on the scale, and this one was no exception.

The boxers, looking much like any group of young men you might see hanging around the street corners of Philadelphia's blue-collar neighborhoods, patiently waited their turn at the scales while their trainers shot the bull.

The scale itself is an ancient Fairbanks on wheels, just like the one you see in those old photographs of Joe Louis weighing in for his fights with Max Schmeling and Jim Braddock. If the scales could talk, it would be able to tell things about Philadelphia boxing you'll never find in newspaper clippings or *The Ring Record Book.*

Boxing history has been made in this room, but on this damp and gloomy morning, the most exciting thing that happened was one preliminary fighter coming in half a pound over the contract weight. A quick jog around the block took care of that minor detail. By 12:30 p.m. we were back at Peltz's besieged office, counting money and tickets.

"We might have some good fights tonight," Peltz chortled. "I don't even know who's going to win some of these fights."

———

Because of the shoestring nature of the budget, small club boxing lives or dies on the strength of its ticket sellers. A fighter or manager who won't hustle tickets is poison. As an added incentive, Peltz gives fighters a bonus (one dollar) for each ticket they sell.

Kearney attracts the West Philly gambling crowd, and Jim Nichols, who owns several bars in that section of Philadelphia, always sells several hundred tickets whenever "Buttons" is on the card. Peltz is also careful to make sure that at least one white fighter's face appears on the poster, even if he's not topping the bill. On this show, that face belongs to Brian McGinley, a crowd-pleasing banger who Russell half-jokingly describes as "our most popular loser," despite the fact McGinley has won nine of his 13 pro bouts.

In an effort to flesh out the take, Peltz recently started printing and selling programs for a dollar each. To do so, he had to evict a couple of semi-pro writers who had previously hawked their own product. While this seems heartless to some, at this level, every penny counts. Survival of the species is foremost.

The promotion was not the only thing on Russell's mind as the afternoon lengthened and we headed to the site of the evening's entertainment. Gary Hinton, one of the fighters under promotional contract to Peltz, was in Italy prepping for a match with Reyes Cruz for the vacant IBF junior welterweight title. Peltz will be jetting to

Europe to join him the following day and was understandably worried about the recent rash of terrorist attacks.

"I'm not worried," he protested without much conviction. "I look more like an Arab than a Jew."

———

Although a new sign has replaced the old neon mountain encircled by a blue, halo-like cloud, practically everything else about this crumbling edifice remains much the same as when it was built in the 1920s. The Blue Horizon was originally an upscale home and later housed the Loyal Order of the Moose, but these days cabarets and discos sponsored by local social clubs make up the bulk of the bookings.

A flyer taped to the box-office window announced the upcoming appearance of evangelist Rev. Al and the Ink Spots, but it's as a boxing venue that the decaying structure really shines.

There is not a bad seat in the hall, but the front row of the balcony just might provide the best sightlines in all of boxing. The gallery overhangs the ring, placing the fans and fighters on the most intimate of terms. The clientele is highly knowledgeable and unflaggingly the fair, but god help a fighter who fails to give his best. Both praise and abuse shower down on the combatants, along with an avalanche of advice. I don't know whether it's the intimidating crowd, the smallness of the ring, or that their friends and neighbors are in the audience, but the fighters invariably fight their collective asses off at the Horizon. It's a major part of the joint's charm.

———

Peltz has promoted over 20 world title fights, but he's not afraid to get his hands dirty. An hour before the fighters begin to arrive, he's busy setting up press tables and placing flyers on every seat. Anything to gain an edge that will hopefully drive his promotion into the black. At the ticket window, Maureen is busy selling tickets to savvy fans that stop off on their way home from work. If they wait until fight time, the price goes up from $10 to $12.

Around 6:20 p.m., the first fighters and their corner men began to straggle in out of the rain. One of the first nonparticipants to arrive is "KO" Becky O'Neill, the ponytailed sparkplug who used to manage bantamweight champion Jeff Chandler. She brought spicy hoagies for Peltz and Maureen, a staple of Philly's eclectic street-food culture.

Soon the trickle of customers became a flood, as the evening began to take on all the earmarks of an event as much social as it is sporting. It's this aspect of a night at the Blue Horizon and other small-hall venues that make the entire enterprise such a satisfying experience.

When the doors open at 7 p.m., early fans dash up two flights of stairs to claim their favorite seats along the front row of the balcony. Month after month, you see the same folks in the same seats. Many bring food to eat while they wait for the action to start. Others sip from bottles hidden in brown paper bags. Beneath them, in the bowels of the building, the meager dressing rooms are alive with pre-fight activity.

Inside their shabby cubicles, the fighters prepare themselves for battle, while somewhere in the background a tape deck lays down a steady driving beat. Water buckets, lined up like soldiers ready to be pressed into service, cover most of the bathroom floor. The trainers tape hands, grease torsos and hand out of advice. The fighters, for the most part, are quiet, absorbed in their own private pre-fight rituals.

Upstairs, the crowd gradually gained in size and volume. Peltz had already sold over 1,000 tickets and patrons were still coming in. The concession stand is doing a brisk business at 75 cents for a hotdog and 50 cents per soda. Try to find those prices at a casino or Madison Square Garden.

Fight talk is everywhere, mingling the order of the evening. One can see Buster Drayton talking to Boogaloo Watts in one corner of the auditorium, and former lightweight champ Bob Montgomery holding court in another. At around 8:05 p.m., Peltz gives the word, and the first fighters make their way to the ring. The preparation and planning are over. It's fight time.

———

The fights were, for the most part, evenly matched and earnestly contested. The fans had a ball. They laughed when Vinnie Burgese waggled his tongue at the gallery gang after stopping Ted Greer. They lusted after sexy round card girls, Najah and Fatima. They cheered when McGinley hammered blow after blow into Ted Dancey's belly, but they booed Dancey when he quit. They appreciated Howard Stewart's classy inside boxing and applauded loser Treadwell when he gave Kearney a brisk workout in the main event. All in all, the show was an artistic success, but despite a robust turnout of 1,148 (paid), a financial loser.

To facilitate a better understanding of small club promoter's plight, Peltz opened up his books to *The Ring*, allowing the following financial breakdown to be published. More than just a bookkeeping entry, it shows why even seemingly successful club shows are an endangered species without the aid of television:

INCOME:
TICKET SALES:

277 at $12.00	$3,324.00
871 at $10.00	$8,710.00
PROGRAMS: 271 at $1.00	$271.00

EXPENSES:

Kearney's purse	$1,524.02
Treadwell's purse	$1,000.00
Treadwell's travel expenses	$250.00
Treadwell's hotel	$300.00
Preliminary fighters' purses	$3,200.00
Ticket bonuses	$465.00
City tax	$564.45
Exhibition license	$80.00
State tax	$572.90

Blue Horizon rent	$1,088.51
Liability insurance	$425.00
Security (five men for four hours)	$250.00
Ticket taker	$30.00
Round card girls	$125.00
Two pairs of boxing gloves	$140.00
Dressing room attendants	$100.00
Tickets	$90.00
Posters	$403.00
Ad printing	$113.00
Ad placement (newspapers)	$1,017.00
Poster design	$40.00
Messenger service	$16.50
Transportation & entertainment	$25.00
Photographs	$36.41
Program seller	$20.00
Matchmaker	$1,006.01
Videotaping	$100.00
Postage	$99.41
TOTAL EXPENSES:	$13,816.21
TOTAL INCOME:	$12,305.00
NET LOSS:	$1,511.21

————

A few weeks later, Peltz and Hinton we're back from Italy—unscathed by terrorists and with the IBF junior welterweight title in tow. People wondered why Peltz keeps plugging away at the Blue Horizon when even a near-capacity house ends up in the red. His stock answer is that the investment will pay off in the long run because Kearney and some of the others should eventually develop into moneymakers.

But I have a sneaking suspicion that the real reason runs a little deeper than that, to the very heart of his love affair with the sweet science. Besides promoting fights, Peltz is a passionate collector of boxing memorabilia. In a way, the Blue Horizon is the largest piece in his collection.

———

EPILOGUE: Shortly after the Kearney-Treadwell show, which took place on April 22, 1986, the USA Network began broadcasting its Tuesday Night Fights live from the Blue Horizon on a regular schedule. This allowed Peltz to promote there on a profitable basis, and thanks to the TV exposure, the Blue Horizon became one of boxing's most famous venues. The highly successful partnership between Peltz and the USA Network lasted until August 1998, when the network dropped boxing programing.

IMPACT OF A FAILED EXPERIMENT

THE DANGERS OF DAY-BEFORE-THE-FIGHT WEIGH-INS

ORIGINALLY PUBLISHED BY ESPN.COM, MARCH 5, 2014

ENGLISH PUGILIST Dutch Sam stood 5-foot-6, weighed between 130 and 133 pounds, and is credited with inventing the uppercut. Even though he trained on three glasses of gin a day and sometimes entered the ring drunk, according to no lesser an authority than Pierce Egan, Sam was "one of (if not) the best fighting man in the kingdom."

Nonetheless, despite his fighting prowess and widespread acclaim, Sam, who fought from 1801 to 1814, never became bare-knuckles champion. He was a victim of his time, a lightweight living in a heavyweight world.

From the dawn of modern boxing (during the early decades of the 18th century) until the middle of the 19th century, all prize-fighters were lumped together regardless of size. If the same system applied today, Floyd Mayweather Jr. would have to fight Wladimir Klitschko if he wanted to be champion.

It wasn't until 1886 that Jack McAuliffe became the first light-weight champion, knocking out Billy Frazier in the 21st round. By then it was too late for Dutch Sam—he died in 1816.

The advent of weight divisions was intended to ensure, as much as possible, that boxers were evenly matched and that ability, rather than size advantage, would decide the outcome. It was a noble idea and helped shape the sport's development, but the proliferation of weight divisions (now 17 and counting) was no panacea.

True, separate weight classes greatly benefited fighters below heavyweight, and that's a good thing. Even so, the concept also introduced plenty of new problems, some of which threaten to make a mockery of the notion of a fair fight.

The most recent scam is fighters buying their way out of making the contracted weight, as exemplified by the scandalous shenanigans surrounding Saturday's Julio Cesar Chavez Jr.-Bryan Vera match.

To earn the biggest payday of his career, Vera, who has spent the bulk of his career as a middleweight, was forced to agree to a series of increasingly higher weights. And as the fight drew near and it became obvious that Chavez wasn't going to make 168 pounds, the limit was raised to 173 pounds and a portion of Chavez's purse was given to Vera.

The controversy caused quite a stink, reinforced Chavez's spoiled-brat image, and put another dent in the sport's battered reputation—as did the contentious decision in Junior's favor.

Perhaps the most egregious case of pay-to-weigh (or whatever you wish to call it) came when Mayweather gave Juan Manuel Marquez $600,000 rather than shed the two pounds required to make the stipulated 144 pounds before their 2009 bout. As the $300,000 per-pound penalty was written into the fight contract, you can't help but wonder if multimillionaire Mayweather ever had any intention of making weight.

Paying your opponent to gain an unfair advantage is not only poor sportsmanship but also defeats the purpose for which weight classes were created. Although we are seeing more and more of this sort of gambit, it's a symptom of a larger weight-related aberration—the day-before-the-fight weigh-in.

Concerned about dehydrated fighters not having enough time

between the weigh-in and the fight to properly rehydrate, influential ringside physician Dr. Edwin "Flip" Homansky advocated switching to day-before weigh-ins. It seemed to make a lot of sense. There are many medical risks associated with dehydration, including reducing the amount of cerebrospinal fluid in which the brain floats. Insufficient fluid compromises the cushion-effect and the brain's ability to absorb shock.

The Nevada State Athletic Commission saw merit in Dr. Homansky's suggestion and instituted the new day-before policy in the mid-1980s. It wasn't long before virtually all jurisdictions followed suit, but unanticipated complications soon surfaced.

Many boxers abuse the change, taking it as an invitation to drain their bodies to an unhealthy degree to make a weight that is inappropriate for their age and body size. After the weigh-in, these emaciated fighters chug down large quantities of fluids and stuff themselves with food to a point where they are often a division or more over the contracted weight by fight time.

"It has actually become part of the matchmaking process," said Keith Kizer, executive director of the Nevada State Athletic Commission, "with some people not wanting to fight a certain fighter because he is known to put on extra weight after the weigh-in. Or sometimes they'll agree to a fight because they know the opponent will come in depleted."

In many instances, the extra weight gives a fighter a substantial edge over his opponent, such as when Arturo Gatti gained 19 pounds after the weigh-in for his 2000 match with Joey Gamache. Gatti blasted Gamache in the second round, sending him to the hospital and ending his career. On the other hand, when Oscar De La Hoya depleted himself to make weight for his fight with Manny Pacquiao, his rehydration effort failed. He gained only two pounds and was hammered into a humiliating defeat.

"Going back to the morning of the fight would be more uniform," said Homansky, who has changed his mind about the benefits of day-before weigh-ins. "It would decrease abuse. A welterweight should go into the ring not much more than 147 pounds. It's a crime when a kid weighing almost 160 fights somebody weighing 147."

Homansky is not alone in his belief that the day-before weigh-in is a failed experiment and should be abandoned.

"Our sport and our boxers suffer from ill-advised weight loss and weight loss practices," wrote Greg Sirb, executive director of the Pennsylvania State Athletic Commission, in a letter to members of the Association of Boxing Commissions. "By granting them the privilege to weigh-in well before the event we are only encouraging boxers to starve so that they can regain, sometime large amounts of weight, so that by the time the actual competition takes place the true weight class of the boxer becomes a farce."

Sirb is practicing what he preaches and, except for an occasional title fight, holds weigh-ins the morning of the fight. But why aren't other commissions doing likewise? After all, the NCAA has already banned day-before weigh-ins for all collegiate wrestlers.

"Every one of the commissions knows there is a problem, but it's easier to turn a blind eye and pray for nothing to happen that places the sport in a bad light," said Dr. Margaret Goodman, a neurologist and former chairman of the Medical Advisory Board of the Nevada State Athletic Commission. "If there are no deaths, nothing changes."

Then there are business concerns. The day-before weigh-in has become an important part of the promotion. For major fights in Las Vegas, fans stand in line for hours in order to snag a free seat to see their favorite fighters step on the scales. These events have transformed one of boxing's oldest rituals into a pep rally, creating the sort of boisterous scene that garners plenty of media attention and helps market the fight.

Even before the introduction of day-before weigh-ins, making weight was a dodgy part of the boxing culture and frequently resulted in a whatever-it-takes mentality. Unhealthy weight-cutting methods often start in the amateur ranks, where youthful boxers routinely binge and purge, a habit that can quickly become a full-blown eating disorder and carry over into their pro careers.

The improper use of diuretics and laxatives can also be extremely detrimental to metabolism and body chemistry, as are extended stints in the steam room. It's a dangerous game, and fighters who practice extreme weight-cutting techniques are literally flirting with death.

On Sept. 26, Brazilian MMA fighter Leandro "Feijao" Souza died from a stroke while cutting weight for an upcoming contest. Pathologists have yet to establish a definitive link between Souza's weight cutting and his stroke, but aggressive weight loss is known to lower blood pressure, cause kidney failure and lead to unconsciousness.

Any trainer will tell you that the best course of action is for a fighter to get in the best possible physical condition and fight at whatever weight he or she is at that point. Some, such as Bernard Hopkins, have practiced that method with great success over a long period of time, but for most fighters it's not that simple. Opportunity and money have persuaded athletes involved in combat sports that fighting at an inappropriate weight is the way to go, which has resulted in a multi-horned dilemma that undermines what was intended to be the sport's great equalizer.

It wouldn't be a cure-all, but a return to same-day weigh-ins would certainly be a significant step in the right direction. Unfortunately, most commissions lack the resolve to rectify a mistake that was ballyhooed as an innovative safety measure.

If Souza had been a boxer fighting in the United States, his death might have been the kind of tipping point that Goodman suggested it would take to bring back day-of weigh-ins. But an MMA guy in Brazil doesn't cut close enough to the bone, and nothing is going to change anytime soon.

Dutch Sam, who understood how difficult it is to buck the system, would probably just sigh and order another gin.

———

EPILOGUE: Despite the dangers, day-before-the-fight weigh-in continue unabated in most jurisdictions.

CANNABIS IN BOXING

VADA IS THE ONLY ANTI-DOPING AGENCY THAT GOT IT RIGHT

ORIGINALLY PUBLISHED IN *BOXING NEWS*, AUGUST 15, 2019

YOU WOULDN'T THINK Avery Sparrow had just returned from a year's layoff as he shadowboxed and hit the pads. Dressed in a black T-shirt and black tights, his jab darted out fast and straight, often in doubles and triples. He looked graceful ducking and moving laterally, first to his left and then to his right, his combinations were a blur.

The 25-year-old Philadelphia lightweight hadn't wanted to talk about the year he was without a boxing license, which was understandable under the circumstances. His post-fight urine sample had tested positive for cannabis following his second-round stoppage of Jesus Serrano on March 19, 2018. The victory was changed to no-contest and Sparrow's fast-rising career came to an abrupt halt.

With his comeback fight with local rival Hank Lundy just a few days away, Sparrow finally agreed to a private interview at a downtown gym where a public workout was taking place. He was understandably guarded at first, but relaxed when informed the article wouldn't be published until after the fight. He didn't want to be labeled a "stoner" going in.

Sparrow's suspension came at a time when public opinion concerning cannabis use in the United States is undergoing a sea change. Nineteen states and Washington, D.C. have legalized recreational cannabis for adults. According to the Pew Research Center six in 10 Americans support legalization of marijuana and medical marijuana is legal in 37 states.

It is generally accepted that smoking or ingesting cannabis decreases reaction time, disrupts hand-eye coordination and perception, and diverts attention. Therefore, it's the antithesis of a Performance Enhancing Drug (PED). Nonetheless, cannabis remains on the Word Anti-Doping Agency (WADA) and the Unites States Anti-Doping Agency's (USADA) list of prohibited substances for boxers.

"I feel that if it doesn't enhance your performance, it shouldn't be on the banned list," Sparrow said. "I think the sport needs to catch up with the laws. As time goes on it will evolve, but at this point boxing is a little bit behind."

California and Nevada, two of boxing's busiest states, have legal recreational cannabis. Under state law it's in the same category as tobacco and alcohol, neither of which are on the WADA and USADA's banned list.

Neither Bob Bennett, Executive Director of the Nevada State Athletic Commission, nor Andy Foster, Executive Director of the California State Athletic Commission, believes cannabis is a PED. Still, even if they wanted to remove it from the prohibited substance list, they couldn't.

As government employees, it's their job to enforce the state's licensing regulations, which uses WADA's prohibited substance list. In what amounts to bureaucratic chain of command, the United States Anti-Doping Agency (USADA) is a signatory of the World Anti-Doping Code as set by WADA.

Cannabis was legal for many decades in the United States and in the late-19th century it became a popular ingredient in many medicinal products. How it became illegal is a tale of racism, propaganda and politics.

Much like today's so-called immigration crisis at the U.S.-Mexican border, when Mexicans crossed into the United States following the Revolution of 1910, they were greeted by unfounded prejudices and fears.

"Police officers in Texas claimed that marijuana incited violent crimes, aroused a 'lust for blood,' and gave its users 'superhuman strength.' Rumors spread that Mexicans were distributing this 'killer weed' to unsuspecting American schoolchildren," wrote Eric Schlosser in *The Atlantic* magazine. Fake news isn't a recent invention.

Harry J. Anslinger, a J. Edgar Hoover wannabe, was the founding commissioner of the Federal Bureau of Narcotics and drafted the Marijuana Tax Act of 1937. He also used racist language during his anti-cannabis campaign, such as "Reefer makes darkies think they're as good as white men."

The practice of using cannabis as an excuse to suppress certain segments of the population was intensified when President Richard Nixon declared a War on Drugs in 1971. In 1994 John Ehrlichman, Nixon's counsel and Assistant for Domestic Affairs, revealed drugs and drug abuse wasn't the target. It was aimed at the anti-war left and blacks.

WADA, located in Montreal, Canada, was founded in 1999, but it wasn't until 2012 that voters in Colorado and Washington approved ballot initiatives to legalize recreational marijuana. Therefore, cannabis was probably included on WADA's banned substance list simply because it was illegal, not because it could enhance performance.

Even WADA has made a small concession to the change in public opinion and the modifications of the law. It has raised the cannabis threshold to 150 ng/mL, which means nanograms (one billionth of a gram) per millimeter of blood.

The new permissible threshold means that regular smokers would need to stop smoking 28 days before a test, instead of 30.

"It needs to be dropped from WADA and to not do so is unfortunate. All commissions need to stop including it," said Dr. Margaret Goodman, co-founder, along with Dr. Edwin "Flip" Homansky, of the Voluntary Anti-Doping Association (VADA), which was launched in 2011. "VADA removed cannabinoids in 2012. We do not believe they're performance enhancing and should not be included on any prohibited list. Changing the threshold for the labs proves organizations agree."

Due to its state-of-the-art testing procedures, random no-warning testing and independence, VADA is widely recognized as the most reliable anti-doping organization

Many prominent boxers have signed with VADA, including, but not limited to, Deontay Wilder, Gennady Golovkin, Anthony Joshua, Manny Pacquiao, Errol Spence, Oleksandr Usyk, Terence Crawford, Canelo Alvarez, Vasyl Lomachenko, and Nonito Donaire.

One of boxing's most prominent cannabis busts came on October 20, 2000, when Mike Tyson tested positive for marijuana after stopping Andrew Golota. The result was changed to no-contest, Tyson was suspended and fined $200,000.

Today, Tyson is a budding (pun intended) cannabis mogul. In partnership with Jay Strommen and Robert Hickman, he's opened Tyson Ranch, a forty-acre cannabis resort in California City, a town in the Mojave Desert two hours outside of Los Angeles. The ranch also cultivates its own brand of weed.

Tyson readily admits he's used marijuana most of his life and had smoked before the Golota fight, but insisted it was the only time he fought high. He also credits cannabis with helping him come to terms with himself after leading a tumultuous existence for most of his life.

"I like who I am when I smoke. You know what I mean?" Tyson said during a January 2019 appearance on the *Joe Rogan Experience* podcast. "Without weed I don't like who I am sometimes … it makes me nicer. It calms me down."

Of course, a mellow mood is not the mindset most boxers would want when the opening bell rings. It's a fight, not a love fest. Not even Tyson would recommend smoking a joint in the dressing room.

"If you smoke a joint right before the fight, that's wrong because it could affect your performance and you could be injured," said Hall of Fame promoter Bob Arum, a longtime user and cannabis advocate. "But if you smoke a joint a month before the fight who cares, and whose business is it?"

Arum has got a point. The psychoactive effects of cannabis can last up to two days, but that's rare. Nonetheless, traces of it can be found in your body a month or more after use.

According to Verywell, a website designed to provide information to health professional, "some of the THC metabolites (the principle psychoactive elements) are stored in fat and have an eliminations half-life of 10 to 13 days. It takes five to six half-lives for a substance to be almost entirely eliminated."

There's no way to prove or disprove it, but most likely the majority of the boxers who fail a cannabis test probably haven't used marijuana in weeks, maybe not since the start of training camp. When this is the case, the cannabis remaining in their system has been neutralized. No harm. No foul.

Keeping cannabis on WADA's list of prohibited substances also deprives boxers of its medicinal benefits. Although medical science is divided on the matter, there is much antidotal evidence to the affect that marijuana can be helpful in the treatment of post-traumatic stress disorder (PTSD)—a condition to which fighters are unquestionably vulnerable.

Boxing isn't the only sport grappling with changing attitude toward cannabis. Of the three major team sports in the United States, Major League Baseball has by far the most liberal cannabis policy. Testing big leagues baseball players is virtually nonexistent.

"They don't care because professional baseball has long had a public relations problem when it comes to drugs, but these "drugs" don't include weed," writes Jenn Keeler on Wikileaf, an online resource for medical and recreational marijuana patients and consumers. "Most of us are aware of the steroid era — the era when players bulked up and home run totals soared. It's these performance-enhancing drugs that have the league's attention."

Canada has legalized recreational cannabis, so there's little or no infamy associated with the substance in the country that invented the sport. With so many National Hockey League teams and players residing in north of the border testing doesn't make any sense.

Although the National Football League has a reputation for being very conservative, Chris Long, who recently retired after playing in the NFL for 11 years, said, "I certainly enjoyed my fair share on a regular basis throughout my career. Testing players once a year for 'street drugs,' which is a terrible classification for marijuana, is kind of silly because, you know, players know when the test is. We can stop." Whether the publicity Long's revelation generated will lead to a change in the NFL's testing policy remain to be seen.

Nonetheless, if WADA could bring itself to follow VADA's example, boxing would, for a change, be on the leading edge of progress. It's a small thing compared to many of boxing ills, but an easy one to solve.

———

Sparrow's bout with Lundy was the best fight on a good card. Lundy survived two second-round knockdowns to give his young and relatively inexperienced adversary the toughest test of his 11-fight career. There were some lively exchanges, especially near the end of the eighth round, when, much to the delight of the crowd, they traded punches with reckless abandon. The majority 10-round decision went to Sparrow.

Sparrow is a precocious talent with an aesthetically pleasing style. He can't afford to wait for WADA to get its act together. A boxer's career moves a lot quicker than an entrenched bureaucracy changes its regulations. From here on, Sparrow has to be careful and keep a close eye on the calendar.

———

EPILOGUE: In July 2021, the Nevada State Athletic Commission stopped punishing boxers that test positive for cannabis.

Avery Sparrow has fought three times since beating Hank Lundy, losing the first two, but tallying an impressive TKO of Matt Conway on January 15, 2022.

THE HAPPY WARRIOR

MANNY PACQUIAO

THE ROOTS OF HIS LEGEND AND THE SECRET OF HIS SUCCESS

ORIGINALLY PUBLISHED IN *THE RING*, FEBRUARY 2010

IT WAS a sunny June morning in 2002 and the Memphis International Airport was busier than usual. The night before heavyweight champion Lennox Lewis had knocked out Mike Tyson in a fight that was at the time the highest grossing pay-per-view event in history.

As long lines of fans and media members shuffled slowly toward the departure gates, a slender boyish-looking man sat alone, a tiny suitcase at his feet, unrecognized by the crush of travelers. He too had fought the previous evening, savagely knocking out Jorge Eliécer Julio on the undercard, but Manny Pacquiao remain anonymous among the rush of humanity, just another guy waiting for a plane.

Flash forward to the early hours of November 15, 2009, as a gathering of approximately 5,000 revelers at the Mandalay Bay Events Center waited patiently for their hero to arrive. And when Pacquiao bounded onto the stage and launched into an ass-kicking version of *La Bamba*, the crowds went bananas.

If it was not for the bandage wrapped around his head, partially hidden by a small fedora he was wearing at a rakish angle, you would not have known that just a few hours earlier, Pacquiao had engaged in a brutal prizefight with Miguel Cotto. The bruise under his eye had almost disappeared. Maybe the lights and make up had something to do with it.

This wasn't Rinty Monaghan singing "Danny Boy" in the ring after a fight. It was a full-blown production, complete with flashing lights, a crackerjack band and dancing girls.

The juxtaposition of the evening's two events was deliciously surreal. As promised, Pacquiao sang eight songs, some Tagalog and some in English—"so everybody can understand"—ranging from up-tempo rockers to the schmaltzy ballads Filipinos adore.

When he segued into "Sometimes When We Touch," the Dan Hill tune he sang on the *Jimmy Kimmel Live* a few weeks before the fight, the rapturous squeals from the female members of the audience almost drowned out the band.

Boxing's latest savior was celebrating his 50th victory in his own unique manner, and if he didn't sing anywhere as near as well as he fights, nobody cared. They just wanted to be part of the incredible thrill ride that is Manny Pacquiao, a ride that is taken him from abject part poverty in an Asian backwater to the cover of *Time* magazine and the bright lights of Las Vegas.

Who could have imagined, on that long ago Sunday morning in Memphis, that such a thing was possible? Maybe not even Manny dared to dream so spectacularly.

Today he is the centerpiece of a growing economical and political empire, an international personality whose life and exploits have eclipsed the sports page and become the stuff of legend.

Even for the Cotto fight, seen by many as his most difficult challenge to date, Pacquiao's business obligation meant a helter-skelter training camp of barely eight weeks. Nonetheless, he was in magnificent physical condition and seemed as full of energy in the final round as he did in the first.

By the time Pacquiao leaped forward and landed his final two punches of the night in the eleventh round, referee Kenny Bayless was looking for the opportunity to stop the fight. When Pacquiao gave it to him, poor Cotto was mercilessly lowered from the cross, and the Manny Pacquiao bandwagon rolled on.

As improbable as it all seemed seven years ago in Memphis, it's now possible to look back at what's happened. See how all the pieces of this man and the history of his people dovetail together to create the international phenomena he has become.

Of course, none of the incredible fame and fortune would have been possible if Pacquiao wasn't a great fighter. That's the foundation of everything. But it should not be forgotten that he comes from ancient warrior stock. This is something that is often overlooked by contemporary observers, who forget that when Ferdinand Magellan took on the Filipino chief Lapu-Lapu in the battle of Mactan, it was the Portuguese explorer who ended up dead, riddled with poisonous arrows.

Centuries of oppression under the thumb of foreign invaders and corrupt home-grown leaders have not taken away the fighting spirit of the Filipino people. It has instead been sharpened by the kind of desperation that leads to a what-have-we-got-to-lose mentality. And that is exactly the mindset Pacquiao needs to fight with the reckless abandon that has carried him to unprecedented success.

True, he is many years and millions of dollars away from his boyhood days hustling cigarettes on the street. But those formative years, the years of literally not knowing for sure where the next meal was coming from, molded the boy who became the man who now has the boxing world in the palm of his hands.

Manny's sunny disposition and humble demeanor, which contrasts so vividly with his merciless ferocity inside the ring, is also a product of his roots. Among Filipinos, humility and hospitality are the most admired traits, and when Pacquiao told reporters at the post-fight press conference that he thought of himself as an "ordinary fighter," he wasn't kidding.

Sure, he knows he is much more than that. But it took a blatant prod from trainer Freddie Roach for him to admit as much, and even then, Manny acquiesced in a way that paid homage to his teacher not the student.

"You're not ordinary," said Roach.

"Sorry, master," Pacquiao replied, flashing grin of Cheshire Cat proportions. Manny is more than happy to leave the talking to Roach.

Although Pacquiao legend grows with each passing fight, the massacre of Cotto was an outcome that many critics considered highly unlikely.

"Wait until Pacquiao gets hit by a full-fledged 147-pounder," nonbelievers said. "The first time Cotto with his left hook it will be over."

Well, Pacquiao did get hit quite a bit in the early rounds, and Cotto's frightening left hook found the mark more than once. But Manny just blinked and continued to do his thing. Later, he revealed to ESPN's Brian Kenny that Cotto's punches has indeed hurt, but that he pretended they did not.

Pacquiao's eagerness to share his success with his people, while remaining one of them, is an essential ingredient of the mix that creates the magic. When he said he wants to put on a good fight to "make the people happy," it sets him apart from so many sporting prima donnas, who typically have more selfish motives behind their striving.

The commercial spinoffs from Pacquiao's Hall of Fame boxing career now consumes the majority of his time and energy. Dire predictions of being derailed by his lifestyle and/or outside interests have been a staple of media coverage since the beginning of his rise to prominence.

His singing career is a relatively small part of his extracurricular activities. Check out the number of Pacquiao commercials on YouTube. The variety of products he endorses seems endless, Nike, San Miguel beer, McDonald's, Talk and Text, Head and Shoulders dandruff shampoo, Magnolia dairy products—you name it, Manny has probably plugged it. Then there are the movies.

Pacquiao has appeared in seven movies since 2000, starting with secondary roles and gradually progressing to leading-men status in 2005's *Lisensyadong Kamao,* in which he played a boxer whose mother and sister are kidnapped by thugs while he's training for a big fight. In 2008's *Anak ng Kumander*, Manny was a rebel hiding out in the mountains with a band of men wreaking havoc on the crooked officials who oppose the people.

There is a cornball charm to these low-budget Filipino productions, and Pacquiao just might have hit his stride with his latest effort, *Wapakman*. In this flick, he's a superhero complete with a cheesy red costume and numerous superpowers.

While one must suspend all disbelieve in order to enjoy such guilty pleasures, in the boxing ring, the critics have retreated and their skepticism replaced by incredulity.

If, as the bean counters insist, a fighter is to be measured by the amount of money he generates, the extraordinary pay-per-view buy rate for the Cotto fight put Pacquiao at the elite level. According to HBO the fights sold approximately 1.25 million pay-per-views, roughly 200,000 more than Floyd Mayweather-Juan Manuel Marquez fight in September. Moreover, the live gate, created by a capacity crowd of 16,200 at the MGM Grand Garden Arena, was $8.8 million, which topped Mayweather-Marquez by around $2 million.

Many people who care about him wish that Pacquiao would slow down, stop spreading himself so thin and abandon his political aspirations. But that's not about to happen, not yet anyway. Right now, the Pac-Man express is going so fast, he couldn't get off if he wanted to. Pacquiao's destiny is rushing full speed into the unknown—all we can do is hold on tight and enjoy the ride.

———

EPILOGUE: The Cotto knockout was Pacquiao's last great performance. He went 12-5 in his next 17 bouts. One of those losses —the December 2012 split decision to Tim Bradley—who he subsequently beat twice—was a horrendous decision. Pacquiao retired following his decision loss to Yordenis Ugas on August 21, 2021

BELTING PAC MAN IN THE PHILIPPINES

FROM BOXING AND POLITICS TO COCKFIGHTS AND ZOMBIES

ORIGINALLY PUBLISHED IN *THE RING*, SEPTEMBER 2004

THEY KICKED the zombies out of Manila's North Cemetery so I could visit Pancho Villa's grave. But that was just one event in a series of surreal occurrences that marked a marvelously madcap trip to the Philippines, a beguiling land where boxing is still front-page news and Manny Pacquiao is an even bigger star than Oscar De la Hoya is in the United States.

The chief purpose of my visit was to present Pacquiao with *The Ring* magazine featherweight championship belt. I also wanted to pay homage to Filipino legends Pancho Villa and Gabriel "Flash" Elorde. But the trip soon turned into an over-the-top production, and less than five minutes after the plane landed at Ninoy Aquino International Airport, I was muttering to myself what would soon become my mantra for the entire visit: *I can't believe this is happening.*

My first hint that I wasn't in Las Vegas or Atlantic City was when I was whisked through customs and escorted to the VIP lounge while somebody fetched my luggage. Meanwhile, the video crew that would shadow me throughout the week documented every move. Except for the TV cameras, this must have been how it was for Nat Fleischer in the 1950s and '60s, back when the founder and first editor of *The Ring* toured Asia.

For me, however, it was a unique experience, unprecedented in my two terms as editor-in-chief. In a little more than a week in the Philippines, *The Ring* garnered more media attention as it would in a year in the United States.

I should hasten to add that none of the hoopla that surrounded my visit had anything to do with me personally. True, *The Ring* name still had a certain cachet, and I was its representative, but it was Pacquiao's tremendous popularity, unparalleled in his homeland since Elorde held the junior lightweight title in the 1960s, together with the distinctive character of the country and its inhabitants that combined to create an extraordinary happening.

Fueling the buzz was the fact that there was a general election coming up, and every politician wanted Pacquiao in his or her corner. It made sense, and regardless of any ulterior motives, there's no denying the genuine pride and affection for Pacquiao that's shared by poor and powerful alike.

The man who set the wheels in motion for the trip was Ted Lerner, *The Ring*'s Philippines correspondent, who has lived there for more than ten years. Although the story soon took on a life of its own, Lerner somehow managed to maintain a loose grip on the proceedings as the media caravan careened through Metro Manila the next several days en route to the climatic "belting" ceremony at Malacanang Palace. It was an unforgettable ride.

Everything is so exaggerated in the Philippines, going there is like stepping into the pages of a comic book. But if you can abandon yourself to that screwball spirit, it is an exhilarating experience. You have to go with the flow and savor the culture in all its beauty and craziness.

Metro Manila is a teeming caldron of more than 10 million people, and life bubbles over onto the streets in dazzling diversity. The Filipinos are a nation of entrepreneurs, and people set up shop wherever there's available space: on the sidewalks, in the street, wherever they can find a spot to do their thing. It's all about survival.

You'll see a vendor frying fish balls next to another cooking corn on the cob, and a few yards down the road a couple of guys are fixing transmissions on the sidewalk. Moneychangers and girlie bars are everywhere, and everybody us selling something or another. No wonder a freewheeling enterprise such as professional boxing has flourished there since the early years of the 20th century.

As the guest of Manila Mayor Lito Atienza, we were headquartered at the magisterial Manila Hotel, a distinction shared with General Douglas MacArthur, who was bivouacked there during his stint a commander of U.S. armed forces in the Far East during the 1940s. Even though the smiling guards at the gate wielded sawed-off shotguns, the Manila Hotel still exudes old-world charm and is a relative oasis of serenity in a city bursting with activity.

The golden era of Philippine boxing was the 1960s, when Elorde held the 130-pound title for more than seven years. His title-winning bout against Harold Gomes at the Araneta Coliseum (15 years later, the site of the "Thrilla in Manila" between Muhammad Ali and Joe Frazier) drew a crowd of 36,402. Elorde, along with Villa, are the only two Philippine boxers enshrined in the International Boxing Hall of Fame, and by all accounts "Flash" was a wonderful human being beloved by all, even by some of his ring victims.

Driving through Sucat the day after my arrival, it was hard to believe that it was cattle-grazing country when Elorde purchased a piece of property with his ring earnings. These days, urban sprawl has made Sucat pretty much indistinguishable from any part of Metro Manila. But the Elorde Sports Center is still an intrinsic part of the neighborhood, featuring an eclectic mix of boxing, cockfights, billiards, ballroom dancing, and swimming.

Young men who want to become boxers are welcomed into the Elorde fold. They are fed, housed in an on-site dormitory, and taught to box in the gym. All of this is free, providing the boxers work on their craft and help with chores around the complex. In a country with no social safety net, such a program is a blessing, but it's not just boxers the Elorde family is helping. The overall operation requires all sorts of employees, and it's no exaggeration to say that Elorde is still giving back to the community almost two decades after his death.

Lunch with Elorde's widow, Laura, along with other clan members and friends, was a special treat. The Elordes are still very much the First Family of Philippine boxing, and three of Elorde's sons, Bebot, Johnny, and Marty, promote and/or manage boxers.

After lunch we drove to Manila Memorial Park to place a floral tribute at Elorde's tomb. Our tiny graveside gathering brought together people from two different cultures, divided by thousands of miles but united by the common bond of boxing. It was the sort of moment that reminds you how righteous the sweet science can be when practiced by a man of Elorde's enduring class and character.

The senses are continually bombarded with the jarring juxtaposition of life in the Philippines. We went from poignancy of visiting Elorde's final resting place to the visceral world of the "sabong" (cockfights) in the time it took to drive a few blocks. Cockfighting is a national pastime and is essential to the financial wellbeing of the Elorde Sports Center. I lasted about an hour, which was long enough to see about ten chickens meet their fate. Roy Jones would have loved it, but I probably won't go again.

The next stop on that memorable Saturday afternoon was the Wild Card Gym. Not the one in Hollywood run by Pacquiao's trainer, Freddie Roach, of course, but a new state-of-the-art facility in Sucat, named after the original. Rod Nazario, Pacquiao's business manager, owns the gym. Pac Man's brother Bobby Pacquiao was there, busy prepping for an upcoming defense of Philippine junior lightweight title. Manny, however, was still in Davao City in Mindanao (the Philippines is made up of more than 6,000 islands), which quickly became the subject of consternation.

Pacquiao was supposed to already be training for his May 8 bout with Juan Manuel Marquez, but there were suspicions the featherweight champion was otherwise engaged.

"I called him on his cell phone, and I could hear the pool balls

194

clicking in the background," said irate journalist Ronnie Nathanielsz, who produces sports documentaries for Viva Entertainment and writes for the *Manila Standard*.

Nathanielsz has covered Pacquiao since his days as a preliminary fighter and has an obvious affection for him. Still, he pulled no punches in his next column, writing he was " … dismayed by the behavior of the rash young man from General Santos City who has been losing money at pool to regular hustlers, spending long hours and nights instead of training."

The media blitz began in earnest Monday morning with a press luncheon, hosted by Ali Atienza, the mayor's son and chairman of the Manila Sports Council. When *The Ring* belt was displayed, you would have thought it was the Holy Grail. The photographers surged forward en masse, strobes blazing. The next morning photos of the belt were plastered all over the newspapers, and you couldn't help but wonder how long the alphabet gangs would survive if *The Ring* championship policy received that sort of coverage in the Unites States.

After the press conference, Nathanielsz took us back to his office and showed tapes of Pacquiao's early fights. If you think Pac Man is reckless now, you should have seen him when he first turned pro. Raw, wild, and usually leading with his chin, the teenage Pacquiao overcame his deficits with boundless enthusiasm, backed up with a paralyzing punch. It was easy to understand why Filipino fans loved him from the start.

The following day I was a guest at the monthly Philippine Sportswriters Association Forum, along with Nazario and Celso Dayrit, president of the Philippine Olympic Committee. There are a least twenty daily newspapers published in Manila, which prompts fierce competition and a style of reportage that frequently veers toward sensationalism. The headline "Ring Editor Warns Pacquiao: Be Sharp For Marquez Or Else" had already appeared in one news-paper, but on this occasion most of the serious grilling was directed at Dayrit.

From the PSA Forum at the swank Manila Pavilion, we segued to the seedy Sampaloc area, location of the fabled L & M Gym. I had a pretty good idea of what to expect, but this third-world sweatshop was even grimier than anticipated. While dozen or so fighters toiled in a sweltering, airless room akin to a torture chamber, we joined the taciturn Nazario (clearly the Alpha male of Philippine boxing), giggling gym proprietor Moi Lianez, gofer Jerry Garcia (honest), the ubiquitous Nathanielsz, and several others in the air-conditioned office.

Sitting alone at a small desk in the corner was Erbing Jardenil, an ancient matchmaker who thumbed through a tiny, tattered notebook, a worried look on his wizened face, presumably trying to find the right pairing for an upcoming card. A couple of dusty trophies sat on the floor, a few faded photographs hung on the wall. Typically, none of the regulars in the office seemed to be paying attention to the fighters visible on the other side of the window that divided them from the gym.

We still hadn't seen Pacquiao, but Nazario assured us he was flying from Mindanao that evening and would be on hand for the next day's festivities. Besides playing pool, the champ's arrival had been delayed when his wife's uncle was killed in a road accident.

Like most famous boxers, Pacquiao was being pulled in several different directions at the same time, and everybody in the boxing community knew that the sooner he got out of the Philippines and into Roach's care the better. But before leaving for California, Pacquiao had a date with Philippine President Gloria Macapagal Arroyo and me at the palace the next day.

The first order of business Wednesday morning, however, was a courtesy call at Manila City Hall. Lerner told me that Mayor Atienza had been a *Ring* magazine reader since boyhood, so I knew we had something in common, but was unprepared for the mind-blowing reception that greeted us. The moment our van came to a halt and the door slid open, a thirty-piece band began to play. It was all starting to seem like a movie.

As we stood in the sunny courtyard listening to a spirited selection of vaguely familiar tunes, another vehicle rolled up, and out stepped Pacquiao. Suddenly, there were people everywhere. "Manny! ... Manny!" they screamed, rushing forward, attempting to get a glimpse of their idol.

We were quickly escorted inside, up a flight of stairs, and into a crowded reception room, where Mayor Atienza, his son, Ali, and a gathering of perhaps a hundred people waited. After some brief remarks by the mayor, I was presented with the key to the city.

"This key will open all doors in Manila, even the bank—if you care to invest," said Atienza, a well-practiced smile on his face. Did he really think boxing writers have money to invest?

Word had filtered down that President Arroyo would not wait if we were late, so there was a mad dash down the stairs, through a mob of fans, and back into the van. With the mayor's vehicle in the lead, our small motorcade roared off behind a motorcycle escort, which immediately disappeared into traffic, leaving us to fend for ourselves. But thanks to our driver, Boy (that's a name in the Philippines, not an indicator of age or a pejorative), we made it to the palace on time.

Once inside the beautiful Malacanang Palace, we were briefed on protocol as other guest arrived, and a few minutes later I was in the receiving line, shaking hands with a beaming President Arroyo. Soon it was time for the "belting," a term I first heard from Hermie Rivera (the manager of former WBA bantamweight and WBC featherweight titleholder Luisito Espinosa) who was working for the Office of the Press Secretary and our entree to Malacanang.

After an introduction from Nathanielsz and opening remarks by Mayor Atienza, I strapped the belt around Pacquiao's waist. When I raised his left arm in the traditional victory pose, Pacquiao raised President Arroyo's arm, a gesture that was intended as a sign that he was supporting her bid for another term.

All life is so interwoven in the Philippines it's almost impossible not to get caught in its web of political intrigues. For instance, Nazario's wife, Justice Minta Chico-Nazario, had been nominated for the Supreme Court, only to have her nomination recalled amid allegations that she had originally gotten it through what *The Philippine Star* called the "Pacquiao connection."

Still, politics aside, it's not often the leader of a country takes a positive interest in boxing, and it was gratifying to see the sport honored in such an opulent setting. Nobody puts on a "belting" like the Filipinos.

Later that day we struggled through a monumental traffic jam to Quezon City (one of the eleven cities that make up Metro Manila) for a late-afternoon get-together with one of the Philippine's leading captains of industry, Jorge Araneta, owner of the Araneta Coliseum.

Araneta, a slender, ethereal-looking man, received us in his penthouse office, which afforded a panoramic view of the city as the setting sun turned the sky a brilliant orange. It was Araneta's arena, of course, that hosted the legendary "Thrilla in Manila" in 1975. He'd maintained a keen interest in the sport throughout the ensuing decades and spoke enthusiastically about Pacquiao and lamented the passing of big-time boxing at the Araneta Coliseum, which today is the home of basketball, beauty pageants, and other forms of popular entertainment.

Nevertheless, when Nathanielsz suggested that perhaps he should become the business manager of a hot young prospect he knew of, Araneta smiled and said, "Why not?" So perhaps Araneta's formal involvement in boxing is not over. His roots go back to the days when five-figure boxing crowds at the Coliseum were routine, and if anybody has the juice and financial wherewithal to bring big-time boxing back to the Philippines, it's Araneta.

In the meantime, the best Filipino boxers, like Pacquiao and so many others, will have to go to the United States to earn big money. It seems a cruel irony that fighters from a country that loves boxing have to travel to one where the sport has been reduced to cult status in order to maximize their earning potential. But facts are facts, and there's no escaping the harsh reality that the average annual income for a Filipino is roughly $1,030.

———

By now you're probably wondering what happened to the zombies. Well, originally, I thought visiting Villa's grave would be a relatively simple act. But it seemed the old flyweight champion's burial place had fallen into disrepair since he died in 1925, and the City of Manila wanted to fix it up before I paid my respects.

The restoration was finally finished, and the day after Pacquiao's belting, we set off early, picking up a floral wreath on the way. I also purchased a number of newspapers and couldn't help but notice a front-page story in one of the tabloids headlined, "Zombies Evicted From Manila's North Cemetery."

It turned out that these were not the living dead of Haitian and Hollywood fame, but rather homeless people who lived in the cemetery. Admittedly, nowhere in the article did it mentions that they were being expelled on my behalf, but considering the great length the city has already gone in preparation of my visit, I'm pretty sure it wasn't a coincident.

The surrealism reached new heights when we spotted a banner stretched across the top of the gate, welcoming me to the cemetery. I just hoped nobody was expecting me to join Villa as a perpetual guest.

Waiting for us at Villa's grave were Emmanuel R. Sison, secretary to the mayor, several other city employees, a small crowd of about 50 onlookers, Nathanielsz, his camera crew, and, believe it or not, another band.

Villa was looking better than he had in decades. The life-size bust that sits in front of his tomb has been spruced up, but they'd used a shade of paint that made him look like a white guy. Still, it was the thought that counted, and the considerable effort the city had gone to was touching. If nothing else was accomplished by my visit to the Philippines, it was good to know that I had helped resurrect the memory of Asia's first world champion.

Lerner, his wife Aurora, and I returned to the Manila Hotel for my final night in the Philippines. I was half asleep in front of the TV when a face on the screen jolted me out of my semi-slumber.

"That's Carlos Padilla!" I yelped as the man who refereed "The

Thrilla in Manila" broke up a tussle between two housewives over a bottle of rubbing alcohol.

"Take it easy, ladies," crooned Padilla. "There's plenty for everybody."

"They've been running that commercial for years," said Lerner. "I think he made it soon after the fight."

Padilla's commercial was the final boxing-related episode of my Philippines sojourn. A few hours later I was on a jet headed for home, the past eight days tumbling around my brain like socks in a dryer. Originally, I'd been concerned about displacing the zombies, but Lerner assured me they'd probably be back living in the cemetery long before my plane reached the shores of America.

————

EPILOGUE: I returned to the Philippines in 2019 and attended two boxing events. First was a card promoted by Pacquiao (who was on hand) at the Resort World Hotel in Pasay City. Two nights later, it was the 19th Gabriel Elorde Banquet of Champions at the swank Okada Hotel in Paranaque City. Sadly, my friends Ronnie Nathanielsz and Hermie Rivera have both died since my first visit, in 2004.

LEGENDS OF THE RING

A GOD AMONG MORTALS

MEMORIES OF MARVIN HAGLER

Originally published in *Ringside Seat*, Spring 2021.

IT WAS a difficult decision to make, play softball with my buddies from work or watch Marvelous Marvin Hagler challenge middleweight champion Alan Minter on television. The thorny issue was settled when a teammate somehow jury-rigged a small TV to the battery of his car, which was parked on the stretch of grass where we played.

For some inexplicable reason that autumn afternoon in 1980 was the first thing that flashed through my mind after learning Marvin had died, unexpectedly, March 13 at the age of 66.

Maybe it was because he made his bones fighting a series of badass Philly middleweights at the Spectrum, located almost within home run distance of where we clustered around a middle-aged Chevy with a black and white TV on its roof—an echo of the time when folks huddled around a radio to listen to Joe Louis fight.

Our game wasn't delayed too long. Hagler, a savvy, ambidextrous

southpaw with a jackhammer punch, stopped Minter in the third round. The quick demise of the Brit sparked a disgraceful racist-fueled riot fermented by drunken thugs among the sellout crowd of 12,000 at London's Wembley Arena. A fuselage of beer bottles came crashing into the ring like mortar shells and there were no foxholes in which to hide.

The image of five men, including Hagler's trainers and co-managers, Pat and Goody Petronelli, forming a human shield over a kneeling Hagler had a quasi-religious look to it, the Martyrdom of Saint Stephen, maybe. But it was beer bottles instead of stones, and a flying wedge of police rushed Marvin out of the ring to safety.

What a shitty way to start what turned out to be a magnificent six-year and seven-month title reign. What happened in London only added to the bitterness that Hagler seemed to wear like an extra pair of fists. Who knows when it began? Was it as a child when the tenement his family lived in was destroyed in the Newark Riot of 1967, or was it when his mother moved the family to Brockton, Massachusetts, where getting beaten up in a street fight led to a boxing gym?

Bitterness and anger can eat you alive, but it can also be the generator that drives your ambition. The difference between the two is discipline and balls enough to go for what you want, and Hagler had plenty of both.

He brandished the chip on his shoulder like a cudgel, bashing down his opponents and the doors of the boxing establishment. In those days Hagler was far from a glad-hander and rarely let his guard down inside or out of a boxing ring, as I discovered the first time we met.

Hagler was in Philadelphia for one of his fights. Promoter J Russell Peltz invited me to have dinner with him, Goody, and Hagler at the hotel restaurant where they were staying. We were there at least an hour, probably more, eating, drinking, and chatting. Everybody except Marvin, that is. He was just eating. The best we got out of him was "hello" and "goodbye," plus a few grunts and noncommittal nods.

It would be years before Hagler became champion, but he was too stubborn and had too much belief in himself to give up. Beating up anybody they put in front of him was easy, cathartic, and a way to pay the bills. The hard part was keeping the faith, but like a true zealot he did. There was never a doubt in his mind that he could destroy the other 160-pounders out there. It was just that his train was a longtime coming.

The Minter fight was the beginning of a reign of terror in which Hagler successfully defended the title 12 times. Roberto Duran was the only challenger to hear the final bell.

Marvin never stopped grinding after becoming champion. His pride wouldn't allow it, so he pushed harder, refined his craft and never stopped testing himself. Film and photos of Hagler doing road-work in a Cape Cod blizzard, ice on his beard, steam issuing from his nose like a warhorse, is now part of his legend.

Hagler's Q-ratings and paychecks rose exponentially with every defense. His ferocious demeanor and merciless destruction of those who dared challenge him became must-watch TV. He would have fit right in with warriors from Hannibal and Shaka Zulu to Tom Molineaux and Peter Jackson. Yet he still endured snarky comments from certain members of the media who never seemed satisfied. They called him "Mediocre Marvin" and "Marginal Marv," and it pissed him off.

On the other hand, he'd attracted an ever-growing fan base and was closing in on the pinnacle of his career, the iconic war with Thomas "Hit Man" Hearns.

It took place April 15, 1985, during my first full year as editor of *The Ring*, a stroke of luck that put me ringside for their three-round apocalypse. On fight week there was a buzz that tingled right down to the soles of your shoes and made you feel like you were walking on air in the center of the universe. There was nowhere else on earth I'd rather have been, and I think most everybody else felt the same way.

The first round is widely considered the greatest three minutes in boxing history. My story read, "If Marvin was possessed, as many claimed he appeared to be, it was possession tempered by several decades of grueling work and dedication to his trade. For as primitive as Hagler's attack may have seemed to the uninitiated, it was not the wild assault of a maniac, rather a controlled onslaught of a passionate warrior."

In the third round, a snarling Hagler, blood dripping down his face from an eye cut suffered in the first round, "turned Hearns into a horizontal zombie, lashing out with a vicious right. The blow struck Hearns on the temple with such impact, Tommy was sent stumbling backward across the ring. Another right kept Hearns going backward, and then after missing with a left hook, Marvin applied the finisher, a flush right to the cheek." He'd savaged the Motor City "Hitman" and left his critics dumbfounded.

It wasn't until a couple of days after he splattered Hearns that the true measure of Marvelous Marvin Hagler's spectacular victory really hit home. I had returned from Las Vegas and was sitting in front of the television, allowing some silly sitcom to gradually lure me to sleep. But before Morpheus could carry me away to the Land of Nod, my attention was galvanized by the sight of Hagler's face filling the TV screen.

He was munching on a slice of pizza while somebody laid down some tasty blues licks on the guitar. After savoring a mouthful, the undisputed middleweight champion of the world smiled and said, "I was thinking, 'I wonder what old what's-his-name is having tonight.'" Then, stifling a chuckle, Marvin nailed the punch line as deftly as he nailed Hearns ... "Probably soup." He had achieved recognition from a far more powerful entity than all of boxing's sanctioning bodies put together—Madison Avenue.

Success softened Hagler outside the ring. He was rich and had nothing more to prove. One day, my daughter, who was around eight years old at the time, was pestering me while I was trying to beat a deadline. Giving her the old, "this-is-how-I put-food-on-the-table-and-a roof-over-our-head" line wasn't working, so I came up with something new.

She knew who Marvin Hagler was, so I gave her a magazine with his photo on the cover and said, "Why don't you draw a picture of Marvin? If you do a good job, I'll send it to him." About an hour later she presented me with a colored portrait of the middleweight champ, complete with his championship belt and shaven head. It wasn't bad for a little kid. You could tell who it was, and most of the coloring was within the lines. I dutifully mailed her masterpiece to Hagler and pretty much forgot about it. About two or three months later, my daughter received a letter from the champ. He thanked her for the drawing, told her to work hard in school, and listen to her father. When I told her Saturday that Marvin was gone, we talked about that drawing, a small kindness that made his death seem more personal than just the passing of a famous person you admired.

After the glory of the Hearns fight, there was a demanding knockout victory of John "The Beast" Mugabi, which, along with the Hearns fight, seemed to take a lot out of Hagler. It sure looked that way in his next and final fight, the controversial loss to Sugar Ray Leonard on April 6, 1987. The debate over who really deserved the decision was more intense than the fight and continues until today, an evergreen argument that will never be settled.

I'm not sure who won matters that much at this point. Hagler has come to represent something more than a great champion, and an International Boxing Hall of Fame inductee. Other qualities overshadow his enviable record of 62-3-2 (52), his Fighter of the Year awards in 1983 and 1985, and the millions of dollars he earned in the ring. He became the standard bearer for a time when boxing seemed somehow purer. Not the business side so much, but the fighters. Hagler was the real thing, a god among mortals who once walked among us.

FROM KID AZTECA TO CANELO ALVAREZ

THERE'S NOTHING QUITE LIKE A MEXICAN BOXER

ORIGINALLY PUBLISHED BY ESPN.COM, MAY 3, 2017

IT STARTED around 1918 in the bordellos of Tampico and other port cities along the Gulf of Mexico. Sailors and fishermen would set up improvised rings, where men would fight for drinking money, wrapping napkins around their hands for protection and passing the hat afterward.

These unsupervised brawls were not only popular they were dangerous, which led to the formation of Mexico's first boxing commission, in Tampico in 1921. From this crude beginning, boxing quickly spread throughout the country and flourished, fertilized by a macho culture not long removed from revolution.

The latest manifestation of Mexico's enduring love affair with "boxeo" takes place this Saturday at the T-Mobile Arena in Las Vegas, when native sons Canelo Álvarez and Julio César Chávez Jr. do battle in a 12-round super middleweight bout (164½-pound catch weight) broadcasts by HBO PPV.

There's nothing quite like a showdown between two Mexican boxers to divide a nation's loyalties. Alvarez is a big favorite with the oddsmakers, anywhere from -550 to -900, but the rooting sections won't be as one-sided come fight time. The Chávez name still carries a lot of weight in Mexico

The scene and setting have changed tremendously over the decades. Álvarez and Chávez are fighting in a state-of-the-art venue, and they will be paid millions of dollars, not coins in a hat. But the soul of Mexican boxing has remained unaltered, immune to the lure of trappings and treasure. It is innate. It is of the heart.

It is also the reason we look forward to their fights with such anticipation. Mexican fighters at almost every level come with a guarantee. In shape, out of shape, it doesn't matter. They will give you everything they've got. It's the only way they know.

Revolutionary Emiliano Zapata was preaching to the choir when he said, "It's better to die on your feet than to live on your knees." The sons and daughters of the Mexican Revolution who threw off the yoke of oppression had been on their knees so long, they knew he spoke the truth.

Mexico's first boxing star was Kid Azteca, a native of Tepito, known as "Barrio Bravo," the same fierce Mexico City neighborhood that would also give us Marco Antonio Barrera, Rubén Olivares, Carlos Zárate and Ratón Macias.

Azteca's real name was Luis Villanueva Páramo. He had black curly hair, a broad nose and a wistful smile. The left hook to the liver was his specialty, and he is as responsible as anybody for popularizing the signature punch of Mexican boxing.

The boy who became Kid Azteca was born during the revolution, but the exact date varies, depending on the source. It's generally agreed, however, that he was around 13 years old when he made his pro debut in 1929, losing a six-round decision to Pancho Aranda for which he earned 4 pesos.

Azteca lost to the same guy again in his second fight, but he couldn't afford to quit. Besides, Mexican fighters don't back down, and they don't quit. It's part of the code. Azteca embraced the message and became a legend.

His 252-bout career spanned five decades and encompassed a remarkable 16-year reign as the welterweight champion of Mexico.

He fought on both sides of the U.S.-Mexico border and beat Filipino fighter Ceferino Garcia (twice) and Fritzie Zivic in nontitle bouts. But it was his unprecedented term as Mexico's welterweight champion that defined him—until it suddenly didn't.

El Conscripto (Tomás López), another Mexico City fighter, finally ended Azteca's tenure as national welterweight champ. They had a five-fight rivalry, with Azteca holding a 3-1-1 advantage when all was said and done. But El Conscripto's only victory came in their fourth fight, Jan. 28, 1950, when he stopped Azteca in the 10th round, ending an extraordinary streak that began Oct. 23, 1932.

Kid Azteca's best years were over by then, but the arrival of TV in the 1950s created a fresh start. He was already famous, but instead of thousands, millions now saw his fights. It made him a bigger star than ever. He appeared in Mexican potboilers such as "Kid Tabaco" and "Guantes de Oro" and hung around with Cantinflas. His likeness graced a 24,000,000-peso lottery ticket.

Best of all, his TV ratings were so high he was able to cruise through the backstretch of his career beating obscure opponents. Such was the Mexican people's love for their enduring hero.

Azteca and other top Mexican fighters of his era, including Juan Zurita, Chico Cisneros, Baby Arizmendi and Rodolfo "Chango" Casanova took the sport from humble beginnings to a world-class level. And just as important, they set the standard for what a Mexican fighter is all about.

It's a reputation that has spread around world, a badge of courage respected by all. For many non-Mexicans, it's something to aspire to. British junior lightweight Michael Armstrong changed his last name to Gomez and called himself "The Irish Mexican." Gennady Golovkin likes to fight "Mexican style."

For Mexicans, it's just who they are. The generations of fighters who came in the wake of Kid Azteca and his contemporaries have not only carried on the tradition, they've enhanced it.

Rubén Olivares, another Chilango, turned pro three years after Azteca retired and eventually became a central figure of a period considered the last Golden Age of California boxing.

With his snaggletooth smile, party-hardy lifestyle and paralyzing left hook, Olivares was a perfect fit for L.A. in late 1960s and 1970s. His three-fight rivalry with fellow Mexican, Chucho Castillo, was arguably the high point of the era, an orgy of action that was the envy of the boxing world. Olivares won the first and the third, and a combined audience of more than 53,000 reveled in the glory of it all, setting new indoor gate records.

The dynamics of the various rooting interests among people of Mexican heritage are often delineated by geography. Boxers from outside the Distrito Federal generally hate fighters from Mexico City. The rivalries between Mexican Nationals and Mexican-American are particularly intense, and it's not unusual to see Mexican-Americans cheering for the boxer from south of the border.

Oscar De La Hoya said he was surprised when fans booed him during his 1996 bloodbath with Julio César Chávez. The old "Lion of Culiacan" almost bled out before it was stopped in the fourth, but he was still No. 1 in the hearts of Mexicans fans regardless of where they lived.

Interestingly, Julio César Chávez did not have significant fights with a Mexican adversary after winning a vacant junior lightweight belt from Mario Martinez in 1984. He went where the money was, and who can blame him? But Marco Antonio Barrera, who will be joining Chávez as a member of the International Boxing Hall of Fame in June, participated in one of the most celebrated rivalries of the new millennium.

Barrera's three showdowns with Érik Morales were paeans to savagery, especially the first one in February 2000, when they went at each other with unrelenting fury. Barrera deserved that win, but they gave it to Morales, who should have won the second but didn't. Barrera won the rubber match fair and square. The first fight is often mentioned when people talk about the best fights they've ever seen.

If further proof is needed of the vital role Mexico plays in U.S. boxing, I give you the magnificent first three fights between Israel Vázquez and Rafael Márquez, which took place between 2007 and 2010.

Officially, they ended even at 2-2, but their final fight should never have been sanctioned. Vázquez's eyes were so severely damaged winning two of the first three fights, he wasn't fit to box in the fourth. But he knew he would never fight again and needed that final payday.

In the end, it cost him his right eye. Márquez was also spent. He lost four of his next six fights, three by knockout, and packed it in. They would probably both still do the same thing if they had to do it all over again. Most fighters would.

On Saturday, Álvarez and Chávez will be measured against a fighting tradition passed down from the days of Kid Azteca. Chávez has faltered in the past, and this is probably his chance to prove himself. He doesn't even have to win to do so. He just has to remember where he came from.

———

EPILOGUE: Álvarez won a unanimous 12-round decision, wining every round on every official scorecard. Chávez Jr. showed heart lasting the distance.

BENNIE BRISCOE

A PERSONAL REMEMBRANCE

ORIGINALLY PUBLISHED IN *THE RING*, APRIL 2011

I CAN STILL SEE him in my mind's eye, his trademark shaven head shining in the lights as he jogged down the aisle to the ring, the crowd cheering every step. The anticipation was palatable: You knew that if Bennie Briscoe was on the card, you were going to see a *real* fight. Somebody was going to get hurt.

The first fight I covered for *The Ring* was Briscoe's seventh-round TKO of Luis Vinales on October 11, 1972. Almost 40 years later, on January 10, 2011, I attended Bennie's funeral service at the Deliverance Evangelistic Church in North Philly. It was a bittersweet occasion that scrambled my emotions in unexpected ways.

As I paid my final respects, it was hard to reconcile the wax-like figure in the coffin with the flesh and blood man who struck fear in the hearts of a generation of middleweights. His death didn't come as a surprise; I knew he'd been ill for a couple of years. But that didn't stop a little piece of me dying along with him.

Bennie was my favorite fighter. Not the best I've seen, but my favorite, nonetheless. For me, he was also the strongest symbol of the wonderful decade of the 1970s when Philadelphia boxing was basking in the rays of its last golden era.

That was before everybody had cable TV and before casino gambling in nearby Atlantic City stole the boxing spotlight away from Philadelphia. It was also a time when the sport depended on the live audience to generate virtually all of the revenue, and Briscoe became the city's top attraction among a field teeming with tough and talented prizefighters.

It didn't start that way, but Bennie outlasted his contemporaries, and, along the way, became a beloved figure in a hard-to-please city, where just being good at your job was never enough to win the hearts of the people.

There was, however, something about Briscoe that struck a chord that resonated from ghettos to the Main Line and all the blue-collar neighborhoods in between.

It started, of course, with his fierce, uncompromising fighting style. Bennie chugged irrepressibly forward, walking through his opponents' offerings like a man brushing aside a swarm of gnats. And when he got within range, "Bad" Bennie unleashed vicious, arching blows, any one of which could end a fight.

He was a crippling body puncher and ruthless in-fighter. If he got a man trapped in a corner and worked him over, the guy might never be the same fighter again. Briscoe had what old-timers called "heavy hands." And even a friendly tap on the upper arm would still hurt the next day. I know from firsthand experience.

Briscoe's utter lack of pretension, juxtaposed against his fearsome ring persona, were a perfect match for a shot-and-beer city like Philly.

Bennie would never shake an opponent's hand before a fight, and win or lose, would never say a bad word about him after it was over. His battle plan was always the same: Get in shape and try to stop the other guy. He stood between rounds instead of sitting on his stool and was never in a bad fight. We loved him for that and more.

He was a genuine badass, but a badass with a generous heart for everybody except the boxer in the other corner. At the memorial service, Briscoe's brother, Archie Glenn said, "If Briscoe had a million dollars, he wouldn't have a dime. He would give it all away. He knew what it was like to be hungry."

Although he had his final fight in 1982, Briscoe was not a forgotten man when he passed on December 28, 2010. The Philadelphia fight fraternity turned out en masse to say goodbye to a fallen hero. Joe Frazier was there and so were Larry Hazzard and Bobby "Boogaloo" Watts. Willie "The Worm" Monroe was one of the pallbearers. A number of Briscoe's victims were on hand, including Eugene "Cyclone" Hart and Kitten Hayward. Former WBA light heavyweight titleholder Eddie Mustafa Muhammad flew in from Las Vegas to pay tribute to the man who had beaten him in 1975.

When Hall of Fame promoter J Russell Peltz spoke so movingly of the fighter who "made him," it was impossible to keep the tears from welling up. But in an attempt to honor Bennie's incredible toughness, I held them back and went the distance without needing one of the tissues the church ladies were handing out.

If you had to sum up Briscoe in a short, declarative sentence, I'd go with what veteran cutman Milt Bailey said when someone asked him to describe the fighter whose corner he had worked in rings around the world.

"He's 100 percent man," said Bailey. Amen to that.

After the casket was sealed and the large crowd shuffled into the lobby, I knew for sure that if a man such as Bennie Briscoe could die, my secret hope of immortality was as ephemeral as the chilly breeze that blew as his remains were loaded into a hearse.

DICK TIGER

A HERO WORTHY OF THE NAME

ORIGINALLY PUBLISHED IN *RINGSIDE SEAT,* NUMBER 12, FALL 2020

"As you get older, it's more difficult to have heroes, but it's just as necessary."

— *Ernest Hemingway*

IT WAS love at first sight. Not the romantic kind, the kind kids have for their heroes. Our heroes change as we age, but the early ones stick, not as prevalent as when they were new, yet still there, still part of you. Dick Tiger has been part of me since I turned on the television the evening of April 12, 1961 to watch ABC's *Fight of the Week*.

I'd never seen Tiger or his opponent box before, but just their names were enough to push my anticipation level from, "I can't wait until I get my driver's license" to "I can't wait until I get laid."

Dick Tiger vs. Spider Webb. Damn! What 15-year-old schoolboy could resist a 10-rounder between an apex predator and a venomous, eight-legged creepy-crawly?

There were never wild tigers in Nigeria, where Tiger was born

Richard Ihetu on August 14, 1929, or anywhere else on the African continent. But if anybody deserved such an awesome name it was he. Straight out of Amaigbo and ready to kick ass.

"He was so ripped, so beautiful, so strong," said Ron Lipton, Tiger's sparring partner and friend. "What I call couplings, his lower back, legs and knee joints were like the Terminator's."

Physical aesthetics have always been a significant part of hero worship, a phrase coined by Scottish man of letters Thomas Carlyle in 1841. Comic book superheroes from Mighty Mouse to Batman are usually broad at the shoulders, narrow at the waist, and covered with balloon-like muscles. Even Popeye the sailor man is buff after inhaling a can of spinach.

Body type doesn't mean much in boxing, knowing how to fight is what counts. Of course, it doesn't hurt if a boxer looks the part and fights the way he looks. With Tiger what you saw was what you got. His gladiatorial aura was as real as the left hooks that put Webb down three times before the carnage was stopped in the sixth round.

I was a Tiger devotee from that moment until now, nearly 50 years after his death in 1971 at the age of 42. And yes, he was a striking-looking man. I spent two week's allowance on an 8 x 10 glossy from *The Ring* and hung it on my bedroom wall.

My father had told me about Joe Louis, Sugar Ray Robinson, and Archie Moore. His father regaled me with yarns of Henry "The Game Chicken" Pearce, "Gypsy" Jem Mace, and Peter Jackson. But I discovered Tiger. True, he had already fought 56 professional bouts before squashing Spider Webb, but that didn't matter, not to me, not then.

I watched alone that night and Tiger was mine, a hero like so many of his kind, destined for triumph and tragedy. Nothing is free in the hero or boxing racket, and the risk-reward factor is rolling-paper thin.

Tiger's life mirrored the classic hero journey, a quest fraught with challenges that test men's souls. You could say the same of most boxers, I suppose, but it's a matter of degree. Tiger was warrior writ large, a man unto himself who fought valiantly in the ring and stood with his people during their darkest hour.

He was born in Amaigbo, a village in South Eastern Nigeria, widely regarded as the cradle of the Igbo civilization. His mother, Rebecca, believed her son was the reincarnation of her fearless warrior father, Ononiwu. Maybe she was right. After all, we've all inherited some of our grandparents' genes.

Dick moved to bustling Aba (a town about 60 miles from Amaigbo) with his brothers, where he worked as a delivery boy, pushing a handcart during the day and going to school at night. It was in urban Aba that Tiger came to believe that success went to the strong. He was a formidable force at the chaotic communal water pump and a feared street fighter.

It was reading a newspaper article about Nigerian boxers immigrating to England that caught Dick's attention. The sport quickly became his focus, the vehicle that propelled him through a short but incredible life.

My father and I watched together on January 20, 1962, when Tiger turned Florentino Fernandez's nose into a glob of gore, forcing the Cuban left hook artist to quit at the end of the fifth round.

"I bloody well wouldn't want to fight him," said my father, who learned to box in a church basement, where the village vicar taught lads the basics.

I remember him taking me to a large empty gym in Bristol when we still lived in England. The dust particles that danced where the sun shone through the windows emphasized the ghostly ambiance that haunts empty buildings. The gym was soon to be torn down, and I'm pretty sure we were there to say goodbye. Little did we know that less than 200 miles to the north in Liverpool there was the man we would be watching on TV, seven-years later and an ocean away.

Tiger had followed fellow Nigerian and future featherweight champion Hogan "Kid" Bassey to Liverpool, a city with large black and mixed-race communities. If a boxer was good enough, Liverpool could serve as a bridge to the big money in the United States. After

17 pro fights in Nigeria and 28 in the U.K., Tiger sailed for New York in May 1959. He was 30 years old and just getting started.

After struggling initially in the U.S., Tiger went on a remarkable run, beginning with a 10-round decision over previously undefeated Gene "Ace" Armstrong in September 1959. It built from there, with victories over future middleweight champion Joey Giardello (who he would eventually fight four times), two-time New York Golden Gloves champ William Pickett, popular slugger Henry Hank, super slick Holly Mims, as well as Webb and Fernandez. Much of the streak was televised on national TV, and the Madison Square Garden brass was so impressed with Tiger's popularity they raised his fee to $10,500 per fight, more than twice the going rate and the equivalent of more than $92,000 today.

Media hacks considered Tiger an exotic oddity and couldn't resist asking ludicrous questions about Africa. Tiger was offended by their ignorance but seldom showed his displeasure. Instead, he created a collection of retorts to deflect the most common affronts. When asked about cannibalism—yep, they actually asked that—he'd reply, "We quit that years ago when the Governor General made us sick."

When the press grew tired of what Tiger referred to as his "Tarzan image," they switched to making jokes about his frugality. They couldn't fathom the mindset of a Nigerian man born into a family of subsistence farmers. They seemed baffled by a fighter who didn't blow his money faster than he earned it. Writing about a guy who sent his money home to his wife didn't sell newspapers.

The only flashy thing about Tiger was a perfect set of teeth, which he put to good use during photo shoots. He was a well-mannered, soft-spoken gentleman who wore the same black homburg hat and old overcoat for years and was known to carry his boxing kit in a brown paper bag. Between training sessions, he would wash his clothes just to keep busy.

Boxing fans didn't give a damn about Tiger's laundry habits, street clothes or what he did with his money. All they cared about was good fights, and Tiger delivered. He fought with a kind of looming inevitability, stalking, stalking, poker-faced, eyes blazing.

It's easy to love a fighter like that.

Tiger finally got an overdue title shot at National Boxing Association middleweight champion Gene Fullmer, October 23, 1962, at chilly Candlestick Park, home of the San Francisco Giants. I couldn't attend the closed circuit telecast because there was school the next day, so early the following morning I sprinted to the nearest newspaper box and fed coins into the slot. Relief replaced anxiety as I read the Associated Press version of Tiger's 15-round unanimous decision victory. Nowadays, all I would have to do is reach for my phone. I wouldn't even have to get out of bed. That's a good thing I guess, but the newspaper-box runs are the ones I remember, and it would be tough to top that crisp autumn morning when I learned my hero had prevailed and all was right with the world.

———

Tiger was 34 when he became champion, not old exactly, but certainly not young. The next eight years was a maddening cycle of success, failure, and rebirth. Like an African Odysseus, his voyage home was long and perilous. True, Tiger didn't have to deal with a pissed-off Cyclopes or flesh-eating Laestrygonians, but the middleweight division was menacing enough.

Fullmer, a career-long brawler, turned cutie in the rematch and held Tiger to a draw in Vegas. The fight sucked, or as Tiger put it, "We both boxed like amateurs, not champions." Even so, a fair number of people thought Fullmer won, including old mashed potato-face himself. In fact, he was so sure that he could beat Tiger, he agreed to another fight, this one in Nigeria.

The third fight, which proved to be Fullmer's last, took place on August 10, 1963, in front of a crowd of approximately 30,000 at Liberty Stadium, located in Ibadan, the third most populous city in Nigeria. Some have claimed it was a forerunner of "The Rumble in The Jungle," but it was more a homecoming celebration. Even

Fullmer said he had a great time until the fight started. He took a terrible beating and his manager, Marv Jenson, stopped the fight at the end of the seventh round.

————

Nigeria was an artificial country created by British colonialist in 1914. When it gained its independence in 1960, long-time tribal rivalries were rekindled. The persecution of Igbo in northern Nigeria escalated and pogroms, led by the Northern Army, killed tens of thousands of Igbo, leading to a mass exodus of upward of a million people to the Igbo-dominated east.

Tiger had returned to Aba by the time Biafra declared independence on May 30, 1967, and on July 15, he announced, "Nigeria is dead. I am a Biafran"

The civil war between the secessionist state of Biafra and the government of Nigeria was a hideous mismatch that defined Tiger almost as much as his boxing career. I vividly recall photographs of horribly emaciated Biafran children, with bloated bellies and toothpick legs. Before the war ended between 500,000 and two million Biafran civilians died of starvation.

As a lieutenant in the Morale Corps of the Biafran Armed Forces, Tiger toured military bases, where he developed fitness courses for the troops. He was also probably Biafra's most visible representative to the outside world, defending the cause in frequent interviews with the western press.

Tiger probably realized he was being used, but it must have seemed insignificant compared to the appalling things he'd witnessed. A bomb dropped on a residential neighborhood a few blocks from his house, killing 15 people. There was an even worse incident in the nearby town of Ogui, where the marketplace had been bombed. Tiger and some of his neighbors rushed to help and came upon a scene of unspeakable carnage, stinking of burning flesh. Around 100 people died there that day. At one point, Dick stashed his wife, Abigail, and family in Portugal to keep them from harm's way.

Simultaneously fighting on two fronts is complicated. Tiger was scheduled to defend against Roger Rouse in November 1967 in Las Vegas but was trapped in Biafra. The borders had been sealed by federal troops, so Dick snuck out by following a dangerous bush path to Cameroon and the Portuguese-controlled island of Sao Tome. From there he flew to Lisbon and then on to Vegas. Stopping Rouse in the 12th round was the easy part.

Tiger lost control of his Nigerian businesses during the war, his investments were in limbo, and he needed money. There were several proposals, but the $100,000 he could earn defending the 175-pound title against Bob Foster was by far the best offer.

The 6'3" Foster was so much taller than the 5'8" Tiger, some-body joked, "Face to face, they looked like Wilt Chamberlain and Flip Wilson." But there was nothing funny about Foster's left hook. He put Tiger down for the 10-count in the fourth round with a doozy.

Tiger was four months shy of his 39th birthday when Foster knocked him cold, and it was generally assumed the end of the line was near. It still hurts me to see the photographs and videos of the execution-style ending. Chilling stuff, especially when a forever favorite is getting splattered.

But nobody believed in Dick Tiger more than Dick Tiger.

———

On October 25, 1968, a delirious crowd of 13,201 at MSG watched Tiger trade knockdowns with Frankie DePaula, a mobbed-up, lights-out puncher from North Jersey. It was one of those is-this-really-happening experiences. Tiger was down twice in the second round and DePaula twice in the third. It was gloriously savage, and at the end of 10 rounds, Tiger won a unanimous decision.

The thriller with DePaula was exactly what Tiger needed to stay relevant after the Foster disaster. The Garden matched him with reigning middleweight champion Nino Benvenuti in a non-title bout on May 26, 1969. The Italian busted his right hand on Tiger's head in the first round and seemed to lose heart. Tiger fed him a steady diet of body punches the rest of the way and won a unanimous decision.

A points-win over Andy Kendall in November was the last time Tiger's hand was raised in victory. Eight months later, on July 15, 1970, he lost a decision to Griffith in an uneventful match between a pair of aging ex-champs.

It was over, but Tiger didn't know it. He continued to train in the hope of obtaining another payday, but nothing worthwhile was forthcoming, so he took a job as a guard at Manhattan's Museum of Natural History that paid $96 per week.

"He was lonely living in New York," said Lipton. "I could feel it and see it in his eyes. He worried about the war and how they were killing people over there. It was almost like what happened in Rwanda. Even if I touched on that subject, his whole facial expression would change to grief-stricken sadness."

The last time Lipton saw his friend was at the museum.

"He seemed to have dwindled down," said Lipton. "It hurt to see him like that. Jesus Christ, to think of him up in the ring as one of the greatest, strongest middleweight champions."

My hero's journey was almost at an end. The war at home was over, and Tiger accepted defeat gallantly. But the worst was yet to come. He was diagnosed with no-hope liver cancer, and, with the assurance of the Nigerian government that he would have safe passage, returned home to die. It happened on December 14, 1971, at St. Anthony's Hospital in Aba. He had a hell of a sendoff.

"His body laid in state at the mansion in Aba. Outside, every day, queues of mourners filled Cameroon Road, patiently waiting their turn to file past his coffin and pay respect," wrote Adeyinka Makinde in his excellent biography *Dick Tiger: The Life And Times Of A Boxing Immortal*. "The funeral service was held in Amaigbo. Cars, buses, and mopeds choked the expressway that led out of Aba, and the cortege travelled at a snail's pace. In Amaigbo itself, a crowd estimated at 15,000 thronged the hot and dusty road that led from to the local Anglican Church to the place of burial. Every vantage point from buildings to tree branches to the roofs of vehicles was taken as they struggled to glimpse the coffin."

———

I had never been to the United Nations before, but there I was standing behind a podium, looking at a couple of hundred Nigerian faces. They appeared to be very serious, stone-faced, sitting up straight, inscrutable. Before I began my mini-tribute to Dick Tiger, I tried to make a joke by saying it was nice to see so many smiling faces. Nobody laughed.

It was 2002, and I was at the U.N. for the book launch of *Dick Tiger: The Life & Times of Africa's Most Accomplished World Boxing Champion* by Damola Ifaturoti, a Nigerian living in the United States. He wrote the book because he was troubled by the fact that many Nigerians, especially school-age children, had never heard of Tiger. Lingering animosity by the establishment was part of the problem, but that was beginning to soften.

Ifaturoti's book is a slim, straightforward account of Tiger's life perfectly suited for young readers. It was published by Sungai Books, which specialized in such. In 2004, Makinde's comprehensive biography was published, another step toward restoring Tiger to his rightful place in Nigerian history.

That 15-year-old boy who fell in love with Tiger the first time he saw him on TV is an old man now. But that boy is still alive in my heart, a reminder that we need heroes first and foremost because they help define the limits of our aspirations.

———

EPILOGUE: Tiger was posthumously inducted into the International Boxing Hall of Fame (1991), The Ring magazine's Hall of Fame (1975), World Boxing Hall of Fame (1987) and Nigerian Boxing Hall of Fame (1987). He was The Ring magazine's Fighter of the Year in 1962 & 1965 and the Boxing Writers Association of America's Fighter of the Year 1962 & 1966. The Tiger-DePaula match was The Ring magazine's 1968 Fight of the Year.

JOLTIN' JEFF CHANDLER

THE PERSONIFICATION OF A PHILADELPHIA FIGHTER

ORIGINALLY PUBLISHED IN *THE RING,* SEPTEMBER 2000.

"Jeff was the most talented fighter, both physically and mentally, I ever promoted."

—J Russell Peltz

WHEN IT CAME time to have his fist cast in plaster during the International Boxing Hall of Fame's induction weekend in June, former WBA bantamweight champion Jeff Chandler, who fought out of an orthodox stance, insisted they immortalize his left hand.

"It's gotta be the left hand," said Chandler as he prepared to plunge his ball-up hand in a bucket of goop that's used to make an impression that would later be filled with plaster. "I'm a Philadelphia fighter. Philly fighters are famous for the left hook, and I had a pretty good one."

The fans close enough to hear Chandler on that sunny afternoon in Canastota, New York, laughed, and a ripple of approval spread through the crowd. Some of the same folks who had cheered Chandler on to victory at the old Philadelphia Spectrum and various Atlantic City casinos were on hand, and they hadn't forgotten the greatness that once made him the highest-paid bantamweight in history.

"You tell 'em, Jeff," yelled one guy in his 40s, wearing a faded "Joltin' Jeff Chandler" T-shirt that had to be at least 16 years old. "You knocked a lot of guys out with that hook."

Suddenly, after more than a decade-and-a-half of anonymity, Chandler was back in the spotlight, surrounded by well-wishers and a jostling pack of autograph hounds, being ushered from one event to the next by the IBHOF staff, a celebrity again—if only for one magic weekend. His reappearance as a public figure was amplified by the fact that he had disappeared from view so abruptly after his last fight, April 7, 1984. Most fighters do a slow fade. Chandler went from world champion to virtually an invisible man in just a few months.

The bare facts are common knowledge: Chandler underwent cataract surgery shortly after losing the 118-pound title to Richie Sandoval, which required plastic lenses in both eyes, and immediately announced his retirement. No hesitation. No comeback. It was a shockingly swift end to a brilliant career that had seen the wiry, whippet-like Chandler who turn pro after only two amateur bouts and won the WBA title in his 25th pro fight, knocking out Julian Solís on November 14, 1980.

Twelve fight (nine of them successful title defense) later, he was gone, a fantastic fighter who had, essentially, become a phantom overnight. Now, there he was again, rescued from obscurity by a call from the Hall. It was a call Chandler was never sure was coming until Ed Brophy, executive director of IBHOF, dialed his number in mid-January.

"When Mr. Brophy called, I was ready to jump through the ceiling," Chandler told the *Philadelphia Daily News*. "I really wasn't expecting it at all."

Naturally, Chandler, 43, has changed a bit since his fighting days. His beard has turned gray, and he normally wears thick bifocals, but he can't be more than 10 pounds over his old fighting weight, if that.

And the pride that took him to the top of his profession is still intact, the same pride that is partly responsible for his disappearing act. Like most stories, the tale of Chandler's quick demise and retreat from public view has many layers, several of which have remained behind a veil of privacy until the compellingly candid interview he granted *The Ring* on Hall of Fame weekend.

Maybe the best way to understand what happened to Chandler is to start at the end, on October 10, 1984 (the day he underwent the surgery that saved his eyesight and ended his boxing career) and work backwards. The procedure came as a total surprise to the triumvirate most closely associated with his career: promoter J Russell Peltz, manager "KO" Becky O'Neill, and trainer Willie O'Neill, Becky's husband. None of them knew in advance Chandler was going to have the operation.

It was not, however, a lack of trust or respect that kept Chandler from telling the people closest to him what he was going to do. In fact, it was the complete opposite.

"Me and Russell, we didn't talk like we should have," Chandler told *The Ring* as he sipped his breakfast coffee in his Canastota hotel room. "Russell and I were always on the same page about things, and I was concerned that if I sat down with Russell, it would cause me to postpone the operation, put it on the back burner for a while. My concern, my mother's concern, and my doctor's concern was that the progression of my cataracts had gone a long way since 1982 [when he was first diagnosed with the condition]. They didn't think it was a good idea to wait another day, much less get in the ring again and spar. Me and Russell were so close, I figured that if we sat down and talked about it, I would change my mind."

While the cataract operation was the ultimate cause of Chandler's retirement from the ring, his decline as fighter began several years before the eye ailment reach a critical stage. In September 1981, Chandler was placed on six-month's probation after being arrested for a small amount of marijuana and cocaine. It didn't seem like a particularly big deal at the time, and certainly didn't appear to affect his performances inside the ring.

The drug bust had occurred in June, a little more than a month before Chandler stopped Solís again in a rematch, taking out the Puerto Rican ex-champ in half as many rounds as it took to win the title. But what was assumed to be an occasional recreational use of a controlled substances was rapidly becoming a serious problem. Today, Chandler is willing to admit that drugs played a major role in his fall from grace.

"I'd be a fool to try to downplay it," he said. "It wasn't my only problem, but it was the majority of it. It was never a venture to make money off of. I had a problem with the consumption of drugs. I had no problem with the sale of drugs. It was never on my mind to sell anybody any drugs. I was a user."

His use increased between March '82, when he knocked out local rival Johnny Carter in defense of the title, and October of the same year, when he stopped challenger Miguel Iriarte in his next fight.

"It happened when I had that seven-month layoff between fights," said Chandler. "The was no fighting going on for me at the time, just partying. When the fighting started up again, it stared to affect my career, and it definitely affected my mindset. I wasn't as much into the art of boxing as I was before."

Still, for the most part, Chandler continued to perform extraordinarily well. He turned back the challenge of hard-hitting Gaby Canizales in March '83, winning a 15-round decision in impressive style. Then, following a non-title win over Hector Cortez in May, Chandler lost a 10-round split decision to Oscar Muniz in another non-title bout. It was an ugly fight that brought considerable criticism from many quarters, including fans that turned against him when he clowned and taunted Muniz in a losing cause.

When they were rematched in December with the title on the line, Chandler said he'd taken Muniz lightly the first time and has learned a lesson.

"I've got a whole lot to thank Oscar Muniz for; it woke me up," he said. "That loss brought me back to my senses."

Judging by the way he chopped up Muniz for a seventh-round TKO, Chandler had indeed leaned the error of his ways, and at the time, few expected it would be his last successful defense. But the end was rapidly approaching, accelerated by a combination of drugs, medical problems, and an inner battle aggravated by both. He knew his cataracts were progressing and would eventually kill his career, but he didn't know when, and it was eating him up inside.

"I was a confident fighter all of my career," said Chandler. "When I stepped up to take the challenge, I was confident. I felt that I could win every fight I stepped into. But suddenly there was feeling of not being sure. I felt that there was a crack in my armor. I wasn't the iron man I'd always been."

Taking solace in drugs obviously wasn't the answer, and although it eased the pain for a while, it also hastened the inevitable. But not all of the pain was mental. Chandler injured his shoulder training for the Sandoval fight, ironically, while practicing the left hook of which he is still so proud.

"The Sandoval fight was on a Saturday," said Peltz. "I went down to Atlantic City on either Wednesday or Thursday. Jeff and Willie had been training there for a while. I was in my room, and Willie (who died in 1995) walked in and said, 'I've got bad news. Jeff can't fight. His left shoulder hurts so much, he can't even put his shirt on by himself.' We went to the doctor, and he gave Jeff a shot of cortisone, and then he could move his shoulder. Jeff was afraid he'd be stripped of the title, so we went ahead with the fight anyway. I didn't know at the time that he'd been hurt several weeks earlier. I don't think he won more than two rounds. They stopped it in the 15th round."

Like so many boxers, Chandler, who finished with a 33-2-2 (18) record, has struggled to find a place for himself in the world after boxing, and to a degree, he's still fighting that battle."

"That was a craziest situation I've ever been in," Chandler said of his instantaneous transformation form world champion to ex-boxer. "Being champion of the world was something I took great stock in. I had been setting myself up to be champion from the very first day I walked into the gymnasium. That was the itinerary from the very beginning. We were in the gym to train to become champion. It wasn't just to be a fighter. I wanted to be the best."

For a short span of time, that's exactly what he was—an aggressive, mercury-quick, resourceful boxer who punched in sharp combinations. But although he was a thinking fighter, Joltin' Jeff possessed the hard-edged grit that personifies a Philadelphia fighter. When it came to go toe-to-toe, he never backed down and seldom came away second best. Thankfully, some of those same qualities helped him keep going when the cheering stopped.

"I had three children, so I had a job I could get into," he said. "I had something to take my mind off of what was in the rearview mirror. I had something to consume those moments when there was no boxing.

"I've taken care of the dollars well, very well for a fighter. All the back bills were paid. We're talking about 2000, and we're still holding on to some of that. Regardless of what anybody might think or the look I might be giving, I'm still okay."

And the drugs?

"You're always recovering, but I have no problem with it at all," said Chandler. "I feel good about that. I don't look to do it. People don't look to me to do it anymore."

On Sunday, June 11, Chandler stood on the podium during the induction ceremony, his two sons. Jeff Jr. and Julius, at his side, and basked in the glow low of three standing ovations. "This is my proudest moment," he told the cheering crowd. For the person who has known him the longest, however, just the fact that he is alive and not behind bars was more than enough.

"As a teenager, I was coming up pretty rough," said Chandler. "I was gang warring in my high school days, and my mother once said that I would be dead or in jail before I was 21. I've beaten that already, 43 is more than twice 21. I've already whupped that, and it's not over yet."

―――――

EPILOGUE: Chandler now lives in Delaware. In 2006 he was inducted into both the Pennsylvania and New Jersey Boxing Hall of Fame and made an appearance at the annual Briscoe Awards. When I next saw Chandler, his health had declined to a point that he didn't know who I was.

EMANUEL STEWARD

THE WIZARD OF KRONK

Originally published by Grantland.com. October 26, 2012

It was too late by the time I arrived at the Montgomery County Boys Club—I'd just missed a historic gym war between two boxers who would eventually be enshrined in the International Boxing Hall of Fame. Thomas Hearns was still in the ring having his headgear removed and Matthew Saad Muhammad (then Matthew Franklin) was sitting on the apron unwrapping his hands. Both were scuffed up, breathing hard and drenched in sweat. While I had no way of knowing at the time, there was another future Hall of Famer in the gym that day: Hearns's trainer, Emanuel Steward.

When news of Steward's death Thursday at the age of 68 plunged the boxing world into a state a grief, I couldn't help thinking back to the spring afternoon in 1979 when I first met Steward. He was warm and friendly, eager to talk about the zipper-thin puncher he had brought to Philadelphia to fight at the Spectrum. Hearns was riding a 17-fight knockout streak and was expected to make local journeyman Alfonso Hayman number 18, but it didn't turn out that way. Hayman lost every round on every card but was still standing at the final bell. The Philly faithful booed Hearns and cheered Hayman, but Steward was unfazed. He understood that Philadelphia was a lot like his hometown of Detroit—a shot-and-a-beer city passionate to a fault when it came to its sporting heroes.

Hearns wasn't Steward's first titleholder; that honor belonged to Hilmer Kenty, who stopped Ernesto España to win the WBA lightweight title in May 1980. Less than eight months later, Hearns almost decapitated Mexican slugger Pipino Cuevas to take the WBA welterweight title in front of an ecstatic crowd at Detroit's Joe Louis Arena.

By then, Steward's Kronk Gym, located in the basement of a city-owned recreation center, was a veritable fighter factory, cranking out contenders and champs like a Motor City assembly line. A former amateur boxer, Steward got his start working with amateurs, and when the time was ripe, he introduced the best of them to the professional ranks with uncommon success. The parade of champions rolled on and on. Milton McCrory, Jimmy Paul, and Duane Thomas all won titles before the end of 1983. Eventually the Kronk brand grew to the point where Steward opened a franchise in Tucson, Arizona.

He often said that he was just as proud of the job he did managing his fighters as he was training them, but aside from his business acumen and his technical understanding of the sport, another quality made Steward exceptional. Emanuel had that rare ability to make everybody he met feel special. He had a knack for remembering something about you that linked you to him in a personal way.

Decades after the fact, he enjoyed reminding me of the voiceovers I used to do for an obscure and long-defunct UHF television show called *Cavalcade of Boxing*. He was a boxing writer's best friend, as available to a cub reporter as a major media outlet, generously giving his time and virtually always returning phone calls. It was that same giving quality that endeared him to his fighters.

"I stayed in Detroit at one of Emanuel's homes at the tail end of my career and he made me part of his family," recalled former WBA light heavyweight titleholder Eddie Mustafa Muhammad the day

Steward died. "We had a great time together. Emanuel liked to cook, but he was more than that; he was [a] chef and very proud of his cooking. We used to sit around talking about boxing, and he talked a great deal about the art of self-defense, hitting and not getting hit. A lot of the things he taught me I've passed on to the fighters I'm training. More than anything else, Emanuel was a man of integrity."

I was ringside on April 15, 1985, the night Marvin Hagler decimated Hearns in one of the most savage fights of the gloved era, and I can't forget the look of anguish on Steward's face as Tommy fell to the canvas under Hagler's finishing barrage. It was the look of a man who had witnessed his son's tragic downfall and couldn't tear his eyes away from the heartbreaking aftermath. But Steward bounced back — resilient as ever — and stayed with Hearns to the end, even though he must have wished the curtain had come down on the Hitman's long goodbye much sooner.

As Kronk's original stars began to fade, Steward took on the role of a hired gun, traveling from town to town to ply his trade. He became the trainer of choice for flagging headliners in search of new answers to old problems. When Riddick Bowe took the heavyweight championship away from Evander Holyfield in 1993, it was Steward who guided Holyfield to victory in the rematch. When Frankie Randall handed Mexican icon Julio Cesar Chavez his first loss in 1994, Steward helped Chavez win the rematch.

Not all of his reclamation projects were major players. Shortly before his death, Steward resurrected the career of Cornelius "K9" Bundrage, a journeyman from *The Contender* in need of a payday and running out of time.

Perhaps the finest feat in the Wizard of Kronk's bag of tricks involved the old switcheroo. After training Oliver McCall for his upset knockout of Lennox Lewis, the defeated Englishman hired Steward to train him. While working with the 6-foot-5 Lewis and, later in his career, Wladimir Klitschko, Steward showed a touch of genius, becoming the first trainer to teach truly big men how to fight tall. After decades of lumbering heavyweights such as Jess Willard and Primo Carnera, Steward transformed the athletic but unrefined Lewis into the best heavyweight of late 1990s and early 2000s.

I visited Lewis at his Pocono Mountains training camp in June 2003 when he was getting ready for what turned out to be his final bout, a blood-smeared TKO of Vitali Klitschko. A lot of people mistook Lewis's shyness for arrogance, but once he knew you and let his defenses down, he was a sociable-enough fighter. After much gentle prodding from Steward, Lewis, who was not yet in prime condition, finally agreed to pose for photographs after the day's work was finished and darkness enveloped the wooded hills outside the gym.

As I watched Emanuel bandage Lewis's hands, our conversation strayed from boxing to politics. The man who taught men to inflict severe bodily harm on others voiced his disgust with the war in Iraq, shaking his head in dismay at the folly of it all. The carnage in the Middle East was beyond comprehension for somebody who had launched his career trying to save young men from the lethal streets of Detroit.

After learning of Steward's death, boxing photographer Will Hart called me to commiserate, and we talked about old times with Emanuel. He told me about a package he received in the mail many years ago: "I had met Manny when I went to Detroit to cover a fight in 1986, and about two weeks after I returned, I got a size 38 Kronk boxing team jacket in the mail. It was the gold-and-red vintage one with blue letters and leather sleeves. It even had my name embossed on it. At first, I couldn't figure out why he had sent it, but then I remembered telling him that it was my birthday. When I wore that jacket, people actually stepped aside to let me pass, figuring I was some kind of badass. After much searching, I dug it out of the closet tonight. It was a struggle getting it on, but even more trouble getting it off, because I'd gone from a size 38 to 42. But if it still fit, I'd still be wearing it."

I too was the recipient of many acts of kindness from Emanuel. The last one came during my final year as editor of *The Ring* magazine. He wanted to tell me how much he liked a piece I'd written but said that he had lost my number and didn't know how to get in touch with me. So he went out of his way and called my colleague Eric Raskin to get my number. When we finally spoke, what he said meant more to me than any paycheck I earned in my career.

If I had a Kronk jacket, I'd find a way to make it fit.

THE REBIRTH OF STANLEY KETCHEL

BOXING IS AN ART FORM

ORIGINALLY PUBLISHED BY ESPN.COM ON OCTOBER 2, 2015

I WENT SEARCHING for Stanley Ketchel on a recent September afternoon, an excursion that took me to the backstreets of Philadelphia's Port Richmond section, where abandoned railroad tracks hint of a time when its location on the banks of the Delaware River made it a major terminus.

Today, gentrification is nibbling away at the traditionally working-class neighborhood but has not yet reached the old industrial area, where weather-beaten warehouses from a bygone era still house an eclectic assortment of businesses. It was in one of these buildings that I found the "Michigan Assassin" looking as formidable as ever.

He appeared larger than life, standing like Superman, arms folded, looking into the distance, an enigmatic expression on his face. Ketchel, the erstwhile middleweight champion of the world, dead since October 15, 1910, had been resurrected in bronze.

His earthly remains were interred at St. Adelbert's graveyard in Ketchel's hometown of Grand Rapids, Michigan, where he was given a grand sendoff, complete with a military band, flower girls and a white horse-drawn hearse.

Ketchel's metaphoric rebirth took place at Port Richmond's Independent Casting more than a hundred years later, with far less pageantry but no less devotion.

When I arrived, sculptor Ann Hirsch was watching the foundry's patina artist, Melanie—baseball cap on backward and goggles firmly in place—wield a blowtorch and apply the finishing touches to the statue.

In a few days, Ketchel would be headed home once again to Grand Rapids, but instead of a grave, his destination would be a place of honor, a perpetual reminder of the iconic fighter who was only 24 and still world champion when a bullet in the back ended his tumultuous life.

Art doesn't come from a mold. It comes from the heart and mind of the artist. Hirsch was a boxing neophyte when she received the commission from the Grand Rapids Community Legends Foundation to create the Ketchel sculpture. The foundation, established and funded by philanthropist Peter Secchia and headed by Joseph Becherer, is a long-term plan to erect 25 statues in Grand Rapids of notable figures in the city's history.

"Some people call me a method-actor sculptor," Hirsch said. "I do a lot of research before I start. I make the person very real in my mind's eye. That's what guides me when I sculpt."

Before Ketchel, the only athlete that Hirsch had sculpted was NBA legend Bill Russell, so she immersed herself in boxing in preparation for her mission. It proved a revelatory journey into a world that has changed little since the first decade of the 20th century, when her subject once rode down New York's Fifth Avenue, wearing a pink dressing gown and tossing peanuts to the cheering multitude.

"My grandfather was a crazy boxing fan, but I'm not generally a sports fan," Hirsch said. "I appreciate athletes, but, for me, boxing has been the most incredible discovery. One of the first things that struck me about boxing is that it's an art form. I love it."

Despite the difference in their crafts, Hirsch found herself simpatico with those who toil between the ropes.

"Boxers are very much alone in the ring," she said. "It's a weird comparison, but as a sculptor alone in the studio wrestling with my art, I really relate to that."

Reading everything about Ketchel she could get her hands on was just the start of Hirsch's education. She wanted to know how boxers move, how they learn their trade and what makes them tick.

"ESPN boxing editor Andres Ferrari helped me with research," she said. "He shared his boxing passion and knowledge with me and introduced me to Donegal middleweight boxer Jason Quigley and a number of Massachusetts fighters, including Mark DeLuca, Danny 'Bhoy' O'Connor and Ryan 'Polish Prince' Kielczweski."

Hirsch attended a fight card at the Barclays Center last August, when Danny Garcia fought Paulie Malignaggi and Danny Jacobs fought Sergio Mora, and witnessed boxing's spectacle firsthand. But it was at the Somerville Boxing Gym, near her home in Cambridge, Massachusetts, that she gained her greatest insights.

"I walked in off the street, and they welcomed me with open arms from day one. Boxing people are some of the warmest, most loyal and kindest people I've ever met," Hirsch said. "The first day I was there I was getting hugs. Where else does that happen?"

Her host was Norman "Stoney" Stone, who was best known as the bellicose manager-trainer of heavyweight John Ruiz, but apparently is putty in the hands of a female sculptor.

"I love that man," Hirsch said. "He's really funny. He likes to bust your chops. After I visited the gym, he came to my studio, which was probably difficult for him. It's so outside of his comfort zone."

Boxing soon became Hirsch's new comfort zone, and the next step was to channel all she had learned into the creation of the sculpture.

Unlike so many boxing sculptures, Ketchel's does not show him in a boxing stance, fists raised, ready for combat.

"I wanted people to see a different side of boxing, to suggest the man first, before the boxer. I want people to know how real he was," Hirsch said. "He's got arms crossed. It's kind of a stare-down, kind of a threat. Ketchel had what is known as controlled rage as a boxer, and it's almost like he's saying, 'I'm controlling myself because when I uncross my arms, I'm going to raise some hell.'"

Born Stanislaus Kiecal, Ketchel certainly raised a lot of hell both in and outside of the ring. People used to tell him how he would turn white with anger when he fought, but that was all talk as far as Ketchel was concerned. He just did what came naturally, which was to keep throwing punches until the other guy was comatose. His reputation for viciousness, first established in hobo camps across the West and later reinforced in the ring, was well deserved.

After leaving home as a teenager, he settled for a while in Butte, Montana, a wide-open, freewheeling town crawling with miners, cowboys, gamblers and prostitutes. The town teemed with dance halls, saloons and seedy theaters, all intent on relieving the miners and cowboys of their hard-earned pay. After drinking and gambling, the most popular form of entertainment was boxing.

Ketchel was hired by the Casino Theater for $20 a week to take on all comers. "I hit 'em so hard that they used to fall over the footlights and land in people's laps," he liked to brag.

Ketchel had his first official bout in May 1904, against Kid Tracy, scoring the first of 49 knockouts he would tally in his 64 professional bouts. By 1906, he'd racked a long string of conquests and outgrown Butte. If he wanted to be champion, he'd have to move to California, then the center of big-time boxing.

It took him a while to obtain his first match on the West Coast, but once he got started Ketchel became the sensation he always knew he would be. He knocked out Jack "Twin" Sullivan in the 20th round on May 5, 1908, at the Mission Street Arena in Colma, California, to claim the middleweight title.

Ketchel was champ during America's White Hope era, an infamous search to find a white heavyweight capable of beating black heavyweight champion Jack Johnson. It proved a fool's errand, so Ketchel, already widely acknowledged as a special fighter, stepped into the breach against Johnson despite being at a 35-pound disadvantage. He was knocked out cold in the 12th round.

Although Ketchel still held the middleweight championship, some of the spark seemed to go out of him after the loss to Johnson. He fought just four more times, knocking out Jim Smith on June 10, 1910, at the National Sporting Club in New York City in his final fight. Four months later, he was dead, shot by Walter A. Dipley while vacationing on the Missouri ranch of longtime friend Pete Dickerson.

Ketchel and Dipley had quarreled over Dipley's girlfriend, Goldie Smith, and although what really happened that day depends on whose story you believe, both Dipley and Smith were convicted of murder in what amounted to a kangaroo court. They received life sentences, but both were eventually released. Dipley served 24 years before being freed because of failing health and died less than five years later.

How good was Ketchel?

Nat Fleischer, editor and founder of *The Ring* magazine, considered him the greatest middleweight of all time. Films of Ketchel's fights with Billy Papke and Johnson, however, showed him to be little more than a wild swinger with a knockout punch in both hands. He looks raw and clumsy compared with today's fighters, but that's not a fair comparison.

A fighter can be accurately measured only against the best of his time, and outside of Johnson, Ketchel was the best fighter of his era. In his 2006 book, *Boxing's Greatest Fighters*, historian Bert Sugar listed Ketchel 19th, ahead of such celebrated modern boxers as George Foreman, Joe Frazier and Sugar Ray Leonard.

According to David Mayo, who covers boxing for the *Grand Rapids Press*, "The only tangible memorial to Ketchel is a historical marker near the intersection of Bridge Street and Stocking Avenue." That situation was rectified on Oct. 2, when Hirsch's sculpture was unveiled on Bridge Street in the city's historically Polish section.

"Boxers are intertwined with history and have an important story to tell," Hirsch said. "There is a very strong Polish community in Grand Rapids, and Ketchel was their first champion. I'd like people who don't know about boxing or Ketchel to see the piece and become interested by wondering, 'Who is this guy?'"

Ketchel never fought an official bout in his hometown, just a three-round exhibition in 1909. But he did fight twice in Philly, against fellow legends Sam Langford and "Philadelphia" Jack O'Brien, in venues just a few miles south of Port Richmond, another Polish-American enclave where he emerged anew from a crucible of fire, ready to take another bow.

————

EPILOGUE: Ketchel was inducted into the International Boxing Hall of Fame in 1990. In 2005 James Carlos Blake published a critically acclaimed novel titled, The Killings of Stanley Ketchel.

CARLOS MONZÓN

HIS ONLY FIGHT IN THE UNITED STATES

Originally published by ESPN.com, June 30, 2015

CARLOS MONZÓN WAS a pungent mix of primal power and urbanity —a badass playboy just as comfortable chilling with the jet set on the Riviera as he was hanging out in the slums of San Javier, Argentina, that spawned him. But he looked different from the cheap seats at Madison Square Garden than he did on television. The bright lights and distance emphasized his stick-figure physique—all legs and arms.

But it was Monzón, all right. His regal bearing and mop of black hair were unmistakable. As were his black trunks imprinted with "Fernet-Branca," the potent liqueur so popular in his native Argentina

It was 40 years ago—June 30, 1975, to be precise—but you don't forget the only time you see a fighter like Monzón box live. I was only a cub reporter, so I didn't even apply for a media credential. Instead, I went with my buddies and watched from the gods.

It turned out to be Monzón's only fight in the United States, the once-in-a-lifetime opportunity to witness this unique, albeit contro-versial, champion. His eventual fall from grace was as tragic as his

249

rise had been triumphant. And although we didn't know it at the time, the arc of his life had already passed its apogee and begun its descent.

When Monzón arrived in New York City to fight Tony Licata he had not lost in more than 10 years and had been champion since November 1970. His prestige was such that it seemed more like a royal visit than a fight, especially with his glamorous consort, actress/model Susana Giménez, in tow.

"Monzón was in the middle of a torrid romance with Susana," said Carlos Irusta, Argentina's leading boxing journalist. "They met a year before when they made a movie, *La Mary*. They fell in love, and he started to live in Buenos Aires, not in his hometown of Santa Fe. And when Carlos went to New York to fight Licata, Susana went with him."

Monzón's wife, Mercedes Beatriz, best known as "Pelusa," was almost as volatile as her husband. When she learned of the affair, she confronted

Giménez at a theater where her rival was working and yelled, "Carlos is mine!" as she sprang at her husband's paramour.

"They kind of had a brawl," said Irusta. "It was no secret that Susana and Carlos were dating. Some months before, they went to the Tamanaco Hilton hotel in Caracas, Venezuela. It was supposed to be a secret rendezvous, but Susana let the press know. It wasn't long after Monzón returned home from the Licata fight that divorce proceedings between Carlos and 'Pelusa' began."

New Orleans native Licata, who fought out of Tampa, Florida, lived in a different world than Monzón, a world devoid of glitz, flashy women and six-figure paydays. He was a popular, workaday boxer fighting his way up the rankings under the guidance of Lou Viscusi, a veteran manager who had, shall we say, connections in the right places.

Licata was the son of an Italian father and a Chinese mother, whose uncle, Ralph Chong, had been a decent middleweight. Tony was a slick, quick craftsman in the manner of other New Orleans cuties such as Willie Pastrano and Ralph Dupas. He'd built a record of 49-1-3 (20 KOs) en route to a title shot, and his only loss (by majority decision to Ramon Mendez) had been avenged.

Regardless of his respectable credentials, few gave Licata a chance. He was bolder than Pastrano and Dupas and wasn't averse to trading when he thought he could get away with it, not a good thing when your punching power is average at best and you're in there with one of the greatest middleweights of all time.

I had met Monzón briefly at the Boxing Writers of America Association's 1972 awards banquet, where Carlos was honored as Fighter of the Year.

The champion stood alone, acknowledging well-wishers with bored indifference, but as I approached, he cracked a smile

I thought for a nanosecond it was for me, but it wasn't. The smile was for Philly middleweight Bennie Briscoe, who was just behind me. They had fought twice in Buenos Aires, a draw and a decision for Monzón. The 25 hard rounds they'd shared had forged a bond only fighters can really understand.

Licata was tough but not as tough as Briscoe. Nonetheless, he proved a brave and determined challenger. Tony took a pasting pretty much from the start, but always flurried back when things looked the worst. Monzón administered a steady beating, catching Licata coming and going with heavy blows.

Even so, it was the challenger's plucky stand against supposedly overwhelming odds that stood out. Despite an occasional roar of "Argentina," it was when Licata fired back that the crowd of 13,496 erupted.

None of Licata's punches appeared to hurt Monzón, but as the rounds ticked by, two questions demanded answers: What was keeping Licata upright, and why couldn't Monzón close the show? The champion's infatuation with Giménez was clearly a factor. Even Monzón admitted that.

"When I was in the ring, and I saw her at ringside, cheering and shouting, I tried to make the best fight of my life," Monzón revealed in his autobiography, *Mi Verdadera Vida* [My Real Life]."

In that, he failed. The supremely confident champion had

predicted it wouldn't go past the fifth round, but despite being hammered around the ring, Licata was defiantly upright and ready to go when the bell rang for the sixth.

If Monzón was frustrated, he never showed it. He remained outwardly composed and kept the pressure on and the punches flowing. After absorbing a spiteful beating in the ninth, Licata finally caved in the 10th, dropping to his hands and knees after taking a wicked right.

Licata was up by the count of five but looked perilously vulnerable when referee Tony Perez turned Monzón loose. A pair of malevolent left-right combinations landed flush, and Licata dipped down to one knee. He instinctively popped right back up, but Perez waved it off at the 2:43 mark and guided the blurry-eyed challenger back to his corner.

Licata fought on with middling success until 1980, but even in defeat, the Monzón fight had been his finest hour.

Once the ring announcer made it official, Monzón walked to the ropes, blew a kiss to the crowd and thrust both arms into the air. The victory earned him the cover of *Sports Illustrated*, headlined "Monzón The Magnificent," but the magazine was a bit late on the uptake.

By then, Monzón was 32 years old and the attrition of 97 professional fights was beginning to show. Considering his hedonistic lifestyle, which included chain smoking up to 100 cigarettes a day, it is remarkable that Monzón accomplished so much and stayed on top for so long.

There were three more successful title defenses after Licata, two against the murderous-punching Rodrigo Valdes, and then Monzón was done. A knockdown he suffered in the second Valdes fight convinced Monzón it was time to quit. He announced his retirement in August 1977, still the undisputed middleweight champion, and remained a hugely popular figure in Argentina for some time to come.

But the inner rage that fueled Monzón's boxing career was toxic outside the ring and eventually consumed him. According to writer Dan Colasimone,

Giménez " was another of Monzón's lovers whose face sometimes bore the bruises of his violent domestic outbursts."

When she left him, Monzón's downward spiral accelerated.

"He drank a lot, and you could say he was a violent drunk," said Irusta. "I believe that when he was unable to express himself with words he would respond with violence. The difference in the ring was that it was his work, and he channeled all his aggression."

Accounts of exactly what happened in the early hours of Feb. 14, 1988, are many and varied. But they all end the same way—with Monzón's common-law wife, Alicia Muniz (mother of his son Maximiliano), lying face down in a pool of blood, two stories below the balcony of a house in Mar de Plata. Monzón claimed she fell, but forensic evidence showed that she had been strangled before her fall.

On July 3, 1989, Monzón was found guilty of murder by a three-judge panel and sentenced to 11 years in prison. Six years later, he was given a one-day furlough for good behavior. In the evening of Jan. 8, 1995, while driving back to prison, Monzón rolled his car and died before help could arrive.

Shortly thereafter, Giménez invited "Pelusa" to appear on her TV show, where the two women professed their love for Carlos and cried together.

———

EPILOGUE: Monzón, considered one of the greatest middleweights of all time, was inducted into the International Hall of Fame in 1990. In 2017, Carlos Irusta published a comprehensive, Spanish-language biography, Monzón: La Biografia Definitiva. *In 2019 Netflix produced a series about Monzón called* Monzón: A Knockout Blow, *actor Jorge Roman in the title role.*

Licata died on May 22, 2008, at the age of 56.

LUNCH WITH CARMEN BASILIO

HE GREETED EVERYONE AS AN OLD FRIEND

ORIGINALLY PUBLISHED BY ESPN.COM, NOVEMBER 7, 2012

THERE WAS a time when you were nobody in boxing until you'd had your pocket picked by Carmen Basilio. This is a story about the day I joined that not-so-exclusive club and the man who initiated me, the great old fighter who died Wednesday at age 85.

It was October 2000, and I was killing time in my hotel room until the Rochester Boxing Hall of Fame banquet that evening. Then the phone rang. It was Tony Liccione, president of the RBHOF, with an offer no journalist or boxing fan could ignore

"How would you like to have lunch with Carmen Basilio?" asked Liccione. He didn't have to ask twice. Within a few minutes, I was in a van with a small group of chattering fight freaks on my way to Basilio's home.

By the time I began watching Basilio on TV, he was washed up. I vividly recall the conclusion of his June 1960 rematch with Gene Fullmer. Basilio, blood streaming down his gnarled face, had taken a hideous beating, but he just kept coming forward because that's all he knew how to do. Finally, in the 12th round, referee Pete Giacoma had seen enough and stopped the fight. Basilio was enraged and shoved the ref away, yelling obscenities and demanding that he be allowed to keep fighting.

In his mind, Carmen was still the fighter who had captured the welterweight and middleweight championships during a legendary career. But that Basilio was gone, worn to a nub by more than 70 pro bouts against the very best fighters of his era. All that was left was a bag of guts and an indomitable fighting spirit.

The van pulled up to the curb of a modest home on a pleasant residential street in Rochester where Basilio had lived since 1985. His wife, Josie, met us at the door and showed us to the basement stairway. There in the pine-paneled recreation room was a bespectacled man in his 70s with a sly grin on his face and a sparkle in his eyes—the man who had beaten the incomparable Sugar Ray Robinson.

Carmen greeted everyone as if we were old friends, and in a way we were. Those who love the sweet science feel a connection with its heroes, a bond forged by history out of admiration, respect and a certain kind of awe for what these larger-than-life men have accomplished. For an individual who had achieved so much in his fighting career (1949-61), Basilio was as unaffected and down-to-earth as he must have been as a boy, picking onions in the fields of upstate New York.

"Help yourself," Carmen said, indicating a long table filled with homemade food (prepared by Josie) and several jugs of wine.

What followed were several unforgettable hours. Carmen engaged each of us in conversation and at some point, managed to remove almost all of our wallets, one by one, totally undetected. Then, before you knew it was missing, he would sidle up to you and innocently ask if the proffered wallet looked familiar. Carmen kept us laughing with a series of ribald jokes that grew funnier as the wine flowed. Finally, after a little prompting, he agreed to show us a film of one of his fights.

"I'm gonna show you my fight with Art Aragon," he said. "He had a smart-ass mouth, so I enjoyed beating the crap out of him."

As the black-and-white picture filled the screen, there was

Carmen as he looked in 1958, muscles taut, his black hair dripping with sweat as he ripped into California's original "Golden Boy." He provided tough-guy commentary as we watched him punch Aragon around the ring, and he seemed to take great glee in reliving the moment. The uncompromising fighter who hadn't thrown a punch in anger in almost four decades was still alive inside of Basilio, and I liked him all the more for it.

As we reluctantly filed out of his house, Carmen sat at the kitchen table signing photographs of himself in his prime, making sure he spelled everyone's name correctly. He made an inexcusably crude joke about mine, but I instantly forgave him. That evening at the banquet, Carmen recited the same jokes he had told that afternoon in his basement, but even those of us who had heard them earlier that day couldn't help laughing again.

Thanks, Carmen. Thanks for everything.

JAKE LAMOTTA

THE RAGING BULL RAGES NO MORE

ORIGINALLY PUBLISHED IN *BOXING NEWS*, SEPTEMBER 28, 2017.

THERE'S a blurry video popping up on the Internet for months now, a bare-chested old man throwing slow-motion punches in a dimly lit room. It looks like he's in a dream and perhaps he was, maybe dreaming of past glories, maybe trying to find out if he's still got it.

Jake LaMotta died on September 19 at the age of 95 and shadow boxes no more. He was one of the last remaining links to another time, a time when Joe Louis was the heavyweight champ and every man wore a hat. The old scoundrel had outlived them all and now he's gone.

In his fighting prime LaMotta was an imposing presence. He had a chunky physique, accented by slabs of muscle plastered across his hairy chest and broad back. He wore a leopard-print robe and when the bell rang he went about his business with reckless belligerence. Nobody had an easy time with LaMotta, not even Sugar Ray Robinson.

His life outside the ring was as turbulent as his fighting style. The son of an abusive father, LaMotta grew up poor, street smart, and wild. He spent time in a reformatory for youthful offenders but didn't reform.

LaMotta abused women, including his wives, and beat a man so severely during a robbery that he thought he had killed him, an event that haunted him for years. Guilt was the catalyst of his intractable fighting style. Jake felt that he did not deserve to live.

That version of the "Bronx Bull" was just a memory when he strolled into *The Ring* magazine's Manhattan editorial office one summer day in 1985. He was wearing a striped polo shirt and a wry smile. Except for a receding hairline and a few extra pounds around the middle, he looked pretty much the same as during his fighting days. A live-in face like Jake's is something you don't forget and his low rumbling growl of a voice was instantly recognizable.

LaMotta, who celebrated his 63th birthday the following month, was in a good mood. He had just learned that he had finally been voted into *The Ring's* Boxing Hall of Fame, 30 years after his last fight. The former middleweight champion and the first man to beat Robinson had been denied the honor for so long because he'd thrown a fight with mob-managed "Blackjack" Billy Fox.

It was hypocritical to blackball LaMotta when other fighters who had been involved in fixed fights were already enshrined, including George Dixon, Abe Attell and Kid McCoy. It seems that LaMotta's real sin was admitting his transgressions. He did so in 1960 before a U.S. Senate sub-committee investigating organized crime's influence on boxing. One gets the feeling that boxing's establishment would have preferred he kept his mouth shut.

Despite all the punches he'd taken in 106 professional bouts, LaMotta showed no ill effects of his former occupation. His answers during a wide-ranging interview that day were thoughtful, candid, and at times humorous. He had been eking out a living as a stand-up comedian and couldn't resist throwing in a little shtick when asked if he had any regrets.

"I would have never gotten married," he said, laughing. "No. No. I got something out of each of each marriage. Theresa, my present wife, we're very compatible. Each night when we go to bed, we both get headaches at the same time."

Getting married was one habit LaMotta never kicked. When he died due to complications from pneumonia, he was married to his seventh wife, Denise Baker.

LaMotta's rise from poverty began when he turned pro on March 3, 1941. By the time he fought Fox he'd already beaten Fritzie Zivic, Tony Janiro, Tommy Bell, Holman Williams, Lloyd Marshall, Bob Satterfield, José Besora, and Robinson. Nevertheless, his refusal to cooperate with organized crime, which had a stranglehold of much of boxing at the time, was a problem he couldn't solve with a punch in the mouth.

"I was the uncrowned champion for five years," said LaMotta. "Nobody wanted to give me a shot ... but time was running out. I was getting a little too old. I wasn't as good as I used to be. I had to make a decision. Either I lose the fight to Fox, or I don't get a chance to fight for the title. They offered me $100,000. I turned them down. I didn't need the money. All I wanted was a Chance to fight for the title."

Even after LaMotta allowed Fox to stop him, it wasn't until June 16, 1949 that he got the promised title fight against reigning champion Marcel Cerdan. The defining moment came in the first round when LaMotta, who was notorious for his uncompromising fighting style, threw Cerdan to the canvas with what historian Bert Sugar called "as pretty a hip roll as ever seen in a wrestling bout."

Cerdan injured his left shoulder when he fell, making him virtually a one-handed fighter. The Frenchman struggled on until the end of the ninth round but didn't answer the bell for the 10th. LaMotta had finally fought his way to the top of the boxing world, but he had to give the Mafia $20,000 to cement the deal. The only money Jake made that night was what he won betting on himself.

There was supposed to be a rematch, but Cerdan died in a plane crash on his way to New York from his home in France.

LaMotta made two successful defenses in 1950, a 15-round decision over Tiberio Mitri and a knockout of Laurent Dauthuille in the waning moments of the 15th round. Behind on points, LaMotta staged a furious last-gasp rally, knocking out the French challenger at the 2:47 mark. It was quintessential LaMotta and Fight of the Year.

LaMotta's joke about fighting Sugar Ray so many times he was surprised he wasn't diabetic is a classic, but there was nothing funny about their six-bout series. Even though Jake only won the second fight, all six were hard fought and the fifth a split decision. A sixth with the title on the line was a natural.

Robinson and LaMotta faced each other for the final time on February 14, 1961 in front of a packed house at Chicago Stadium. The champ went after Robinson in his usual swarming, roughhouse manner, while Sugar Ray backpedaled and countered. It was "guile versus guts, head versus heart, and combinations verses courage," wrote Sugar.

LaMotta was in the fight for the first eight rounds, but Robinson started to pull ahead in the ninth. From then until the bout was stopped in 13th round, LaMotta took such a terrible beating that the fight became known as the St. Valentine's Day Massacre, named after the gangland murder of seven men on the same date in 1929.

Jake was famously still on his feet when the fight was stopped, helpless but still on his feet. It was a badge of honor for LaMotta, but just another night's work for his legendary chin.

LaMotta never fought for the title again. His courageous stand in the final Robinson bout took everything out of him. He lost three of his next seven fights and retired after Billy Kilgore outpointed him on April 14, 1954. As you might expect adjusting to life after boxing was even tougher than fighting Robinson.

"I was a little like Dr. Jekyll and Mr. Hyde. When I was involved in the boxing business, I was one character. When I went home to my kids, I was another character," said LaMotta. "After my career was over, I still had two characters and I had to get rid of one of them. I was frustrated. Before, I used to take it out on my opponents. Then I started taking it out on my wives."

It was the beginning of a downward spiral that resulted in LaMotta severing six months on a chain gang in 1958 after being convicted of introducing men to an underage girl in a Miami night-club he owned. There were many lean and unhappy years after he was released. The bit parts in movies and public appearances dried up. It got so bad that one Christmas he wandered the street of New York with just 35 cents in his pocket, ashamed to go home because he couldn't afford gifts or a tree.

Things took a positive turn in 1970 when his autobiography, *Raging Bull: My Story* (ghosted by Joseph Carter and Peter Savage) was published by Prentice-Hall. The hard-hitting, tell-all book was well received, and in 1980 was turned into a movie directed by Martin Scorsese and starring Robert DeNiro as Jake. The juicy role earned DeNiro an Academy Award for Best Actor.

The movie portrayed LaMotta warts and all, emphasizing his volcanic temper, including roughing up Vikki LaMotta (portrayed by Cathy Moriarty) who was his wife at the time he won the title.

"That was exaggerated," said LaMotta. "I was a jealous guy and belted my wives a couple of times, but if I really belted them, they wouldn't be alive."

The movie put LaMotta back in the spotlight, Sentiment about him, at least among boxing fans, had clearly mellowed. When he was introduced at Madison Square Garden before Marvin Hagler-Mustafa Hamsho in October 1984, Jake received a tremendous ovation.

"It made me feel good," said LaMotta. "The reason for that is that the American people, and maybe the whole world, are for the underdog. They figure I was the underdog."

Shortly after the interview, *The Ring* held a luncheon In Manhattan where LaMotta was officially inducted. He wrote about it in the final chapter of his second book, *Raging Bull II* (ghosted by Chris Anderson and Sharon McGehee).

"And now, 36 years after I win the title, I finally get inducted into *The Ring* magazine's Boxing Hall of Fame … I guess it took a more forgiving generation to recognize my accomplishments in the ring in spite of what I had to do get my rightful shot at the title.

"I stood outside the small midtown restaurant having a smoke before I went inside to accept my plaque. It wasn't the Hall of Fame room at Madison Square Garden, but it was good enough for me."

The decision to give LaMotta his due wasn't universally popular, but five years later he was among the inaugural class of the newly opened International Boxing Hall of Fame in Canastota, New York.

For all the pain and misery it can cause, boxing is one place where even a man like Jake LaMotta can find a measure of redemption.

THE PEOPLE'S FIGHTERS

THE LEGENDS OF CUBAN BOXING

ORIGINALLY PUBLISHED BY ESPN.COM, JUNE 12, 2018

FIVE MEN SIT around a small table on a beach in Havana, Cuba, talking and playing dominoes. There is a relaxed seriousness to their conversation as they speak of their role in a sociopolitical experiment that has shaped their lives and the lives of their fellow Cubans.

These men are not social scientists, politicians or soldiers. They're boxers who, in their youth, brought glory to their country through the strength of their fists and the intensity of their pride. Five living witnesses to the rise of the Cuban school of boxing, a product of the Cuban Revolution that became the dominant force in amateur boxing.

The men and their conversations serve as bookends to *The People's Fighters: Teofilo Stevenson and the Legend of Cuban Boxing*, the Olympic Channel's new documentary, produced by Frank Marshall and directed and narrated by Peter Berg.

"It's the story of Cuba seen through the lens of boxing, which became a much bigger story than just about boxing," said Marshall, producer of such modern classics as *Back to the Future*, *Raiders of the Lost Ark* and *The Color Purple*.

The dominoes-playing caballeros are Emilio Correa Sr., Jorge Hernandez, Armando Martinez, Jose Gomez, and Rolando Garbey. They are 65, 63, 56, 59 and 70 years old, respectively. Except for Garbey, they all won Olympic gold. The elder statesman of the group won silver in 1968, bronze in 1976, and eventually became a Team Cuba coach.

The sculpted bodies of their youth are gone, replaced with wrinkles, gray hair and grandpa physiques. Even so, the fighting spirit that once made them national heroes still smolders inside, as does the pride in their homeland and accomplishments.

These wise old heads, along with other Cuban voices, anchor the film and provide a first-hand and candid account of the turmoil and triumph that has been their lives.

"That was the greatest thing about it," Marshall said. "After being closed off for so long, they really had an opportunity to speak their minds. That was the best thing about it. It was wonderful. Ten years ago, I could not have gone there."

Berg, whose directing credits include *Friday Night Lights*, *Lone Survivor* and *Patriots Day*, juxtaposed footage of both boxing and the Cuban Revolution, creating a montage indicative of how integral they were to each another.

Tanks rolling through the street of Old Havana; young boxers toiling in the gym; troops wading ashore, rifles held high above their heads; a Cuban boxer kissing a gold medal he won in a foreign land; Castro greeting him at the airport upon his return—all signposts of a time and place gone by, when lessons should have been learned but were not.

There's even a weird clip of Castro, a notorious publicity hound, lighting a cigar for ABC Sports' Keith Jackson at the end of an amateur tournament in Havana.

That was during a brief honeymoon period, shortly after the overthrow of America-backed dictator Fulgencio Batista in 1959 and before the Bay of Pigs fiasco in 1961. Then came the Cuban Missile Crisis and the severing of diplomatic ties between the island nation and Uncle Sam.

Seeing the rapturous reception Soviet leader Leonid Brezhnev received on his arrival in Cuba is a reminder of how hot the Cold War really was, and how sports were often a proxy battlefield.

Thanks to considerable support from the Soviet Union, Cuba continued to churn out high quality boxers regardless of the political climate and American embargo. Chief among them was Stevenson, a handsome 6-foot-5 heavyweight with lights-out power in his right hand. He was the perfect centerpiece for Castro's goal of turning Cuba into an athletic juggernaut.

Those who have not seen the freakish power in Stevenson's right hand are in for a treat. The documentary celebrates his dominance with footage of Teofilo dispatching U.S. hopefuls Duane Bobick, Tyrell Biggs and John Tate with alarming ease.

Rather than the thundering herd of a Joe Frazier assault, Stevenson's finishing touch was as precise as a Zen archer's arrow. Frequently a single blow was all he needed. The men he beat to win three consecutive Olympic gold medals (1972, 1976, 1980) knew the right hand was coming but couldn't do anything about it.

Stevenson and Castro made quite an odd couple. Fidel was El Capitan, a bearded firebrand and leader of the Cuban Revolution, a mesmerizing extrovert with messianic leanings. Teofilo was El Gran Campeón, a humble man born into a family of modest means in Puerto Padre. He had smoldering good looks and was able to smite his enemies without a smidgen of hate in his heart.

"We all compared ourselves to him" said Hernandez. "I wanted to be like Teofilo Stevenson."

"He was a blood brother to all Cubans," said Correa Sr.

One of major strengths of *The People's Fighters* is allowing the story to be told from the Cuban point of view. Berg's narration is smooth and informative but never presumptuous. The opinions are those of the people on the ground, the ones that count, the real stars of the film.

The United States considered Cuba's cozy relationship with the Soviet Union a threat, but things looked different to Cubans desperate for the bare necessities.

"The Soviets lent us a hand and respected Cuba's sovereignty," said journalist Rudens Temba. "The Soviet Union was Cuba's best friend in the 1960s, 1970s and 1980s. Its economic support allowed the country to survive."

The film also offers diverse viewpoints about the much-touted match between Stevenson and Muhammad Ali. It was a hot topic after the Cuban's success at the 1976 Olympics, but never got past the talking stage.

When the Soviet Union collapsed in 1991, Cuba's economic pipeline was turned off, and the country was plunged into a depression they call the "Special Period." It was a situation that eventually led to many of Cuba's finest boxers leaving their homeland to seek political asylum and turn professional. Some went to Europe, but most found their way to the U.S. where they have met with mixed fortunes.

Stevenson died in 2012 due to a heart attack at the age of 60, a beloved hero honored almost as much for rejecting the lure of capitalism as for his ring exploits. His heavyweight successor, Felix Savon, also won three Olympic gold medals and opted to stay in Cuba, rejecting lucrative offers to fight Mike Tyson.

"Sometimes it's hard for somebody not from Cuba to understand that back then we all fought out of conviction for revolutionary principles," said Juan Hernandez Sierra, two-time Olympic silver medalist. "We had high ideas."

Today's ideas, personified by Julio César La Cruz, are different.

"Personally, my role models are boxers who, for one reason or another, are not in Cuba." said La Cruz, winner of light heavyweight gold at the 2016 Rio Olympics. "Back in the day we competed for honor, for our colors, for our flag above anything else. Nowadays people think differently—and, of course, making money is good."

Money remains a problem for the old champions on the beach. In their time they were the best at what they did, now they struggle to survive on an inadequate monthly stipend.

"It doesn't cover the cost of life," Martinez said.

"It's not enough, but without it we'd be screwed," Gomez said.

The Lara cars (1950 vintage American vehicles brought to Cuba before the revolution) the government gave them are plain worn out.

"From the bottom of my heart I can say that I love my car because it is a good car," Gomez said. "But it is tired. It can't fight anymore."

The houses they received are also in a state of disrepair, one so decrepit the roof recently collapsed.

"We are not criticizing the revolution," Martinez said. "We love and defend the revolution, but there are certain things that could have been done differently."

In closing segments of the documentary, film footage of the old boxers in their primes are shown, followed by shots of them mimicking the way they looked back then. For a few fleeting moments they were the people's fighters once again. And then it was time to go.

As they walked away with backs to the camera, some of them arm in arm, you knew we would never see their likes again.

———

EPILOGUE: On 30 September 2018, Felix Savón, 51, was reportedly arrested in Cuba on accusation of raping a 12-year-old boy.

IRON MIKE

WELCOME TO THE TYSON ERA

CAN ANYBODY BEAT HIM?

ORIGINALLY PUBLISH IN *THE RING*, MARCH 1987.

ONE CAME AWAY from Mike Tyson's second-round annihilation on Trevor Berbick feeling you had seen a pivotal episode in boxing history, a match to be remembered, not for the fight itself, for there was none, but for the historical significance of the moment. Like Dempsey's cruel demolition of Willard, Louis's battering of Braddock, and Marciano's come from behind KO over Walcott, Tyson knockout of Berbick ushered in a new boxing era—the Tyson Era.

What went down at the Las Vegas Hilton Center seemed more like an execution than a boxing match. Tyson disposed of Berbick with all the subtlety of a slaughterhouse worker wielding a maul. So precise was his violent dismissal of the WBC titleholder, the question on everyone's lips was, "Can anybody beat him?"

It is a query that could keep arenas full and television ratings soaring for a long time to come. For Tyson not only wins, he does so in a manner that stirs something dark in mankind's soul. Call it bloodlust if you will, but any way you say it, it spells box-office bonanza.

Although few were foolhardy enough to pick Berbick to win,

most observers agreed that Trevor would give the 20-year-old dread-
nought a bruising welcome to the championship ranks before
succumbing to the drive and enthusiasm of youth. But the "Fighting
Preacher" didn't have a prayer. Tyson reduced his participation to a
cameo role, a mere prop in a drama that saw "Iron Mike" become the
youngest fighter in boxing history to win even partial recognition as
the world heavyweight champion.

If there are still some who doubt Tyson's authenticity, they
belong among those who believe the world is flat and the moon
made of green cheese.

With the first step easily accomplished, Tyson is well on his way
to the undisputed heavyweight title. By the time you read this, he
will be back in Las Vegas prepping for the next step in his quest.
Once again, the fight will be hosted by the Las Vegas Hilton, but in a
specially constructed outdoor stadium large enough (15,000 seats) to
accommodate Tyson's growing legion of fans.

The near-capacity crowd all 8,743 at the posh Hilton Center was
star-studded with celebrities from all walks of life. High-priced ticket
holders rubbed elbows with the likes of Kirk Douglas and Mr. T,
while those in the bleachers craned their necks to catch a glimpse of
fistic nobility ranging from Muhammad Ali to Hector Camacho, the
only fighter who drew boos when introduced.

Such distractions were essential during the quintessential Don
King undercard, a travesty that threatened to set new standards for
diabolical matchmaking.

The challenger made his entrance first, ducking between the
ropes as the crowd roared its approval. For the first time in his career,
Tyson was not completely bare-chested. He wore a towel over the
upper portion of his torso but remains faithful to his trademark no-
socks look. He wore black trunks in defiance of the Nevada commission, which upheld the champion's prerogative to pick the color of
his trunks. Berbick chose black in an attempt at one-upmanship, but
Tyson accepted the $5,000 fine and also wore black trunks.

Although Tyson was obviously the fans' favorite, Berbick also
had support. A smattering of yellow and green Jamaican flags could

be seen waving bravely throughout the arena as Trevor made his way to the ring. His incongruous calf-high black socks prompted one ringsider to note that, "Between them, there was not a decent pair of hose."

Ring announcer Chuck Hull—he of the snazzy tuxedo and Conway Twitty hairdo—introduced the combatants, referee Mills Lane gave them their last-minute instructions, and at the sound of the first bell, the fight was on.

As expected, Tyson attack immediately, throwing himself into the fray with vehemence. It was, however, a more controlled fury than Mike had displayed in the past. He seemed to have achieved a new level of discipline at exactly the moment he needed it most.

The scheduled 12-round bout was only seconds old when Tyson connected with his first punch. His hand speed was astonishing for a man his size, and he had a little trouble beating the taller Berbick to the punch.

"People talk about Mike's punching power," said Jim Jacobs, his co-manager. "But it's his speed. Nobody ever sees the punch coming."

At first, Berbick seemed to absorb Tyson's bombs well. There was even a brief cause for hope among his followers when he hit Tyson with a clubbing right to the head. But the rally was short lived. After a quick clinch Tyson resumed control, connecting with an assortment of blows to the head.

Near the end of the first round, Tyson landed a short left hook to the head that sent Trevor stumbling backward across the ring in obvious distress. Berbick survived the moment, but the respite was fleeting. Tyson was closing in again when the round-ending bell interrupted his assault.

Berbick wobbled to his corner with a quizzical look on his face. Never the most mobile of heavyweights, he had opted to slug it out with Tyson, a decision he would regret.

"I made a silly mistake," Berbick said. "I tried to prove my manhood with him in the early rounds."

Unfortunately for Berbick, there were to be no later rounds in which to make amends for his rocky start. Tyson had been training for this fight for most of his life and had vowed to leave the ring either champion or dead.

"I refused to get hurt. I refuse to get knocked down. I refused to lose," he declared. "I refuse to leave the ring alive without the belt."

Against such fanatical determination, Berbick was practically helpless. In the second, Tyson immediately picked up where he had left off the previous round.

There was something terrifying about the way Tyson went about his work. It was like watching a jaguar take down its prey. There was no hesitation or doubt, just an explosion of violence, the outcome never in doubt.

As Berbick frantically sought shelter along the ropes, a particularly nasty right to the noggin sent him crashing to the canvas like a man whose legs had been jerked from under him by an invisible rope attached to his ankles.

Showing more valor than common sense, Berbick quickly scrambled to his feet by the count of three. As Lane administered the mandatory eight count, Berbick stared blankly into the referee's face, the picture of a wounded animal awaiting the hunter's final bullet.

Tyson displayed remarkable control going for the finish. Instead of struggling for punching room when Berbick wrapped him in a series of bear hugs, Mike patiently waited for the referee to do his job. Then, with his hands free, he lashed out with lethal concentration, nailing his adversary with the kind of combinations unseen since Joe Louis ruled the heavyweight domain.

"I was throwing, what can you say, hydrogen bombs," said Tyson. "Every punch with murderous intentions."

Then the inevitable happened.

Tyson sank a right into Berbick's left kidney and followed with an economical left hook that nailed Berbick high on the temple, just in back of his ear. There was a split-second pause as the shockwave traveled from Burbank's cerebrum to his legs, then, the circuit complete, he toppled over on to his back.

There followed a tragic-comic tableau that bore testimony, not only to Tysons punching power but also to Berbick's courage. The stricken champion knew he had to try to regain his feet, but his legs simply would not obey the message his brain was sending them. On his first attempt to rise, he flopped over sideways and fell partially through the ropes, he tried again and floundered grotesquely in the opposite direction, finally coming to rest in the arms of Lane, who stopped the fight 2:35 into the second round.

Flush with victory, Tyson was quick to pay tribute to the late Cus D'Amato, who rescued him from reform school and molded him into the kind of fighter capable of winning a piece of the heavyweight championship after only a 20-month apprenticeship as a professional prizefighter.

"Without Cus, this never could have happened," Tyson said.

When someone wanted to know what D'Amato, who maintained Mike was a future champion from the beginning of their relationship, might've said had he lived to see his prophecy fulfilled.

"He would be downstairs making my breakfast as always," Tyson said, "and I'd be afraid to go down for all the criticism."

We will never know what faults, if any, D'Amato would have found with his protégé's title-winning performance, but Berbick was certainly in no position to search for imperfections.

"You saw it. I fought a stupid fight," Berbick said. "He is a very hard, very sharp puncher. I never saw the punch that put me down. I think he has a very good chance to become the undisputed champion."

To his credit, Berbick did not use his legal problems as an excuse. On the Tuesday before the fight, Trevor and his lawyers spent five hours in court seeking to forestall a Nevada judge from attaching $495,000 of his $2.1 million purse. After several days of wrangling, judge Dale Guy ordered the writ of attachment, but also ordered the plaintive, promoter Thomas Pendergast of Texas, to put up a bond covering the same amount until another hearing could be held to settle the dispute.

Tyson's problem, if indeed it can be construed as a problem at this early stage, is of a different sort. Less than three hours after his triumph, fans were lined up 20 deep at the door of Mike's invitation-only victory party. Security was already having great difficulty controlling the mini-mob when a cry went up.

"He's coming out!"

As the new WBC titleholder emerged from the celebration, well-wishers and media types immediately surrounded him. Mike squinted in the blinding glare of the television lights as a reporter shoved a microphone in his face. Two burly companions did their best to protect him from the crush of humanity, but it took a flying wedge of the hotel security guards to guide him to safety.

At this juncture, there doesn't seem to be a heavyweight around capable of defeating Tyson. But from now on fighting will probably be the easiest part of his life. Fame and fortune has ruined many fighters, and some cynics, desperate for a pessimistic angle, hinted it also might be Tyson's downfall. But Mike shrugged off such notions as easily as he vanquished Berbick.

"I am the youngest heavyweight champion, and I am going to be the oldest," said Tyson.

———

EPILOGUE: The Tyson-Berbick fight took place on November 22, 1986. Berbick, who fought on until 2000, was living in Jamaica when he was bludgeoned to death by Harold Berbick (Trevor's nephew) and Kenton Gordon in October 2006. Both were convicted of the killing (over a land dispute) and sent to prison.

"I HATE EVERYBODY"

MIKE TYSON'S JAILHOUSE INTERVIEW

ORIGINALLY PUBLISHED IN *THE RING*, WINTER 1994

THE INDIANA YOUTH CENTER is located off Route 40 in the town of Plainfield, about 25 miles outside of Indianapolis. There's a cornfield on the other side of the road, and except for the barbed wire topped fence and guard towers, it looks more like a rural high school than a penitentiary. The IYC also happens to be the residence of America's most famous prison inmate this side of O. J. Simpson.

Michael Gerald Tyson, former heavyweight champion of the world and self-proclaimed baddest man on the planet, has been incarcerated here since March 1993, when judge Patricia Gifford sentence him to six years for the 1991 rape of an 18-year-old beauty pageant contestant. Under Indiana law, Tyson must serve half of his time before becoming eligible for parole. Despite a series of appeals on his behalf by high-powered attorney Alan Dershowitz and rumors of impending deals to spring him, inmate number 922335 remains behind bars. Excluding any unforeseen his occurrences, parole date is May 9, 1995.

Although he was no longer champion at the time of his conviction, Tyson was still widely regarded as the best heavyweight in the world. As far as the public was concerned, his 10th-round knockout loss to Buster Douglas in February 1990 was an aberration, more the result of Tyson's wavering commitment than a genuine erosion of skill. To millions of Tyson devotees around the world, it was just a matter of time before he regained the title he'd squandered. A scheduled bout with then-champion Evander Holyfield was scrapped when Tyson, suffered a rib injury. It is a foregone conclusion, however, that upon his release, "Iron Mike" would have absolutely no problem obtaining a fight (or fights) with any and all claimants to the throne.

The public's appetite has increased, not diminished since he's been locked up. Even though he hasn't fought since June 28, 1991, when he won a 12-round decision over Razor Ruddock, Tyson is still the most famous boxer in the world, with the potential to earn untold millions of dollars.

Yet despite his notoriety, and despite the fact both his ring career and personal life have been scrutinized ad nauseam, Tyson remains an enigma. Is he a barbaric street thug who temperately managed to channel his anti-social attitude into a sensational boxing career? Or is he a lost soul, still searching for love and nurturing he was deprived of as a child growing up on the mean streets of Brooklyn?

Since he's been incarcerated, not much light has been shed on the inner workings of Tyson. The handful of interviews he's granted haven't revealed anything new, and when *The Ring* received permission to visit him in late-August, it was with the understanding it would be a no-holds-barred session. As Tyson put it, "100 years from now, what Mike Tyson was thinking at this time in his life, they can find out by reading *The Ring*."

I met privately with Tyson in a conference room, far removed from the prison population. No guards, no lawyer, just two guys and a tape recorder. Tyson initially seemed a little shy and almost whispered his answers. It wasn't long, however, before he relaxed, and conversation, and occasional laughter, flowed freely.

Tyson maintained eye contact throughout the 90-minute interview and sometimes tapped me on the thigh, as if to make sure I was playing close attention. No topic was taboo; Tyson was unremittingly candid and didn't duck a single question. The result was a shockingly honest look at boxing's most significant figure since Muhammad Ali.

Prison changes people, some for the best, many more for the worse. During our conversation, Tyson, 28, gave the impression of a man looking past the chaos and controversy that has surrounded him, has seen the brutal truth, and is ready to deal with it head-on.

Though Tyson frequently insisted he trusts no one, he paused before leaving the interview room, hand on the doorknob, and looked back over his shoulder.

"Write a good story," he said. "I trusted you."

What better way to honor that request than to let Tyson's own words speak for him.

———

The Ring: Like Muhammad Ali, your boxing career has been suspended for approximately three years during your prime. Do you see any parallels between Ali and yourself?

Tyson: There was only one Ali. There is no parallel. Ali committed himself to something for a reason, and I did mine by making bad choices, not being careful enough, not protecting myself.

The Ring: Ali fought in a different style after he returned from his exile. Will the time you spent away from boxing change your style or affect the way you fight?

Tyson: No, I train every day. I feel better now than at any time in my career. I'm not saying that will make me a better fighter, but I believe it should. I run about eight miles a day. I do my exercises, my shadow boxing, all that I can do.

The Ring: You look pretty light. How much do you weigh right now?

Tyson: Around 214 pounds.

The Ring: You unified the heavyweight title at a time when boxing desperately needed an undisputed champion. Now the title is split again. How much damage do you think splintered titles and the proliferation of weight classes has done to the sport?

Tyson: We have too many weight divisions now, too many titles. That's because boxing has become big business, and that doesn't allow people to become the best possible fighter they can. You no longer have to work as hard to as you used to become champion. You don't even know who the champion is. At one particular time you didn't even have to be a fight fan to know who the champions were because there were only seven of them. Now, you've got 16, 20 of 'em. It's incredible.

The Ring: If I could wave a magic wand and make you czar of boxing, what would be the one change you would make to improve the sport?

Tyson: Boxers would have a pension—a percentage of their money would go for pensions. Boxing is the only sport where anybody can get involved and make money. A fighter, in general, has no other way of making money except to fight. It can take a guy of low circum-stances and put him in the high ranks. But on the other hand, if a guy abuses his skills and neglects them, he can lose the title.

The Ring: When you start fighting again, would you be willing to give a percentage of your purse toward the pension fund?

Tyson: Only if we can organize. Fighters are not educated, academi-cally. We come from a great fraternity of individuals, the Louises, the Nelsons, the Dempseys, the Jefferies. This is a great fraternity of men, and we continue to be decimated. As time goes by, boxing becomes more and more in the doldrums. We have to find something to do because we're going to be extinct. It won't be the American Medical Association—we are doing it to ourselves. People are greedy and destroy themselves. We have greedy bastards, man, some rotten sons of bitches.

The Ring: There have been certain people who have played an important part in both your life and career. Let's play a variation on the word-association game: I'll give you a name and you respond with the first thing that pops into your head. Here goes: Cus D'Amato.

Tyson: An incredible teacher, an incredible man. I believe Mike Tyson and Cus D'Amato had great chemistry. That's the reason Mike Tyson was the fighter he was. He had great chemistry with his trainer, more so than Cus' other fighters that became successful, like Floyd Peterson and Jose Torres. I had more malice in my temperament, and I took orders well. When Cus told me what to do, I had confidence in him and executed what he told me to do.

The Ring: Camille Ewald (Tyson's surrogate mother).

Tyson: A loving lady. A lot brighter than people give her credit for. Everybody was always trying to manipulate her, especially the press. She just had a good heart, and when somebody comes to the door and wants a story, she's not rude, she doesn't fight back. That's because she's used to having Cus to fight for her. She is very kind, and people try to take advantage of her because she's a very old lady.

The Ring: Jim Jacobs.

Tyson: A very different individual, very mysterious. You never knew anything about him. He lived his whole life a secret. No one knew his situation. He always played the role and never got caught up in scandal, because if there was a scandal, you have to be investigated.

He never allowed himself to be in that position. No one ever knew him.

The Ring: Did you know him?

Tyson: No, I never knew him.

The Ring: Bill Cayton.

Tyson: Bill Cayton is crude and sophistic at the same time. His main objective is Bill Cayton. I don't take it personally, like I once did when my feelings were hurt. But I put myself in that position by trusting him.

The Ring: Kevin Rooney.

Tyson: Kevin Rooney? *(long pause)* This is a difficult one. We used to have a lot of good times. It's sad it had to end the way it did. I was doing my thing. He was doing his own thing. He got caught between something he shouldn't have been caught between. He believed he had more power than he actually did. He believed he was in a situation to stay forever. But that wasn't necessarily true. I was only with him because of Cus. He doesn't understand that Bill Cayton and Jim Jacobs didn't want him to be my trainer. They wanted Eddie Futch to train me. But I was loyal to him because I knew if Kevin didn't train me, what else was he gonna do. He wasn't that successful as a fighter.

The Ring: Steve Lott (An employee of Jacobs and Cayton and one-time roommate of Tyson).

Tyson: Very cordial, a very diplomatic kind of guy. But Steve is a businessman. I like Steve a great deal. We all have our own little way about what we want in life. Steve attacks what he wants in life, and I respect him for that. But sometimes there are complications. I'm not saying there are now, and you never know what will happen when I get out. But I would hate to be on the bad side of him because I really like Steve. I really like him.

The Ring: Jose Torres.

Tyson: An opportunist. For some reason he never liked me, though he pretended to be my friend for many years. I had a lot of respect for him, and I couldn't believe he did the things he did. Then again, I always felt he envied me. It still hurts today that he wrote a book about me that was nothing but lies. I still haven't said anything disrespectful about him because I believe I'm better than that. But he hurt my feelings.

The Ring: HBO is making a movie about you based on Torres' book. Do you have any thoughts about that?

Tyson: Well, the movie is a bunch of lies, and that's what Jose wrote, a bunch of lies. He asked me one time, and I said, "Yes, you can write a book about me." I was a young kid, 20, 21 years old. He discussed something about pain, and how I like to hurt women, which wasn't necessarily true. I said that when I was younger, I loved to inflict pain. He walked around with a tape recorder trying to discuss these things that were damaging. But I wasn't talking about women. When I was fighting, I wanted to hurt the guy. I wanted to break him up. And I got this from the old fighters because they said what they were going to do to a guy. And I'm living back in their time, and I'm not thinking about having some kind of fear for the media. I'm not thinking about becoming a corporation and making commercials. I don't give a damn about Pepsi-Cola. I think about Joe Gans and Battling Nelson. Those were guys I really admired. If those guys told me, "Fuck Pepsi," I would say "Fuck Pepsi." That's what I was into back then. I wasn't thinking about how my life depends on some corporation sponsoring me. That's not where I'm at.

The Ring: So you're saying when you gave Torres permission to write a book about you, you were still kind of naïve?

Tyson: Very much so. I trusted these guys. I never knew the things he did. I never knew that at one time he was going around saying that Cus stole his money. These guys, Floyd Paterson and Torres, did things to Cus I never even knew existed. I understand that things happen, just like with me and Kevin. But Cus always talked about these guys highly and about what great fighters they were. Then, when I found out from writers and other people, I thought, *Holy Moses, Cus never said bad things about these guys.*

The Ring: Robin Givens.

Tyson: We were two young people who weren't supposed to be married in the first place. We weren't ready for marriage, and we got caught up in the whole situation of being who we were. She got caught up in being who she was because she was with me. I don't have any hard feelings for Robin. We were two kids. Things happen. She did things I truly didn't like and don't agree with, but what can I say? When it's all said and done, we're all dead anyway. I don't want to be her friend. I don't want to hug and kiss and be cordial with her, but I have not anything bad or good to say about her.

The Ring: Don King.

Tyson: Don King is a good man. Don King is a businessman. Don King sometimes gets caught up in being so suspicious of everybody. I think that sometimes he even distrusts his friends. I think that just the life he lives. I don't think he trusts me totally.

The Ring: Is he paranoid?

Tyson: Paranoid! Anybody in the boxing business deserves to be paranoid. You have no other choice because being in boxing is like being in the mob. I'm your friend, and then tomorrow I'm your enemy. It depends on what you say and do.

The Ring: Gregory Garrison (special prosecutor in Tyson's rape case).

Tyson: Gregory Garrison is an opportunist. But I was in a situation where I couldn't win. It's like I'm fighting you and your whole family. You and I are fighting in your backyard with the whole family—and they have shotguns. And you expect to win? Give me a break.

The Ring: Vincent Fuller (Tyson's defense attorney)

Tyson: You know what I think? I think these guys really believe I raped this chick. I think I had to convince them that I was innocent. It was a disgusting display of legal tactics. I didn't know anything about legal stuff. The only thing I knew was that Don said these were good guys. I didn't know anything. I didn't know about F. Lee Bailey. We're blind to everything in this world until it happens to us. If you miss a light or your brakes go on you, and you hit someone and kill them, you were blind that could ever happen to you. You depend on your car. You say, "My car never did this to me before." Then it lets you down one time. But now you're not blind. You're in jail and you *know* anything can happen to you.

The Ring: Patricia Gifford (judge in the rape trial)

Tyson: I think this is her claim to fame. She wants everybody to know she put Mike Tyson in jail. She could be a judge for 20 years, and the only thing people know about her is that she put Mike Tyson away.

The Ring: One gets the clear impression that you still think you got a raw deal. Is that an accurate description of how you feel?

Tyson: Absolutely, man. Everyone fucked me. If you want to get right down to the nitty-gritty, the judge fucked me because she doesn't have anything better to do but put a famous guy, who she knows is innocent, in jail. If I was guilty, she would have given me 60 years. If all 12 jurors felt I was guilty, I should have been given the maximum.

The Ring: Do you feel that racism played a role in your conviction?

Tyson: Man, racism is just so prevalent worldwide. Me being who I am, a black man, I said a lot of things that irritated a lot of people at one time in my life. I said things, white people this, black people that. This was an opportunity to dump on me, and if they believe I'm their enemy, they should dump on me, because if they're my enemy I will kill them, too. Okay?

The Ring: Your life has been a series of sensational ups and downs. You went from juvenile delinquent to heavyweight champion of the world. For a while, you had everything—fame, money, beautiful women, and the adulation of millions. Then came your conviction and incarceration. As you look back at this point in your life, what is your biggest regret?

Tyson: I would have never fallen in love.

The Ring: You think falling in love is bad?

Tyson: For me, it probably is. I've never been successful in relationships where you have a deep infatuation for that person.

The Ring: Besides the obvious, what has been the hardest part of being incarcerated?

Tyson: I don't know. It's so crazy, but I think I could do 100 years without flinching.

The Ring: Doesn't the boredom get to you?

Tyson: I used to think it would. When I first came, I used to say, "It's killing me. It's killing me. I want to see my family." But when it really comes down to it, I really don't have anybody I want to go to. I've been alone all my life, and every time I did accept someone in my life, they've fucked me. *(laughs)* Who do I really want to go to? I'll always take care of Camille. Now, she's 90 years old. Come on, odds are not on her side. As long as she's all right and my little daughter is all right, I don't give a damn about anything. Me? My life is useless. I don't care a damn about my life. That's why I'm so successful, because I don't care.

The Ring: Despite your tough-guy image, you're still a human being, experiencing the same emotions as the rest of us. Has there ever been a time when you've been in prison when you broke down and cried?

Tyson: I'd never do that.

The Ring: Why is that? Don't you ever feel sorry for yourself?

Tyson: No, I can't do that. I just feel that everybody is against me. I try not to let myself get angry, and if I cried, I'd get angry with myself.

The Ring: You've been studying the Islamic religion. Has that been a comfort to you?

Tyson: It's helped me a great deal. You know, if it wasn't for Islam, I don't know what I'd be into. I would become part of society in this place. I'd probably be in here with these damned faggots, getting high. Man, I'm telling you, it's a helluva world in here. It's a world within a world.

The Ring: How had Islam helped you?

Tyson: It's given me a great outlook on life. I have to appreciate where I've been, where I haven't been. I could have been somewhere worse. I could have been in Attica. I just praise the Lord that I'm not dead.

The Ring: What about your GED examination? When are you scheduled to take the retest?

Tyson: I don't know. You know, I believe I passed the first time.

The Ring: Are you saying you think the result was rigged?

Tyson: Come on, please. They'd let everyone in here go before they'd let me go. They would keep me in here alone.

The Ring: So you don't think you'll bother taking it again?

Tyson: I may take it. I'm not caught up in no damned GED. I read all these damn books and they drove me out of my mind. I must have read over 100 books. Friedrich Nietzsche, Tolstoy, Alexandre Dumas. It drove me nuts. I'm out of my mind from reading all that shit. It was good stuff, but I never looked at things from that kind of perspective. Nietzsche told me there is no God, there's just super-man. I don't want to hear that crap. Tolstoy told me women ain't shit. Machiavelli told me don't trust nobody. I know that already! *(much laughter)* Don't tell me. I know this.

The Ring: You spent a lot of money on legal fees, unsuccessfully appealing your rape conviction. Do you wish you'd kept the money in the bank?

Tyson: I did the time anyway, right? I'm not tripping on the money. I don't give a damn about money. I just wish I could have given the money to someone who could have used it.

The Ring: There's been a lot of speculation your financial status. A lot of people think you're broke. Is it true?

Tyson: I'm not broke. I'm not Mike Tyson rich, but I can do what I want. I can still buy things I want in prison. I can send money to someone in another country if I want them to come see me.

The Ring: Because you're Mike Tyson, you have the potential to make millions of dollars as soon as you are out of jail and start fighting again. Other inmates won't have the same opportunity to make money. So aren't you really in a different situation from most of the guys in here?

Tyson: Well, if I was that guy and I got this case, I would have got 60 years and nobody would have given a fuck. The world we live in, man, it's incredible. But it's the only world we have.

The Ring: Overall, how would you describe the way the media has treated you throughout your career?

Tyson: They took good shots at me. They got me pretty good. But I'm not an animal. I'm a human being. You, for one, said that. I love my family. I love my daughter. I'm not a child molester. I don't molester my daughter. I don't beat women. A woman may say I beat her, but have you seen Robin Given's face caved in? I hit Mitch Green in a street fight, and you saw what happened to his face. Robin never had no bruises.

The Ring: Is it important to you how the general public feels about you?

Tyson: I don't want anyone to love me. I just want them to respect me. Nobody comes into my face and calls me an asshole or a jerk and violates me without being violated back in return.

The Ring: There has been a lot of speculation about your relationship with Don King. Some people have suggested he filled a void in your life—a need for a father figure. How do you respond to such psychoanalysis?

Tyson: Are any of the people saying that psychiatrists?

The Ring: No, most of them are sportswriters.

Tyson: No, most of them are assholes. *(more laughter)* How can you psychoanalyze somebody? Your job is to write about what you see, not write what you think. They should lose their jobs. I never had a father. So how's he supposed to be my father? What would I know about a father-son relationship?

The Ring: Because you never had that kind of relationship, you were looking for it.

Tyson: That's not true. Okay?

The Ring: Will King be your promoter when you return to the ring? And will his recent indictment for insurance fraud influence your decision.

Tyson: Nothing is going to influence any decision I make, regardless. If I choose him to be my promoter, he's gonna be my promoter. I like Don.

The Ring: When you are released from prison, will you jump right back into boxing or tale some time to relax and hang out?

Tyson: Hey, I've been relaxing for three years. I don't need any more relaxing.

The Ring: There has also been a lot of conjecture about who will train you. Can you give us any insight as to who will get the job?

Tyson: I hate everybody, man. I don't know. I hate everybody because he'll train me today and train another guy to fight me tomorrow. There is no loyalty in this business. This is like the mob, like the highest paid gun. Who gives a fuck about Mike Tyson? Gimme me a break, all right. Who actually cares about my well-being? The people who do are probably not capable of training me.

The Ring: Do you have any comments about the job Teddy Atlas, one of your amateur trainers, did help Michael Moorer win the heavyweight title?

Tyson: Did he help him? Do you believe he helped him a lot?

The Ring: I think he did in the motivational sense. I think he pushed him.

Tyson: But how? It's very difficult to say because the only way you could actually help somebody win is if you're in there throwing punches. The guy always had it in him. I'm sure he would have won it with another trainer. It's just that the other trainer didn't give him the proper insight.

The Ring: But if you give a fighter insight, isn't that helping him?

Tyson: To a certain extent, but trainers get more credit than they deserve. Trainers are glorified cheerleaders, the majority of them, anyway.

The Ring: Are there any active trainers you respect?

Tyson: I don't disrespect anyone. They just get more credit and more money than they deserve.

The Ring: Michael Moorer could very well be one of your future opponents. What is your opinion of him as a fighter?

Tyson: I don't know. I've only seen him fight once or twice. And if I'm in my best shape and he was in his best shape, he couldn't win.

The Ring: Former champion Riddick Bowe and WBC champion Lennox Lewis are soon scheduled to fight each other. Who do you like in that fight?

Tyson: I don't know. I used to like Bowe, but not with the extra weight.

The Ring: What about Lewis? Have you seen him fight?

Tyson: Yeah, I've seen him a couple of times. He looks pretty good. I don't know what the competition is like out there. Sometimes we can think we are better than we really are. I might get out there and be a disaster. I don't think I will be, but I might.

The Ring: Do you have a timetable for your comeback? Will you be ready for a title fight right away or will you want few tune-ups?

Tyson: I just want to relax for just a split-second. Not a month. I just want to relax for a second and think. I'm in here, and it's a totally different atmosphere than it is outside. And I just don't know what to expect yet. I've got to get my life together.

The Ring: What, beside the passing of time, is the biggest difference between the Mike Tyson who was imprisoned almost three years ago and Mike Tyson today?

Tyson: The Mike Tyson who was not in prison and was out on the street being champion loved by everybody, thought everybody was nice. Now, Mike Tyson hates the world. That's just a fact. I hate everybody. I know they say, "No, you can't hate the world, don't be bitter." But I just hate everybody. Well, the majority, maybe 99 percent.

The Ring: Do you feel that you owe boxing fans anything?

Tyson: I'm gonna owe them until the day I die. You always owe those guys. But they don't like you, anyway.

The Ring: It's kind of strange you would say that, because while the establishment put you in prison, there's been a lot of support from the fans. Most of them never turned their backs on you. Doesn't that make you feel good?

Tyson: They do that because they feel sorry for somebody's circumstances. I don't want them feeling sorry for me. I know who I am and what I am. This doesn't trip me out. I understand that people are interested in me for what I do. And they should not expect anything else out of me.

HOW DYNAMITE LIT THE FUSE
OF BOXING'S GREATEST UPSET

ORIGINALLY PUBLISHED BY ESPN.COM, FEBRUARY 11, 2015

"The worst misfortune that can happen to an ordinary man is to have an extraordinary father."

— Austin O'Malley

THE TEENAGER WATCHED with a mixture of terror and awe as his father teetered on the edge of disaster one moment and the threshold of victory the next. He'd seen his father box before. But this was something altogether different, a Rocky movie come to life—the violence so surreal that both the fighters and the crowd were caught up in a trance-like frenzy that seemed to have a life of its own.

As fortunes fluctuated wildly from one extreme to another, the son was sure of only one thing: His father would not quit. How could he? He was Bill "Dynamite" Douglas, a stone-cold badass whose tough love had already set his son on a course that would lead to arguably the greatest upset in boxing history.

Bill Douglas was already 37 and past his prime by the time he fought Matthew Saad Muhammad (then Matthew Franklin) at the

Philadelphia Spectrum the afternoon of Sept. 17, 1977. Their barbaric struggle easily upstaged Roberto Duran's defense of the lightweight title against Edwin Viruet, a humdrum affair broadcast on ABC.

Referees were not as quick to stop fights back then, which was one of the reasons Saad Muhammad was able to build a Hall of Fame career based on his Lazarus-like ability to rally from the brink of oblivion. Against Douglas, however, he needed a little help from an angel wearing a striped referee's jersey.

When Douglas floored Franklin in the fifth, referee Hank Cisco's count was painfully slow, but as soon as the Philly fighter staggered his antagonist in the sixth, Cisco abruptly stopped the fight. Under different circumstances there wouldn't have been such uproar. But considering how many times the ref had allowed Saad Muhammad to keep fighting when he was in trouble, Cisco's action seemed inappropriate at best. Even the most ardent Saad Muhammad supporters were demonstrably unhappy.

"They jumped to their feet yelling and started throwing their programs at the ring," said promoter J Russell Peltz, who was one of Cisco's most outspoken critics.

"My dad was clean robbed," said Buster Douglas, recalling the day, more than 30 years ago, when he sat on the edge of his seat and watched his father trade punches with a legend in the making.

To fully comprehend how Buster Douglas became the unlikely conqueror of Mike Tyson 13 years later, you have to focus on his complicated relationship with his father. Bill was as uncompromising outside the ring as he was inside, a proud man who loved his sons and tried to instill in them the same hard-core values he lived by.

"He was an awesome man, my father, a true warrior," said Buster. "That man was freakin' tough. He was my hero."

Buster, however, was made of different stuff, a gentle soul who would curl up with his dog on the floor and go to sleep. A sensitive child who went to his room and turned up the stereo to hide the sounds of his parents arguing. He had not inherited his father's badass gene, and there was nothing anybody could do about it. Not that his father didn't try.

"Boxing was just the only way he knew of feeling close to his daddy," said Sarah Jones, Buster's maternal grandmother, who raised him the first six years of his life and knew her grandson wasn't cut out to be a fighter.

Nonetheless, the family patriarch was delighted when his youngest son became a regular at the gym. Buster worked hard to please his daddy, but nobody can hide his true character in a boxing ring. There was no getting around it, he lacked the ruthless instincts and self-confidence that his father took for granted. To nobody's great surprise, the clash of personalities eventually caused a temporary rift between them.

The situation came to a head when Buster quit in the corner after just two rounds of his sixth professional fight, against David Bey. His father was so enraged he slapped him right there in the ring for the entire world to see. Bill didn't understand that despite his athletic prowess, Buster was riddled with self-doubt, a character flaw he believes was responsible for all his losses.

Douglas' career continued without his father in his corner. The talent was plain to see, but after losses to Mike White, Jesse Ferguson and Tony Tucker (in a failed bid to win the IBF title), nobody would have guessed Buster would be undisputed heavyweight champion less than three years after Tucker stopped him.

Tyson's life could have probably been different if he'd been the son of a demanding but loving father like Bill Douglas. Tyson's birth certificate lists Jamaican-born Purcell Tyson as his birth father, but Mike grew up thinking his mother's boyfriend, Jimmy Kirkpatrick, was his father. Kirkpatrick was an entirely different kind of role model.

"I desperately wanted to be the son of a pimp because that was a big status [symbol] in my neighborhood," said Tyson during the debut of his one-man confessional, *Mike Tyson: Undisputed Truth*. "[Kirkpatrick] was a fast-talkin' and cool-dressin' [dude] that changed the path of my mother's life. Before long, she was caught up in the street life. She drank to kill the pain. My mother was an addict. That's why I have this addictive personality. When I drank, I drank like she did. I got caught in the gunfire ... collateral damage."

Although everybody knew Tyson was a party animal, the depth of his excess was not fully revealed until he retired from the ring. The ex-champ now earns his living fessing up to every kink in his rush to the bottom.

What made Douglas' knockout of Tyson so surprising to so many was their willingness to believe that "Iron Mike" was immune to the degrading effects of life in the fast lane. The apparent ease with which he dispatched his challengers camouflaged the rot that had set in and gradually drained him of his fighting spirit.

What made it even worse was that Tyson must have known that he was blowing it but didn't give a damn, as long as the party didn't end. Behind the scowling facade lurked a boy acting out his pimp fantasy, a fantasy that was about to be exposed to the merciless light of reality.

Douglas had put together a six-bout winning streak since losing to Tucker, but nobody was getting excited. The general consensus was that the fainthearted progeny of Bill Douglas would submit the first time Tyson administered the appropriate dose of ultra-violence. Some Vegas sports books listed Mike a 42-1 favorite in an attempt to stir up a little action. There were few takers.

Numbers alone seldom get to the heart of the matter. There's usually something else involved, something more personal than stats on a Vegas tote board. In this particular case it was the death of Douglas' mother, Lula Pearl, 23 days before the fight.

The tragedy was the catalyst for Douglas' transformation. His mother was his best friend and biggest fan, the person he called first thing every morning. She was also the buffer between him and his dad in trying times.

Lula Pearl's death galvanized Buster, who, a few days before she died, had assured her that he wasn't afraid of Tyson and would beat him. At her funeral, he looked down at the casket, vowed to keep his promise and headed straight to the gym afterward.

A promise alone, no matter how heartfelt, has never won a boxing match. There's always more to it than that. His father had not only given Buster the tools to do the job but also set an example of how a fighter should behave. Buster had never felt confident enough before to buy into his father's warrior code, but this time the fight stood for something bigger than victory, something even bigger than his father's approval.

Tyson, on the other hand, was uninspired, ill prepared and over-confident. His trainer was Jay Bright, a Cus D'Amato acolyte whose main claim to fame, when they all lived and trained together in Catskill, New York, was his ability to make a tasty soufflé.

The defending champion looked disinterested as he made his ring walk. It's doubtful he was worried about Douglas, a challenger with a spotty record and a reputation for bailing out when things got too serious for his liking. It's hard to imagine how mind-blowing it must have been when Mike realized—probably as early as the first round —that Douglas was in no way intimidated by his fearsome persona and had every intention of trying to rip his head off.

Hugh McIlvanney, the doyen of U.K. sports writers, wrote he had the "bemusing impression that the Tokyo Dome housed a contest between two ringers." In a way, he was spot on.

Where was the pitiless destroyer who had left a trail of comatose fighters strewn in his wake? And who, for cripes sake, was the tall, fluid boxer blunting Tyson's attack with footwork and head-snapping punches?

People watched with incredulity as the fight unfolded, unaware that an unprecedented confluence of circumstances had conspired to turn Douglas into his father. The magic only lasted for one fight, but one fight was all Buster needed to keep his promise to his mother and prove he was a worthy son of a man called "Dynamite."

Tyson, on the other hand, fell victim of the lifestyle of Kirk-patrick, the man he thought was his father and wanted so badly to emulate.

Certain moments of Douglas-Tyson stand out like blood stains on the canvas, vivid reminders of what took place inside the ring the day

Tyson lost his cloak of invincibility: Douglas struggling to his feet after being floored by a right upper in the eighth round, the final sledgehammer blows that drove Tyson to the canvas in the 10th and, perhaps most evocative of all—the erstwhile Baddest Man on the Planet on his hands and knees groping for his mouthpiece.

These enduring images were the final act of a morality play about fathers and sons, defeat and redemption, which had an unforgettable one-night stand on boxing's grandest stage, 25 years ago today.

———

EPILOGUE: Douglas lost the heavyweight championship to Evander Holyfield in his first defense, October 25, 1990, and retired. He made a comeback in 1996, winning eight of nine bouts against limited opposition, and hung up his gloves for keeps in February 1999.

HANGING WITH MR. MIKE

AT HOME INTERVIEW WITH THE BADDEST MAN ON THE PLANET

ORIGINALLY PUBLISHED BY *THE RING EXTRA*, VOLUME II, No. 1, 1996

MIKE TYSON ISN'T who you think he is. And that's not too surprising, considering that the baddest man on the planet is also one of the most reclusive. Except for four fights, a couple of uninformative press conferences, and a handful of perfunctory TV interviews, Tyson has kept an extremely low profile since being released from prison on March 25, 1995. Sure, there was faux pas involving a woman in a Chicago nightclub, but when the Ohio Department of Rehabilitation tightened the terms of Tyson's parole, he became an even more elusive figure.

Fortunately, *The Ring* has been granted far greater access to Tyson than any other member of the print media. He spoke at length with Editor-in-Chief Steve Farhood while in Philadelphia for the Buster Mathis Jr. fight last December, and then graciously opened his Las Vegas home to The Bible of Boxing" on two separate occasions in late June. It was during the course of those visits that Tyson sat down with *The Ring*'s Managing Editor Nigel Collins and gave the interview that follows. Tyson, slightly under the weather and only days away from postponing his fight with Bruce Seldon, gave unselfishly of his time, answered every question with complete candor, and genuinely enjoyed the experience. Collins reports:

"Like most of us, Tyson is a work in progress. Understandably, I found him in a much mellower state of mind than when I interviewed him at the Indiana Youth Center in August 1994. During our Vegas talk, he struck me as an individual in the process of becoming a self-educated man, keenly interested in a wide range of topics, the least of which was boxing. The longer we spoke, the more he opened up and revealed his inner thoughts. Some were predictable, some profound, others outright shocking. And who, in their wildest imagination, would have thought that Iron Mike was a Deadhead!

The Ring: After you knocked out Frank Bruno to regain the WBC heavyweight title, you showed a lot more emotion than you usually do after winning a fight. Can you give us some idea of what you were thinking at that moment?

Tyson: It was just a difficult ordeal. Guys lose a title, then go back and train. Being persistent in training, they win the title back. But I was out of fighting for four years. The only thing I did was calisthenics and running. And I had to come back, in less than a year, to win the championship. I just wanted to do it because there was a lot of pressure on me, more so on me than any other fighters. People expect me to do well. Just give me a break.

The Ring: People hold you to the highest standards.

Tyson: And I'm just not that kind of guy. I'm just a very ordinary person. Even Cus, everybody always put a great deal of pressure on me. And from that experience, I also do it to myself sometimes. I'm my worst critic.

The Ring: But hasn't that pressure molded you into the kind if fighter you are?

Tyson: I don't think so.

The Ring: How important is it to you to unify the heavyweight title again?

Tyson: The only thing I can do is my best. I feel good about myself, and I feel that good things are going to happen with me. Like I say, it's just a lot of pressure that people put on me. But I try my best to avoid the pressure, and just do my job.

The Ring: Do you think that politics among the different organizations will make it difficult for you to win all the belts again?

Tyson: I believe so, yes *(laughs)*.

The Ring: You're one of the most powerful people in boxing. Is there anything you can do to straighten out the situation?

Tyson: I don't know. I'm not too crazy about the boxing business. I just want to fight, and after I'm finished fighting, I don't want to be in this stuff no more. I'd like to come by some of the hall of fame things and some of the awards, but I don't really want to be involved with the fights anymore.

The Ring: The three fights you've had on your comeback have been short and relatively one-sided. All great fighters have had to go up against another great fighter to bring out the best in them. Do you look forward to being in a fight where you've really got to dig deep in order to prevail?

Tyson: I'm not looking forward to it, no.

The Ring: You just want to knock out everybody out quickly?

Tyson: If possible, yeah.

The Ring: Shortly after the Bruno fight, you held a press conference and said you weren't satisfied with your $30-million purse. What was that all about?

Tyson: I had a problem with the cable people. I really don't want to talk about it. I just had a problem with them, those are the people I had a problem with. And sometimes I have a tendency to take my problems out on everyone within my proximity, maybe Don [King] or John [Horne]. It was something that was dealt with, and now I'm happy. I'm feeling much better.

The Ring: Buster Douglas, the only fighter to beat you as a pro, is making a comeback. Are you interested in fighting him again?

Tyson: I never thought about it. If that happens, I'll welcome it. But I'm not the sort of guy who wants revenge. If it happens, it happens. The press would like it.

The Ring: What do you think about IBF super middleweight champion Roy Jones playing basketball in the afternoon and then defending the title at night?

Tyson: I think he's an outstanding fighter and is going to become a household name. He's not a household name yet, and he wants to get to that big payday. Regardless of how good he is, he's still not getting a big payday. Somebody isn't sponsoring him well … because if you see [Oscar] De La Hoya, he has a big constituency behind him. And he's just a little guy. Roy Jones doesn't have that yet. That's because [De La Hoya] has been marketed differently than Roy Jones.

The Ring: Jones claims he doesn't have anybody to fight.

Tyson: That's not true at all, because he's got Nigel Benn, even though he lost. He's got so many guys he can fight. He can fight Virgil Hill.

The Ring: It's been suggested that Jones might even move up to heavyweight.

Tyson: Well, if he wants to fight me, I'm sure he'll find it very stimulating.

The Ring: Do you think it might happen somewhere down the road?

Tyson: I wouldn't have anything to gain. A big, strong bully going up against a good-looking Olympic kid. I'd be totally ominous.

The Ring: Everybody wants to fight Mike Tyson. Even Butterbean wants to fight you.

Tyson: Yeah, I met him. He's a sweet guy.

The Ring: Would you fight him?

Tyson: *(makes a face and shakes his head in a negative manner)* I like Butterbean. I wouldn't want to fight him.

The Ring: Why do you think Butterbean is so popular?

Tyson: He's got balls. You don't have to be a winner, as long as you have balls. Some people have more nerve than common sense.

The Ring: What do you think of women's boxing? A lot of people thought Christy Martin stole the show when she fought on the undercard of your fight with Bruno.

Tyson: I don't mind being second to her. I like her a lot. I take films of her and show them to other fighters. She's amazing. I've seen her do moves that Cus used to show us. I watch her to get my moves back I may have forgotten. You can tell she so intelligent because she will watch other fighters. I've done a move, and then I'll watch her fight, and she'll do the same move *(snaps his finger),* just like she's been doing it every day.

The Ring: Christy's not the only one. There are a lot of good women boxers out there.

Tyson: There are some in the Golden Gloves in New York who are tough. They're gonna get some girls hurt, man. They're gonna get some girls hurt.

The Ring: Do you think they still fix fights?

Tyson: I've got to be careful the way I say this … I think some fighters throw fights. I've seen some fights recently since I've been home. You see guys hit in the shoulder and go down, and these have been rough, tough guys.

The Ring: Has anybody ever asked you to take a dive?

Tyson: I wouldn't do that. I wouldn't do it for a billion dollars. You couldn't live with yourself. But look at Joe Gans. He threw a fight. Jack Blackburn, who was Joe Louis' trainer, said, "I've done a lot of things I'm not proud of in my life, but I ain't never threw a fight." There are some things you don't do, man.

The Ring: Do you enjoy watching sports in general?

Tyson: I'm bored watching sports, and I don't watch boxing that much.

The Ring: Celebrities tend to gravitate toward fighters. Do you enjoy that aspect of fame?

Tyson: I think rich people and people of influence like boxing because that's the only way a person from a horrible social background can be in their presence overnight. Some guy who lived in Brownsville is working hard. Then, one night, he's in the presence of a Russian Czar or the Kuwait dictator, and they admire his skills on one night they view him. But mostly I like everyday people, because that's the people I relate to. But sometimes it's difficult because they don't want to relate to me because of my situation. Some people are star-struck. But a lot of people don't understand. Like if they come in here and see how I live, and they want to go to my other home, they wouldn't understand what it took to get here. They just see the finished results. They don't see the beginning stages.

The Ring: How does a rich and famous person such as yourself know if somebody really likes you or is just a gold digger?

Tyson: I don't think anybody likes me *(laughs)*. I really believe that, because I've seen what money does to people. I remember seeing something about the Gettys on television. And one of the Gettys was dying of AIDS, a young lady. She had a beautiful home and everything, but she wasn't receiving money. And she said, "I don't like money. I've been around money all my life, and if you'd been around money, you'd know what money can do to you. And when she said that, I felt it. [Money] tore her family apart. It takes people who were born together, raised together, and turns them into blood-sucking enemies.

The Ring: That's the flip side of wealth.

Tyson: It's so complicated, and very simple. Come today, gone tomorrow. I fight for everything, but if I was to lose it all tomorrow —what the hell! As long as my kids are in college, doing well and they have their little money, doing their thing. They can decide whether they're going to be a bum or going to be a decent human being. I couldn't decide what I was going to be.

The Ring: Eventually, you had a choice.

Tyson: Well, yeah, when I got to that stage. I'm talking about the beginning of my life. I didn't have a choice. I was going to stay in the ghetto. I was going to involved in crime, and things were going to go wrong. I was going to be locked up. And that happened. Then as time goes on, and I started to elevate my character, I was able to make a choice, either be a decent person or a bum.

The Ring: How has becoming a father for the second time changed you?

Tyson: It's a great deal of responsibility.

The Ring: Does it make you feel any different about yourself?

Tyson: I don't know. It can be a burden because I'm accustomed to a different kind of lifestyle.

The Ring: How much time do you get to spend with your daughters?

Tyson: Rayna, I spend as much time as I can. But with my oldest daughter, Michael, it's kind of difficult because me and her mother have a different relationship than me and Rayna's mother.

The Ring: When you get together with your daughters, what kind of things do you do.

Tyson: Really, not much. I'm not much of a father. I don't call myself some great father. There's no blueprint to being a father. I joke around and play. I take 'em shopping, very insignificant things basically. Because at this stage they're infantile. So there's not much I can discuss with them. Basically, I'm going to try to be a father. Try! I never even tried yet, truly tried. I don't know the first thing about being a father. I've got my pictures here and my pictures upstairs. I send them money because I don't know a thing about being a father. [Monica Turner] better never think about leaving that baby with me *(laughs)*. You know what I mean? I'd be like Susan Smith. I'll put them in the incinerator *(more laughter)*.

The Ring: Have you ever changed a diaper?

Tyson: Never in my life.

The Ring: How about giving her a bottle?

Tyson: Yeah, but I'm not excited about it. I need something more to happen. Say, "Hi, Daddy." Say something. Say you want a car. Let me bribe you for your love.

The Ring: Your kids are going to love you whether you like it or not.

Tyson: You know that's really crazy? How people come over to you, say things, and touch you. When we drive, people be running after the car, jumping on the car. I'm going to tell my kids about this, and they're not going to believe me.

The Ring: Because you're busy training and fighting, you have to delegate a lot of responsibility. Do you know what's going on all the time with your finances?

Tyson: Most of the time, yes. I've been through that situation before when I first started fighting and I was with Jim Jacobs and Bill Cayton. I'm not despotic or anything, but I'm pretty much aware of what's going on. You don't have to be a college grad to understand business. You just have to be an aware person and have the hunger to know what's going on.

The Ring: You've said in the past that people have taken advantage of you. Do you still that way?

Tyson: I just very leery. Everyone uses someone. I mean, I'm using you to get a cover story, and you're using me. But I'd never misuse you, and hope you'd never misuse me. That's the difference, when you misuse one another. That's bad. But there is nothing wrong with using someone.

The Ring: Do you think you are now making better choices about who you trust?

Tyson: Well, I'm all right so far. But I can feel all right, then switch in one minute.

The Ring: Besides the financial rewards, what's the part of boxing you like the best?

Tyson: I don't know. I like the financial rewards *(laughs)*.

The Ring: One gets the impression watching you fight that you're enjoying yourself.

Tyson: It just happens. It's a habit, I guess. I get into it. Once you're under the lights, you're ready to roll.

The Ring: Are there times when you wish that you could stop being Mike Tyson for a little while.

Tyson: Not really. I hate it sometimes, but the reality is that I don't really want that, because I trained all my life for this. I may say I hate myself sometimes, but I'm lying to myself.

The Ring: How come you seem bored at press conferences, like you don't want to be there?

Tyson: I just don't want to get into a pissing contest with you guys. I don't want to get in an argument, because I'm not cool under that kind of pressure. I'm not like I was before, when I could tolerate somebody saying something. I don't do that to anybody else, and I don't tolerate them doing it to me. I don't want any kind of problems.

The Ring: Do you feel you have a bad relationship with the media?

Tyson: I don't talk to them. I never receive anything positive from talking to them. I'm just not interested.

The Ring: Do you feel the media has been unfair to you?

Tyson: Yeah, I believe so. Sometimes I think they have loyalty to other people who don't have my agenda.

The Ring: Do you think some boxing writers on promoters' and manager's payrolls?

Tyson: I was with Jim Jacobs when he used to take a bunch of reporters out to eat. I never saw any money exchanged, but you take these guys out to eat. Cus used to do that in his day, too. I would never do that because that's nor proper.

The Ring: Which bothers you more, when the media talks about your personal life or when they criticize the way you fight.

Tyson: I never take it personal.

The Ring: So why have you decided not to talk to the media?

Tyson: Because I'm not going to give them the ammunition to kill me with.

The Ring: What about the fans? Do you enjoy spending time with them, signing autographs and stuff like that?

Tyson: There's good people out there. I don't care if you've got a billion dollars or two cents. Good people are good people, a bum's a bum.

The Ring: What is the biggest misconception that people have about you?

Tyson: You know … Can I tell you something? I think the biggest misconceptions are what I put on myself. I think people really care. They're happy to see me. They never think, well, *I'm not going to let my daughter sit on his lap.* They always throw their children on me and stuff. The women say, "Meet my daughter. Now there's a woman who isn't going to treat you bad." Or something bizarre like that. They feel more sympathetic toward me than anything. And sometimes I'm offended.

The Ring: Why?

Tyson: Because we're men, and whatever happens, most of the time we bring it upon ourselves. And I just feel embarrassed that somebody has to be sympathetic toward me. I think you should be sympathetic toward cripples and sick people. I'm not weak, and I don't think I should be felt sympathetic toward.

The Ring: In terms of public interest, you're bigger now than before you went to jail.

Tyson: I'm not trying to be big.

The Ring: Was there anything positive that came out of your time in the Indiana Youth Center?

Tyson: I met some good people there, and some of them are never going to come home. They have problems in society, and the things they did which put them in a position where they are never going to come home. It's just an experience, dealing with different kind of people, gang members, Aryan brothers, just different people. It was culture shock.

The Ring: Was it different than you expected?

Tyson: Tremendously.

The Ring: In what way?

Tyson: Discipline mostly. I had to become disciplined. It was a very structured life to be dealt with, and not many people disrespected people there. And when it did happen, there was always a problem. You don't raise your voice at people; you have to respect them.

The Ring: Prison isn't like what you see in the movies.

Tyson: Heck, no. Well, sometimes you hear people screaming. You've got some people into their own thing. You may hear some people scream, people fighting, handling a dispute or something. But the whole nucleus is very subtle. And we look at it like it's every day. Like a guy having sex with another man. You don't trip. Like when I first went to prison, I'm tripping, smelling guy's defecation from having sex or hear a guy make noise. Then it almost becomes like a joke. People say, "Hey you got it today." Or some gay person will be walking out, and guys will be whistling, "Hey, hey, hey. We know what you was doing in there."

The Ring: It sounds like the prison experience made you more tolerant of other lifestyles.

Tyson: Oh, yes, yes, yes, exactly. That's the word I'm looking for, tolerance. At one time I wouldn't want a person who was biting nails, maybe even somebody snoring. I'd be, "What the hell!!" Now, well, that's his problem. Let him deal with it.

The Ring: Were there people in prison who tried to prove themselves by acting tough toward you?

Tyson: We had problems. There are always going to be problems. They try the weakest and the strongest. They always try you; that's just the nature of the beast. But everything turned out okay.

The Ring: You became quite a reader while incarcerated. What have you been reading lately?

Tyson: Any book I can get my hands on. I like history, some economics. It depends on the mood I'm in. I've got a book about John Gotti on my bed.

The Ring: Why are you so fascinated by underworld characters?

Tyson: I think, being from where I'm from, my environment, you can't help being, not in awe, but fascinated by them. Even you, being from Philadelphia, you can't help knowing the history of Angelo Bruno and all those guys. You just can't help that. I had a whole documentary of "Little Nicky" Scarfo [a Philadelphia monster now serving a life without parole]. He's a really interesting person. On one hand, people consider them scumbags; they kill their best friends, killing for power. On the other hand, they make their own rules.

The Ring: And generally, they don't mess with people outside of the organization.

Tyson: That's not true. They mess with whoever they want to mess with *(laughs)*.

The Ring: I guess the biggest change in organized crime is that they started to violate the oath of silence, started to dime each other out.

Tyson: They talked. Can I tell you something? That's the easy way out. You look at these guys, and say, "Listen, the only way to get in is to kill somebody and bring some money to the table." And that's very easy. It's very easy to kill somebody and it's easy to get some money illegally. So they're in the mob now, right? But these guys have never been taught character and perseverance. So as soon as they get in that life, they're gonna tell.

The Ring: Do you see any difference between mobsters, the heads of industry, and the heads of government?

Tyson: One is legal. One is illegal. The only thing that matters is who has the biggest gang. The United States of America has the biggest mob. So they set their own rules. *(Suddenly, Tyson's attention is diverted by something that flashes across a silent wall-sized TV screen on the other the other side of the room.)* Look at that, look at that, Jimi Hendrix! Him and Janis Joplin. I love those two. When I was young, I couldn't stand Jimi Hendrix, because we thought rock-and-roll was white, disgusting, racist. And we never did like him. We were probably drinking or something, and I saw a picture of Jimi Hendrix at my friend's house. I said, "What the hell you doing with Jimi Hendrix hanging on your wall?" My friend was smoking *(makes a sucking noise and pretends he's sucking on a joint)*. They be, "No, no, no. You don't understand. The brother be cool. He's cool." "You serious man?" I'm into disco back then, 13, 12. He says, "No Mike, the brother's cool. You've got to listen. Check it out."

The Ring: What changed your mind?

Tyson: I got older, and listen to that music, and you listen to the pain, sorrow, and happiness, and you understand life better. I wasn't that experienced at that age. As you experience things and you read about this guy and you hear Janis Joplin talking about Bobby McGee, and you think, *Yeah, I'm gonna be all right! Laughs.* I've got some tapes. We should listen some time. I'm gonna tell you something else that's really ironic. I'm just a strange person. But Jerry Garcia, right? He passed away. Every time I've been somewhere, and he had a concert with the Grateful Dead, I'd see people sleeping on the street like vagrants, and these people are working people. These are people who work nine to five at corporations, and they were sleeping on the streets. And I said, "What is this?" And they say, "I'm a Deadhead," And I say, "Oh, yeah, the Grateful Dead are in town." And I ask them if they needed some sodas or anything. These guys were dedicated people to Jerry Garcia.

The Ring: Did you ever attend a Grateful Dead concert?

Tyson: Never had the chance. I so feel bad that I never met him. I wanted to meet Santana, too. Because as I got older, I learned their history, not only the music, and what kind of people they are. That freaks me out. These guys are really revolutionary.

The Ring: You've been talking about how you've matured more, become more accepting and tolerant of things that used to seem strange to you. Why do you think there is still much hatred in our society?

Tyson: Ignorance. Family. Television. Books. I'm just always conscious. If I hear somebody say, "that spic or Jew," I'm very conscious about that guy's feeling toward me. Anytime they say something like, "Yeah, I hate Jews or I hate Spanish or I hate Jamaicans," I know what they think about African-Americans.

The Ring: Considering your background, it would have been easy for you to turn into a racist.

Tyson: I wasn't raised that way. Cus loved all people. You go through stages in your life: White men ain't shit and this and that. Then you go places and experience people, black and white in pain. The pain makes everybody equal. You have to understand in order for me to really be a racist, I would have to be out of my mind. Bobby Stewart *(a white man who trained Tyson when he was incarcerated at Tyron School for incorrigible boys in Johnstown, New York. Cus D'Amato, Camille Ewald (D'Amato's longtime companion and Tyson's surrogate mother)*. I'd have to be a loony tune.

The Ring: Have African-Americans ever tried to play the race card with you, told you that you should disassociate yourself from whites?

Tyson: At one particular time, but they know that they must never disrespect Cus or Camille. Then they would be having no respect for me. They can say anything about anybody else. They can say Rory [Holloway] or John [Horne] are Uncle Toms or something like that. I can handle something like that. I can handle that because they are men, and they can handle it, too, if they are confronted. But if they say anything about Cus or Camille, they know that's total disrespect, and that most likely there's gonna be a problem.

The Ring: You are obviously a much mellower person than you used to be. Does that take the edge off Mike Tyson the fighter?

Tyson: Everybody always says that. But I just think it adds more to it, makes me more relaxed, more at ease. You have to understand, every now and then I get back in that mood where I'm tense and a totally different person.

The Ring: It's often said that there are two sides to Mike Tyson: the laid-back side we are seeing today, and the dark side.

Tyson: There's two sides to you. We all have different sides.

The Ring: The side of you that manifests itself inside the ring, is that your dark side?

Tyson: I don't know about the dark side. It's something I have to do.

The Ring: Cus D'Amato instilled in you a love of boxing. Do you still have that love?

Tyson: I'll fight, but I don't love it as much as I used to do.

The Ring: Does that tell you something?

Tyson: Only God knows, but I don't anticipate fighting much longer. There's a lot of pain in this business.

The Ring: Do you think you can avoid the pitfalls that so many greats have fallen into?

Tyson: I never say what I can do or what I can't do. We just wait. And God willing, whatever happens. I'm prepared for any case, but whatever happens, happens. There is nothing I'm afraid of.

The Ring: What kind of lifestyle do you see yourself when you stop fighting?

Tyson: Messing with my kids. I was saying to Monica, "Do you think we should get married? We're not going to be doing this stuff too much longer, boxing and living lavish and going all around. Eventually, we're to be going have to cool out because it's not going to be worth it anymore. It's getting played out now." And she said, "Yeah, we'll go through that ordeal." She's in her residency now. She is the only woman I know who is very successful. But she's the best for my children, and I just like knowing she's with my children.

The Ring: What about business? Are there certain businesses you're considering getting into after you boxing career is over?

Tyson: There are certain things that people offer me—productions companies and corporations. I just don't know. Even though I fight for money, there are things I won't do for money. Sometimes, I just want to be alone, because I never really had a chance to discover me. When I was in prison, and they were getting ready to let me out, I was telling them, "Listen, you're not doing me a favor," because I wasn't having too much of a bad time in there. I was discovering what I was really all about, and I found I was a pretty decent person. I kind of like myself. I never liked myself before. That's how come I didn't care if I got killed. Because I was trying to kill myself without putting a gun to my head, the way I was living. I wanted to die. I didn't care. But I got to know myself, and I started liking myself.

About the Author

Nigel Collins has been writing about professional boxing for more than 50 years, including two terms as editor-and-chief of *The Ring* magazine. Other platforms include ESPN.com, HBO, Showtime, *Ringside Seat*, *Boxing News*, *KO*, *Boxing Illustrated* and *World Boxing*. His book *Boxing Babylon* was published in 1990. He was inducted into the International Boxing Hall of Fame in 2015. Other honors include the Pennsylvania Boxing Hall of Fame, the Atlantic City Boxing Hall of Fame, the Rocky Marciano Award for "excellence in boxing coverage," and the James J. Walker Award for "long and meritorious service to boxing." Born in England he now resides in the Philadelphia area.